D1626438

CAMBRIDGE MUSICAL TEXTS AND MONOGRAPHS

General Editors: John Butt and Laurence Dreyfus

The series Cambridge Musical Texts and Monographs has as its
centres of interest the history of performance and the history of
instruments. It includes annotated translations of important
historical documents, authentic historical texts on music, and
monographs on various aspects of historical performance.

BACH INTERPRETATION

CAMBRIDGE MUSICAL TEXTS AND MONOGRAPHS

BACH INTERPRETATION
ARTICULATION MARKS IN
PRIMARY SOURCES OF J. S. BACH

JOHN BUTT

CAMBRIDGE
UNIVERSITY PRESS

Published by the Press Syndicate of the University of Cambridge
The Pitt Building, Trumpington Street, Cambridge CB2 1RP
40 West 20th Street, New York, NY 10011-4211, USA
10 Stamford Road, Oakleigh, Melbourne 3166, Australia

First published 1990
Reprinted 1993, 1995, 1997

Transferred to digital printing 1999

Printed in the United Kingdom by Biddles Short Run Books

British Library cataloguing in publication data

Butt, John
Bach interpretation: articulation marks in
primary sources of J. S. Bach. – (Cambridge
musical texts and monographs)
1. German music. Bach, Johann Sebastian,
1685–1750
I. Title
780'.92'4

Library of Congress cataloguing in publication data

Butt, John
Bach interpretation: articulation marks in primary sources of
J. S. Bach / by John Butt.
    p.   cm. – (Cambridge musical texts and monographs)
Includes index.
ISBN 0 521 37239 9
1. Bach, Johann Sebastian, 1685–1750 – Criticism and
interpretation. 2. Music – 18th century – Interpretation (Phrasing,
dynamics, etc.) 3. Music – Performance. I. Title. II. Series.
ML410.B1B9 1990
780'.92 – dc20   89–7141 CIP

ISBN 0 521 37239 9 hardback

Contents

Plates

Preface

Articulation is as crucial to music as it is to speech; without it the most coherent of discourses can be rendered meaningless. It is particularly important in music of the Baroque era in view of the stress laid by composers and theorists on the art of rhetoric, the ability to move and convince an audience. Furthermore, given the relatively narrow dynamic range of Baroque instruments, articulation - the relation in time of each note to its neighbour - is the principal means of expression.

The choice of articulation involves several interpretative decisions which relate closely to how the performer perceives the music and its style. It inevitably involves establishing a hierarchy within the music, not only of how each note relates to its neighbours but also of how groups of notes are defined and which groups and notes within them are of particular importance. These questions of interpretation cannot and should not be answered in a way which excludes other possibilities. However, the choice of articulation and the means by which this choice is made are themselves an art which, like the music itself, can be judged according to certain historical and stylistic parameters. One significant means of establishing such parameters is to study the way the composer interpreted his own music. Since there are no recordings of Bach's own performances - despite several claims of 'authentic' reconstruction - we must return to evidence in the notation.

This study represents an attempt to assess Bach's use of articulation marks - slurs, dots and strokes - in autograph manuscripts, and copies and engravings which passed through his hands. It is hoped that it will provide an insight into both Bach's musical style and the methods by which he composed; it will also furnish the performer with information concerning Bach's articulation style in general (with regard to the conventions of the age) and his use of specific patterns of articulation in various performance media. A central aim of the book is to show that Bach interpretation is a subject which covers history, style, analysis and performance together. The dual role of the *practical* musician of Bach's time as both composer and performer is somewhat foreign to musical life today, so this study attempts to redress the balance.

It is impossible to list or recollect all those people who have assisted me in my research. My immediate thanks are due to Stephen Daw for much help and encouragement with several drafts of this work; to Joshua Rifkin for much lively discussion of articulation and advice in approaching many source problems; to Georg von Dadelsen and Robert Marshall for detailed reports on an earlier version of the thesis; to Malcolm Boyd and Don Franklin for invaluable advice during the process of transforming the work from its original format as a thesis to its present form. I owe the greatest debt to my research supervisor, Peter le Huray, for constant guidance and encouragement over the last six years. His support and friendship have been far more valuable to me than he could possibly imagine.

This work would have been impossible without the help of various bodies. My thanks are due to King's College, Cambridge, for a three-year studentship, to my parents for much support and maintenance throughout my research, to Magdalene College, Cambridge, for a research fellowship. Study trips to the Federal Republic of Germany and West Berlin have been financed by King's College, trips to the German Democratic Republic by the British Council. I am also grateful to the Ministerium für Hoch- und Fachschulwesen and the Nationale Forschungs- und Gedenkstätten Johann Sebastian Bach der DDR for accommodation in the German Democratic Republic, to David Cordier and Karen Williams for several months' accommodation in West Berlin.

The following institutions have been most generous in allowing me access to their collections: Staatsbibliothek Preußischer Kulturbesitz, Berlin/West – Musikabteilung; Deutsche Staatsbibliothek, Berlin/DDR – Musikabteilung; Bach-Archiv, Leipzig; University Library, Cambridge; Pendlebury Music Library, Cambridge University; Rowe Music Library, King's College, Cambridge; British Library, London; University Library, Glasgow. I am particularly grateful to the staff of the Johann-Sebastian-Bach-Institut, Göttingen, for access to photocopies of inaccessible sources, mainly in private possession. Thanks are also due to the other libraries acknowledged in the source list of Appendix 1, which have provided microfilms and copies.

References to works by J. S. Bach in the text are listed by their number in the *Thematisch-systematisches Verzeichnis der musikalischen Werke von Johann Sebastian Bach*, W. Schmieder (Leipzig, 1950). The movement of each work concerned is signified by the numeral after the oblique stroke. The numbering of movements in the larger works such as BWV 207, 232, 244, 245 and 248 follows that of the *NBA*.

A full list of Bach sources consulted and the degree of access gained to the originals is listed in Appendix 1. All abbreviations concerned with the citation of sources are also to be found at the head of Appendix 1.

Abbreviations

AMw   *Archiv für Musikwissenschaft*

BAM   *Bachiana et Alia Musicologica: Festschrift Alfred Dürr*, ed. W. Rehm (Kassel, 1983)

BB   *Beiträge zur Bachforschung*, Nationale Forschungs- und Gedenkstätten Johann Sebastian Bach der DDR (Leipzig, 1982–)

BG   *Johann Sebastian Bachs Werke*, Bach-Gesellschaft edition, 46 vols. (Leipzig, 1851–99)

BJ   *Bach Jahrbuch*

BS   *Bach Studien*, vol. 7 (Leipzig, 1982)

BWV   W. Schmieder, *Thematisch-systematisches Verzeichnis der musikalischen Werke von Johann Sebastian Bach* (Leipzig, 1950)

CM   *Current Musicology*

DDT   *Denkmäler deutscher Tonkunst*, 65 vols., 2nd edn (Wiesbaden, 1957–60)

Dok   *Bach-Dokumente*, 3 vols. (Leipzig and Kassel, 1963, 1969, 1972)

DTÖ   *Denkmäler der Tonkunst in Österreich*, 132 vols. (Vienna, 1894–1904)

EM   *Early Music*

IB V   *Bericht über die Wissenschaftliche Konferenz zum V. Internationalen Bachfest der DDR*, ed. W. Hoffmann and A. Schneiderheinze (Leipzig, 1988)

JAMS   *Journal of the American Musicological Society*

Mf   *Die Musikforschung*

NBA   *Neue Ausgabe sämtlicher Werke*, Neue Bach Ausgabe (Leipzig
         and Kassel, 1954-   )
KB = *Kritischer Bericht* (critical commentary)
ÖMZ   *Österreichische Musik Zeitschrift*
TBSt   *Tübinger Bach-Studien*, 5 vols., ed. W. Gerstenberg (Tros-
         singen, 1957-8)
WF   *Wege der Forschung, Johann Sebastian Bach*, ed. W. Blanken-
         burg (Darmstadt, 1970)

For abbreviations for musical instruments see first page of Appendix 2.

Introduction

Startled by the incredible discrepancies found in the numerous Bach editions,
I decided many years ago to make a thorough study of all the slur material
that has come down to us from Bach's hand, hoping that the answers to
the problems of articulation could be found therein. . . With sadness it
must be said that the result of this investigation, which has cost countless
hours of hard labor, was bitterly disappointing. In contrast to all expectations,
and to the assertions of Schweitzer and Keller. . .it has become apparent
that the cases of concurrence are infinitely less frequent than anticipated.
(Bodky 1960 p. 214)

Bodky's study of articulation, like many previous attempts, generally
relies on collected editions of Bach's works. Were Bodky to have worked
extensively on the original manuscripts, his disappointment would
surely have been even greater since there are so many problems of
legibility and source relationships. Only two certainties seem evident
from a casual survey of the primary sources: many articulation markings survive, in certain works and certain sources at least; many such
markings are problematical at first sight.

Even these two points are significant though, for, if there are many
articulation markings to be found in certain manuscripts and particular works or repertories, they must have had some function in the
original notation and performance of music. Of all the complaints
voiced at the vagueness of Baroque notation, few have registered
the inclusion of too much performance information. Secondly, if these
markings are problematical to us today – and presuming the composer's desire was not to confuse his performers – there must be certain
philological and stylistic conventions which have yet to be fully
discovered.

Given that the markings had a function, is this function worth
studying, particularly in view of the apparent inconsistencies within

1

the markings and the compromises that a modern editor and performer must inevitably make? To answer this question we need to
establish several other points first: (1) Are the markings interpretative –
do they tell us anything about the music, its structure and form which
we didn't know already? If they are technical performance indications,
do they result in an interpretation which the performer would otherwise not have chosen, or at least make a choice from a number of
possibilities usually open to the performer? Did Bach include articulation markings because he could trust few players to interpret his music
correctly? Are they indeed the closest evidence we have of how Bach
performed and 'understood' his own music?[1] (2) Or are the markings
instructive; merely directions to the performer to facilitate performance, helping him to play along fairly conventional lines with a great
amount of leeway in details?

Clearly we must discover how important Bach himself considered
these markings if we are to answer these questions. A study of the
sources and compositional process might reveal his attitude: are the
markings present in the first compositional drafts before the playing
technique is considered? Are they added once the primary task of composition is complete? Does the composer change his mind, or is there a
fixed system of articulation for each motif, or piece, or style?

From this follows the stylistic question of consistency: are like motifs
similarly articulated? For that matter, what *are* like motifs: the same
notes, the same rhythm, the same harmonic context, sequential progressions? Given that motifs or *figurae* in Bach are developed and used
in different ways within the same composition, it may be wrong to
expect exact consistency of articulation. Furthermore, unless certain
philological points are clarified – how, when and by whom the markings were inserted – it is impossible to distinguish intended inconsistency from inaccuracy or indifference.

Two extremes are evident in recent writings on consistency of articulation in Bach and the Baroque style: William Newman (1969)
seems resigned to the inconsistency, incompleteness and inaccuracy of
much of Bach's notated articulation; Dene Barnett (1978) and Graham
Pont (1979) virtually suggest that inconsistency is a virtue, part of the
fundamental spontaneity of the Baroque. Nevertheless it is impossible
to establish any style or quality in any art form without some measure
of consistency – where are we to draw the line? After all, Bach's music
may well be surprising but randomness is certainly not a quality which
is often observed in his output. Was he really so concerned with the

higher order of the universe that he was indifferent to a haphazard approach to performance? Most recent and perhaps most naive among studies taking the notation at its face value is Schestakowa's (1988). Here the writer tries – without any consideration of handwriting, changing norms in Bach's practice, implications of slurs in the various instrumental media – to justify all notated slurs (and their absences) in the autographs of the Brandenburg Concertos. First she observes correctly that the notated slurs are not consistently reproduced for repetitions of the same figuration, considering that such variability is a virtue corresponding to the '"Gemütsbewegungen" in einem Organismus' ('emotions of an organism', p. 317). But, as if squeamish of the implications of randomness, she tries to justify each instance with various contextual circumstances, the choice of which itself seems to be random if not spurious.

At the other extreme, Reinhold Kubik (1986) decides what stylistic and motivic criteria determine Bach's articulation style, establishes what the 'correct' articulation is likely to be for each figure and then, assuming that the original performers would have arrived at the same analytical decisions, he simply ignores markings which do not support his views.

The most experienced and respected German scholars, in particular the two founders of modern Bach research – Georg von Dadelsen (1978, 1980) and Alfred Dürr (1974) – readily admit that considerable problems arise in interpreting Bach's articulation markings and that no edition can reflect the original merely by means of diplomatic transcription, so incomplete and hastily drawn are many of Bach's slurrings.[2] Editorial problems can only be solved with an awareness of the chronology of the markings, a clear tabulation of parallel points within a movement, and thorough knowledge of contemporary performance practice. Both Dadelsen and Dürr apply sound editorial methods to their work, and both conclude that Bach at least intended a rational and consistent system. Dadelsen first notes how Bach's articulation of a particular passage may have altered in the course of time, any inconsistencies which are evident today being the result of a process of change which is only partially completed in the extant autograph (Dadelsen 1978 p. 100). He also observes that autograph material is more consistently marked than secondary copies, a point which he finds lacking in Barnett's arguments. Never does he find evidence that Bach ever intended a specific inconsistency between like voices. He asserts, moreover, that the performers would surely have overcome inaccuracies in the notation with their knowledge of contemporary style and performance practice. This is the conclusion of philological considerations rather than the precondition as in the case of Kubik's study.

While Dürr likewise believes that Bach sought consistency and perfection in performance, he draws attention to the role of improvisation and to the apparent lack of rehearsal in the modern sense (Dürr 1974 pp. 252-3). He suggests that most of Bach's contemporaries would hardly have noticed the inconsistencies and inaccuracies in performance (here articulation is one of several problems: the notes themselves are sometimes copied inaccurately or incompletely in the original vocal and instrumental parts). Although Bach edited performing parts, he evidently did not always have the time or energy to mark recurrent passages consistently. Moreover there is very little evidence that players added to their own parts the sorts of markings or caveats that a modern player would consider essential; their role in the struggle for accuracy and consistency seems little short of irresponsible.

Dadelsen may be correct in observing that most instances of inconsistent articulation are related to minor matters of performance technique, and that markings which relate more to the principal character of the music and its motifs show more sign of regularity and order (Dadelsen 1978 p. 103). In other words there is a distinction between those markings which are interpretative and those that are merely instructive. Another *Neue Bach Ausgabe* editor, Dietrich Kilian (1983), like Kubik takes motivic structure as the starting point for his work. He bases his study on what is actually consistent rather than inconsistent and convincingly shows that certain articulation markings can be related to specific motifs. Furthermore he notes that a particular slurring (where the figuration is more ambiguous) may well derive from its place in the structure and consequently from the relation of patterns to each other in the course of a movement.

Dadelsen concludes: 'Jedoch sei davor gewarnt, aus der Artikulation eine eigene Wissenschaft zu machen: Aus der Nebensache soll keine Hauptsache werden.' ('Be however warned not to make an actual science out of articulation - no fundamental can be derived from a minor matter', Dadelsen 1978 pp. 111-12.) Does this imply that a study of articulation marks is primarily one of a philological nature? It is, after all, hoped that the present study will, through its wide survey of sources, produce some notational norms for Bach's articulation style; an 'articulation register' giving the range of possibilities for each particular slurred pattern. However, it is also hoped that a detailed analysis of articulation marks, in several different categories of primary sources, will reveal them as a significant feature in the identity of Bach's music, one which gives us deeper insight into his compositional style.

While most studies of articulation have been primarily empirical, this survey attempts to show articulation and its notation within the context of Baroque musical thought. Here the relationship between composer and performer is crucial. Who had priority? When? And is it even accurate to make a precise distinction between the two? The atmosphere of rhetoric surrounding education, religion, music and music-making in the Baroque is important here, particularly the role of the performer in realizing the message of the composition, often completing the ornamentation and diminution of the basic musical structure. The close relationship between notated articulation and notated diminution is emphasized throughout this study. This renders the traditional argument as to whether notated articulation relates to 'exceptions' or not redundant; for in terms of Baroque compositional theory, every figure comprising diminution is an 'exception' to the basic contrapuntal or basso continuo skeleton. The very style represents a structure of 'exceptions'.

With these aims and interests in mind, this study is presented in three parts: (1) Fundamentals of articulation: what we know of the stylistic and performance background to articulation in Bach's environment. (2) Articulation marks in the concerted vocal music: the circumstances in which Bach notated articulation, the norms that can be discerned from the sources as a whole. (3) Articulation marks in selected chamber and instrumental works: what Bach marked when he had more time to add detailed articulation instructions; how these markings reveal subtleties in the structure of the music which would not otherwise have been perceived.

Several important works on articulation serve as background to the present study and complement its aims. Ludger Lohmann's general examination (1982) of keyboard articulation in the sixteenth to eighteenth centuries is one of the most perceptive studies to date. Lohmann notes the close relationship between instrumental articulation and speech and expression, showing that the basic principles of articulation are common to all keyboard instruments. His greatest contribution is to outline the grammar of articulation, independent of the concept of 'phrasing', and derived both from the compositional style and the

desire for clarity and expression in Baroque performance. The hierarchies of accent lie behind the principles of articulation and, para-
phrasing Rousseau, these accents can be viewed as grammatical (the
system of metrical stress), oratorical or logical (derived from the sense
and formal structure of the discourse, important notes and cadences,
dissonances etc.) and pathetic (the emphasis of particularly expressive
notes) (*ibid*. pp. 29-88). The grammatical accent rules before 1750
and an extensive study of keyboard fingering shows how the performance technique reflects the standard strong-weak accents within pairs
of even notes ('good' and 'bad' notes).

Although Lohmann generally considers articulation marks to indicate exceptions to the conventions of articulation, he sometimes
accepts that they may indicate or clarify a regular system of accents.
Indeed, he sees this as a primary function of articulation marks in
Bach's pedagogic works.[3] Lohmann considers the concepts of 'legato'
and 'staccato' to be later modifications of the standard metrical hierarchy, legato slurring being derived from ornamental string bowings.
However, he is always at pains to point out the accentual implications
of slurs, the first note of a slur being stressed and the last shortened;
he sees a fundamentally legato style as developing only in the later
eighteenth century, its earlier uses being connected only with a specific
Affekt. Modification of the fundamental articulation dictated by the
grammatical accents might depend on the shape of the motifs, the
Affekt and genre, the acoustics and dynamics and the speed of the
notes concerned; for instance, the second smallest note value is often
articulated more sharply than the smallest note value. The basic conventions of metrical accentuation should never be obscured, however
(*ibid*. pp. 233-328).

George Houle's recent study of metre in music (1987) amplifies many
of the points made by Lohmann. Houle traces the development of the
concept of metre and time signature, the relationship between musical
and poetic metres and the conventions of quantitative metre. This
last section is the most relevant to articulation, defining Lohmann's
grammatical accents in terms of *Quantitas Intrinseca*, the inner length
of notes within their alloted time span (*ibid*. pp. 78-123). The basic
strong-weak pairing of notes throughout the Baroque is reflected in all
instrumental techniques and demonstrated precisely in *La Tonotechnie*
of Engramelle. Unlike Lohmann, Houle continually stresses the difference between articulation achieved through the intrinsic length of
the notes and that achieved by accent. Broadly speaking, accent is

associated with dynamics and is relevant only to the latter part of the eighteenth century.

Although Houle is right to make such a distinction, he perhaps underestimates the role of dynamic accent in earlier music: bow changes and tonguing involve an element of percussion like the consonant of a word. Furthermore, a note stressed by virtue of its length in relation to its surroundings is liable to sound louder.

Josef Rainerius Fuchs' examination of articulation marks in Bach's keyboard music (1985) is the first and largest systematic survey of a portion of Bach's notated articulation, based entirely on examination of the primary sources. He defines articulation as the relative lengths of notes rather than in terms of a basic system of grammatical accents; notated articulation relates to the extremes encompassed by the modern terms 'legato' and 'staccato' (*ibid*. pp. 16-33). Dadelsen's distinction between interpretative compositional articulation markings and instructional technical indications is more difficult to determine in keyboard sources, where slurring is not related to the basic technique (*ibid*. pp. 27-8). Fuchs' study of keyboard concertos where the keyboard part lacks many of the markings found in earlier string versions suggests that markings to be found only in string sources are merely technical instructions (*ibid*. pp. 163-78).

Fuchs adopts a methodology far more precise than in any previous study of articulation; markings are surveyed with regard to: intervals, rhythm, ornamentation and harmony, beaming, metre and accent, group, motif, phrase and theme, performance technique. He also makes a distinction between 'Figurenartikulation' (articulation according to motifs) and 'Grundartikulation' (a predominant style of articulation - *ibid*. p. 57). Several basic principles emerge in Fuchs' conclusion: certain figures and patterns are articulated in similar ways throughout the repertory discussed. However, there are usually several possibilities for one and the same pattern and there is clearly no evidence of the mythical unnotated 'rule' and the notated 'exception'. The reader is warned not to derive a single 'correct' interpretation from Bach's articulation markings, in view of the composer's tremendous variability. Slurs and dots constitute a variable addition that is not grounded in the actual musical substance (*ibid*. pp. 179-81).

Certain principles, then, govern Bach's notated articulation, but the choice of one particular criterion in favour of another appears to be little short of random. Fuchs calls for a more detailed 'articulation register' covering all of Bach's instrumental output, and transferable between all instrumental performance media. The present study it is hoped fulfils this request. Furthermore, through a more detailed study of the sources and the role of articulation marking within Bach's compositional process, the conclusion here derives rather more significance from Bach's notated articulation.

Part I

BACKGROUND TO ARTICULATION IN THE PERFORMANCE PRACTICE OF BACH'S ERA

1

The primacy of singing

'. . .Lehrbegierigen, eine deütliche Art gezeiget wird. . .gute *inventiones* nicht alleine zu bekommen, sondern auch selbige wohl durchzuführen, am allermeisten aber eine *cantable* Art im Spielen zu erlangen. . .' ('Those eager to learn are shown a clear way. . .not only of having good *inventiones* but also of developing these well, and, above all, of arriving at a *cantabile* style of playing. . .', *J. S. Bach: Autograph title page to Inventions and Sinfonias, 1723, Dok* vol. 1 pp. 220-1; italics here, and wherever used in quotations in this work, appear in the originals).

Bach was clearly a demanding teacher: his pupils were expected not only to have musical ideas, inspired by his own example, but also to master the rules of composition and above all perform in a singing style. He was not alone in his emphasis on singing; writers throughout the history of performance criticism have stressed the importance of singing as the basis of all music.[1] Furthermore, in Bach's time singing was very much at the centre of musical thought since it was an essential part of both education and worship in orthodox Lutheranism. In the more modern, enlightenment aesthetic the voice was important both for its alleged 'naturalness' of expression and also for its association with that passport to meaning and aesthetic respectability: the text. Telemann asserts in his autobiography that 'Singing is the fundamental of music in all things' ('Lebens-Lauff / mein / Georg Philipp Telemanns', in Mattheson 1731 p. 170), and J. S. Bach's son, C. P. E. Bach (1753 p. 107), recommends that instrumental melodies be sung through first in order to discover their correct manner of performance. This sounds very like J. S. Bach's advice for the performance of the Inventions, despite the tremendous differences in musical style and aesthetic.

Clearly any study of performance practice, particularly articulation, should take vocal style as a starting point. The role of music and singing in Bach's educational environment provides the most suitable background for an examination of the 'cantabile' style.

SINGING IN THE LUTHERAN TRADITION

Luther's view of music as a supreme gift of God, second only to theology, inspired a rich tradition of church music (see, e.g., *Luther's Works* 1972 pp. 426-9). Music was considered a powerful influence on the emotions and thus performed an exegetic function not unlike that of the sermon (Stiller 1984 pp. 211-23). Thus *Musica theoretica* - part of the *Quadrivium* of traditional Mediaeval education - was soon rivalled and superseded by *Musica practica* (performance and composition), related more to the practical arts of the *Trivium* (especially rhetoric) (Schmitz 1970; Eggebrecht 1970). The first Lutheran school ordinances of Melanchthon and Bugenhagen gave singing an important place in the curriculum for all pupils (Schünemann 1928 pp. 82-4). Cantors - usually ranked third in the school hierarchy - were also specialists in subjects other than music, many progressing to become pastors or rectors; conversely, most other teachers had some proficiency in music and often taught notation and theory (see, e.g., Finkel 1978 pp. 213-18). With the influence of the Italian *seconda prattica*, Lutheran music fulfilled its primary task of communicating meaning and *Affekt* even more successfully. However, this also encouraged the increasing specialization of cantors and pupils to the neglect of the musically indifferent pupils. When, progressively throughout the seventeenth and eighteenth centuries, music was questioned as an essential part of both academic education and worship, the cantor's status dropped, and the cantor contributed less to the academic life of the school (Schünemann 1928 p. 224). Bach's disputes with the rector J. A. Ernesti are ample testimony to the frictions involved (Minear

1975). J. S., C. P. E. Bach and Telemann all avoided teaching Latin. Indeed Telemann - that great advocate of singing and music education - even neglected the general singing lessons (Schulze 1977).

Studies of the background to Bach's education have shown that he undoubtedly benefited both from traditional Lutheran teaching and from the idealist educational reforms of the seventeenth century (Petzoldt 1982, 1985). Luther's catechisms were designed as a basis for religious education and the same question-and-answer style is evident in other school books, noticeably those concerned with the rudiments of music.[2] Rhetoric and logic were also fundamental to the traditional education system and were obviously considered as the means by which the pupils could disseminate their learning and religion (in keeping with Luther's concern to preach the word, through the 'priesthood of all believers').

Music - and especially singing - in Bach's educational environment was a system of communication, transmitting the word of God through its structure and *Affekt*.

THE 'CANTABILE' STYLE

It is all too easy to interpret Bach's exhortation to the 'cantabile' style within the bounds of modern singing technique, in other words an intense legato style with a tremendous dynamic range enhanced by vibrato. In examining singing style in Bach's time we should perhaps begin with the most obvious and certain essentials before inferring other features of style and articulation. The first indispensable feature of singing which sets it apart from other forms of musical performance is the delivery of words.

Mattheson suggests that the instrumentalist must be aware of the advantage words give to singing:

. . .ein Spieler, oder der für Instrumente was setzet, muß alles, was zu einer guten Melodie und Harmonie erfordert wird, viel fleißiger beobachten, als ein Sänger, oder der für Sing-Stimmen componirt: dies weil man bey dem Singen die deutlichsten Worte zum Beistande hat; woran es hergegen bey Instrumenten allemahl fehlet.

(. . .an instrumentalist or one who composes for instruments must observe that which is required for a good melody and harmony even more assiduously than a singer or one who composes for voices, since one has the aid of the clearest words in singing, while instruments are always lacking these.)

(Mattheson 1739 p. 82)

Mersenne suggests that woodwind tonguing creates the same life in performance that words do in singing; playing without tonguing resembles dead or mute things (Mersenne 1636 vol. 1, Wind Instruments 5 p. 235).

The relationship between verbal and musical metre is of particular importance to articulation, especially when the writing is syllabic. With the invention of opera and recitative, *Rhythmopoeia* became a favourite topic of musical discourses (Houle 1987 pp. 62-77). Bacilly (1668) wrote at length about the duration of French syllables in singing; Marpurg (1758) approached vocal composition from the standpoint of poetic metre and syllabic stress. Music itself was also governed by a hierarchy of quantitative stresses inherent in the theory of the two-part tactus (Houle 1987 pp. 78-84). This influenced many other features in the organization of musical structures, not least the preparation and sounding of dissonance. W. C. Printz acknowledged this basic pairing in further divisions of the metre, providing the first account in a compositional treatise of 'good' and 'bad' notes, a concept which had been evident in performance since the sixteenth century (Printz 1696 pp. 18-19; Houle 1987 p. 80). This system needs to be observed 'so wohl wegen des Textes / als auch wegen der *Consonant*ien und *Dissonant*ien' ('on account both of the text and of the consonances and dissonances') (*ibid.* Printz). J. G. Walther – a close associate and relative of Bach – draws heavily on Printz's writing:

Quantitas Intrinseca Notarum (welche auch *Quantitas accentualis* genennet wird) ist diejenige Länge, wenn etliche dem *valore* nach sonst gleich geltende Noten, gantz ungleich *tractir*et werden, also, daß eine gegen die andere ihres gleichen, bald lang, bald kurtz ist. Z.E.

Example A

In diesem *Exempel* sind zwar die Noten, der äuserlichen Geltung nach, einander gleich (weil es neml. lauter Achtel sind) aber der innerl. Geltung nach ist die 1.3.5.7te lang; und die 2.4.6.8te kurtz. Und dieses rühret von der verborgenen Kraft der Zahlen her.

(*Quantitas Intrinseca Notarum* (which is also called *Quantitas accentualis*) refers to those lengths, in the case of several notes of equal value, which are performed unequally, so that these equal notes are alternately long and short. In this example, the notes are, in their outward values, equal with each other (because they are purely quavers) but the inner value is such that the 1.3.5.7th are long, the 2.4.6.8th short. And this originates from the concealed power of numbers.)   (Walther 1708 p. 23)

Writers of treatises addressed purely to practical singing also stressed the importance of metrical accent. J. F. Doles, who came into contact with Bach during his university career, 1739-44, became cantor of the Thomasschule in 1756. His unpublished tutor relates 'good' and 'bad' notes to a strengthening and weakening of the voice ('Stärke und Schwäche der Stimme', Schneiderheinze 1985 pp. 60-1). Similar references are found in the singing methods of Agricola (1757 p. 73), Marpurg (1763 pp. 76-7) and Petri (1782 p. 160). Singers thus sang syllabic music with some regard to the relationship between the stress of the words and the metrical stress of the music. As with speech, the differentiation of strong and weak syllables and notes is achieved both through dynamics and length of notes.

Presumably the metrical hierarchy also influenced the performance of melismas when there was no change of syllable. If Printz is to be believed, articulation was so subtle that the steps between notes in running figures are 'scarcely noticeable' ('Daß man das Schreiten nicht fast vermercke', Printz 1678 pp. 43-4). However, the overwhelming evidence from seventeenth- and early-eighteenth-century sources is that a detached performance of runs had priority over a 'legato' style. Tosi, the writer of the most influential singing treatise of the early eighteenth century, gave clear advice for the standard articulation of *passages* or *divisions*:

3. *Division*, according to the general Opinion, is of two Kinds, the Mark'd, and the Gliding; which last, from its Slowness and Dragging, ought rather to be called a Passage or Grace, than a *Division*.
4. In regard to the first, the Master ought to teach the Scholar that light Motion of the Voice, in which the Notes that constitute the Division be all articulate in equal Proportion, and moderately distinct, that they be not too much join'd, nor too much mark'd.   (Galliard 1742 p. 52)

This view seems in exact accordance with that of Bacilly, writing about French music, over fifty years before: passages should be learned first by practising throat accents as heavily and slowly as possible ('assez lentement'; Bacilly 1668 p. 228). He then mentions another type of passage where the throat accent is not equally applied to each note ('il y a des endroits qui ne demandent pas que le gosier frape avec un soin égal chacune des Nottes'; *ibid*. pp. 234-5). He recommends this particularly for a series of three notes. This somewhat specialized and ornamental performance of passages is likewise specified by Tosi:

5. The second is perform'd in such a Manner, that the first Note is a Guide to all that follow, closely united, gradual, and with such Evenness of Motion, that in Singing it imitates a certain Gliding, by the Masters called a *Slur*; the Effect of which is truly agreeable when used sparingly. . .
7. The Use of the *Slur* is pretty much limited in Singing, and is confined within such few Notes ascending or descending, that it cannot go beyond a fourth without displeasing.   (Galliard 1742 p. 53)

Interestingly, the footnotes added in Galliard's translation link vocal articulation to instrumental and not vice versa: 'The *mark'd Divisions* should be something like the *Staccato* on the Violin, but not too much. . .' (*ibid*. p. 52); 'The *Gliding Notes* are like several Notes in one Stroke of the Bow on the Violin' (*ibid*. p. 53).

J. F. Agricola's footnotes to his translation of Tosi into German (1757 p. 124) are even more informative: in connection with the *marked division*, he states that the vowels on which such passages are made should be repeated gently with as many repercussions as there are notes (in the manner of tonguing for wind instruments and bowing for strings). With smooth passages, only the vowel of the first note is articulated (*ibid*. p. 126).

Agricola also warns against singing all runs in the same way, suggesting that several grades of articulation are necessary:

Viele Sänger haben nur einerley Maaß ihrer Geschwindigkeit, in welches sich alle Passagien schicken müssen, wenn sie gelingen sollen. Ein großer Vortheil nicht nur zur Deutlichkeit, sondern auch zu desto sicherer Beobachtung einer gleichen Bewegung des Tacts, ist es, wenn man von vier oder drei geschwinden Noten, allemal der ersten einen kleinen Nachdruck giebt, welchen ich hier durch Strichelchen andeuten will:

Example B

(Many singers have only one rate of velocity, into which all passages must fit, if they are to be successful. It is a greater advantage, not only to clarity but also to the surer observation of the equal movement of the bar, if one always gives a small stress to the first of four or three running notes, which I will indicate here by small strokes.)   (*ibid*. p. 129)

Exactly the same advice is given by Hiller (1774 p. 178), who succeeded Doles as Thomas-cantor in 1789. Such evidence suggests that runs should be cleanly articulated and bar accents (i.e. 'good' and 'bad' notes) observed.

General comments about singing style in the eighteenth century – other than those relating specifically to passages or divisions – show an increasing emphasis on a fundamentally legato style. Marpurg's comment that one should sustain each note through to the next with no intervening space is echoed in the writings of Doles and Hiller (Marpurg 1763 p. 22; Schneiderheinze 1985 p. 60; Hiller 1774 p. 74). This trend clearly relates to the changes in musical style and aesthetics where concepts such as 'melody' and 'phrase' were increasingly emphasized. We must therefore be wary of assuming 'cantabile' in Bach's music to refer to a continuous legato. The importance of words and the 'grammatical' accentuation of the music suggest that *clarity* is perhaps the major component of the style.

One other feature necessary in singing is the taking and apportionment of breath and this, together with the sense of the words and musical line, contributes to another important element of singing: expression, the oratorical and pathetic accentuation rather than the grammatic.

RHETORIC AND THE RELATIONSHIP BETWEEN COMPOSER AND PERFORMER

Rhetoric was a fundamental of education and humanist thought and is a useful basis from which to study the grammatical and the expressive together. Seventeenth-century rationalism led to the belief that there were finite causes of mood which would eventually be explained rather in terms of the laws of mechanics.[3] There is no certain evidence that every composer followed the same basic rhetorical rules of composition – the numerous writings from Burmeister to Mattheson notwithstanding – but such is the prevalence of rhetorical analogies in treatises that we should expect at least the flavour of rhetoric to be found within the music. This seems even more likely when we consider the reforms of the *seconda prattica* and the musical language of Bach's day: music and its structures were – at least officially – to be subservient to verbal language and expression.

Bach's knowledge of rhetoric and its relation to music is unequivocally recorded by the Leipzig lecturer in rhetoric, Birnbaum, a great supporter of Bach (see Eggebrecht 1970 pp. 269-70; Kloppers 1965

p. 65). Eggebrecht also cites the title-page of the Inventions as a direct allusion to rhetorical art (*ibid*. Eggebrecht).[4] Three levels derived from rhetorical teaching are implied: *Inventio*, *Dispositio* or *Elaboratio*, and *Pronuntiatio* or *Elocutio*. *Inventio* is the basic idea or view to be expressed: this can easily be related to the 'single' *Affekt* traditionally associated with each piece of music, or, in more abstract music, the overriding figuration and techniques involved. *Elaboratio* is the basic skeleton of the piece, its major sections and events. *Decoratio* is the continuation of the same process, adding details and individual words or phrases. *Elecutio* is the performance of the speech (Kloppers 1965 pp. 56-65, 196). Thus he who writes a speech must also deliver it in the appropriate manner and vice versa.

The direct link between musical ideas, composition and performance seems a crucial factor in any study of Bach's performance practice. This is highlighted in the introduction to Printz's *Satyrischer Componist* (1696) and in J. G. Walther's definition of *Musica Practica*:

Die Abtheilung der *Music* ist zweyerley, / nemlich / *Theoretica* und *Practica*. . . .*Musica Practica*. . .bestehet in einer steten Übung, welche machet, daß man die in *musica-theoretica* gelegten *fundamenta* mit Nutzen anwenden und anbringen kann.
Unter diesen sind enthalten
1. *Musica Modulatoria*, welche lehret, wie man wohl singen, oder allerhand *Instrumenta tractir*en kann.
2. *Musica Poëtica*. . .oder die *musicali*sche *Composition*, unter richet, wie man eine liebliche und reine Zusammenstimmung der Klänge erstlich *inventir*en, und hernach aufsetzen und zu Papier bringen soll, damit selbige hernachmahls kann gesungen oder gespielet werden. Und solche Zusammenstimmung nennet man nachgehends einen Gesang.

(Music is divided into two fields: Theory and Practice. . .Practical music consists of a continual practice, which means that one can use and apply the fundamentals laid down in the theory. In this category there are
1. *Musica Modulatoria*, which teaches one how to sing or to play all kinds of instruments.
2. *Musica Poetica*. . .or musical composition, which shows one first how to devise a charming and pure agreement of notes, and subsequently to represent this on paper, so that later the same can be sung or played. And one can furthermore term such sounding together, melody.) (Walther 1708 pp. 14-15)

Bach's testimonials for his more talented pupils suggest that they had acquired equal expertise in composition and performance: F. G. Wild, for instance, learned transverse flute and harpsichord but also studied 'the Clavier, Thorough Bass, and the fundamental rules of composition based thereupon. . .' (*Dok* vol. 1 p. 127).[5] J. C. Weyrauch mastered various instruments, sang and was well versed in the art of composition (*Dok* vol. 1 pp. 135-6).[6] These students thus learned composition through the practical medium óf the keyboard and not as mere academic study.

Not only, then, was it likely that performers had at least an awareness of the process from invention through composition to performance; the performer could also play a substantial role in the *Decoratio* level of the composition. Expression and arousal of the *Affekt*s were inextricably linked with free ornamentation and clearly viewed as a function of rhetoric:

Gleich wie eines *Oratoris* Ampt ist / nicht allein eine *Oration* mit schönen anmutigen lebhafftigen Worten / unnd herrlichen *Figuris* zu zieren / sondern auch recht zu *pronuncijren*. und die *affectus* zu *moviren*. . .

(As with the office of an orator, [performance] involves not only the adorning of an oration with beautiful, charming, lively words and wonderful figures, but also correct pronunciation and moving of the *Affekt*.)

(Praetorius 1619 p. 229)

Praetorius' comments were reproduced exactly by several later writers in the seventeenth century - Herbst (1642/53), Crüger (1660) and Falck (1688) - so they clearly reflect the flavour of German Baroque performance (Allerup 1931).

Printz gives perhaps the most informative account of 'musica modulatoria vocalis'. He demands considerable musical awareness from the performer and a proper knowledge and application of 'figures':

Wir kommen nun auf das achte *Requisitum* eines guten Sängers / welches ist die Wissenschafft , und zierliche *Formir*ung der *Musicali*schen *Figur*en / welche gleichsam das Saltz der Melodeyen sind: Denn gleich wie eine ungesaltzene Speise; also ist eine Melodey ohne *Figur*en wenig annehmlich.

(We come now to the eighth requisite of a good singer, which is the specialist's knowledge and elegant formation of musical figures, which could well be termed the salt of melodies: for like an unsalted dish, a melody without figures is hardly palatable.)

(Printz 1678 p. 42)

Bernhard shows that added coloratura is connected with a particular style of singing, *cantar passagiato*, that associated with the modern *stylus luxurians*, which was essentially an elaboration of the *stylus gravis* of the Renaissance. However, even in the simpler style - *cantar sodo* - embellishment can be added: this includes both features of expression - *piano, forte* - and ornamental figures - *anticipatione*

della syllaba/nota, accentus, etc. (Hilse 1973 pp. 13-14). In his compositional treatises he discusses added figuration under the heading
Figurae Superficiales.

Clearly, then, skilled singers in seventeenth-century Germany played
some part in the *Decoratio* of music, embellishing 'bland' music using
their knowledge of specific formulae or *figurae*. This practice originated in Italy and was greatly emulated by German writers (Neumann
1978 pp. 532-42). The subtitles in writings of Praetorius and his
followers unashamedly stress their reliance on Italian style, offering
instruction in the 'jetzige Italienische Manier'. Publications of music by
Praetorius (*Polyhymnia Caduceatrix*, Frankfurt 1619) and T. Michael
(*Musicalischer Seelen-Lust ander Theil*, Leipzig 1637), cantor at
the Thomasschule, show alternative versions of. certain passages:
coloratura for the more experienced singers and simple versions for
beginners. Michael is somewhat embarrassed at adding coloratura in
print since he considers that embellishment added extemporaneously
by talented singers is always superior (Preface to *Quinta Vox*).

The style of music itself was thus heavily influenced by the coloratura, which was originally the domain of singers. This is made
remarkably clear by J. G. Walther, who draws heavily on the writings
of Bernhard. Walther and Bernhard describe two types of figures:
Figurae Fundamentales and *Figurae Superficiales*. To the former
belong such devices as syncopation, passing notes and fugal style.
However, *Figurae Superficiales*, secondary figures, are regarded as
improvised ornamentation that has gradually been adopted by
composers:

Allein in 15 *seculo*, haben die *Componis*ten allbereit angefangen, eines und
das andere zu setzen, was denen vorigen unbekannt, auch denen Unverstän-
digen unzuläßlich geschienen; guten *musical*. Ohren aber annehml. gewesen:
denn nachdem sie *observi*ret, daß künstl. Sänger und *Instrumenti*sten von
denen Noten hier und dort abgewichen, und also andere anmuthige *Figuren*
angebracht, haben sie solche nachgehens auch gesetzet, daß nunmehr
unsere heutige *Music* wegen Menge der *Figuren* fügl. einer *Rhetorica* zu
vergleichen ist.

(Even in the fifteenth century composers were already beginning to write
one thing or another that was previously unknown, and indeed would have
seemed unacceptable to the uncomprehending but pleasing to good musical
ears; for, when it was noticed that artful singers and instrumentalists diverged
here and there from the notes, and brought in other graceful *figures*, they also
composed such devices, so that our music of today is to be justly compared
with a *rhetoric*, on account of the quantity of *figures*.)

(Walther 1708 p. 152)[7]

According to late-seventeenth-century German theory, then, the current musical style was an extensive elaboration of earlier forms, the composer drawing on well-known figures which had been developed through improvised ornamentation (Schmitz 1952; Neumann 1978 pp. 532-43). When it is considered that Bernhard and Walther viewed the added figures as the elaboration of a fundamental *prima prattica* structure - in other words there is a hierarchy of diminution within the music - and further that such a style resembled a rhetoric, it is not unreasonable to infer that figuration in performance would have been given some form of delineation.

'FIGURAE'

Certainly Printz considered that singers should be aware of the figuration constituting a musical passage. He describes two kinds of *figurae*: *simple figures*, which are not immediately preceded or succeeded by others, and *compound figures*, which are composed of smaller figures in succession. The following comment implies that the performer should somehow mark each figure:

Hier erinnern wir ins gemein / daß eine jede *Figur* ihren manierlichen *Apulsum gutturalem* haben müsse / daß ist / ein Anschlagen / welches in der Kehle gemacht werden soll mit einer natürlichen Geschickligkeit / nicht mit einem garstigen Drücken. . .

(Here we must stress that in general every figure must have its mannerly *Apulsum Gutturalem*, that is, a delineation which should be made in the throat with a natural skill and not with a nasty thrust. . .)

(Printz 1678 p. 43)

J. S. Beyer, writing in 1703, states that the practice of adding coloratura - other than that which the composer has specified - is no longer in use. However, he includes examples of ornamented cadences, 'zum blossen *Exercitio* der Jugend' ('purely for the practice of youth', Beyer 1703 p. 60). Thus singers were still proficient in performing coloratura even if they no longer improvised it themselves.

Even Marpurg, writing over a decade after Bach's death, suggests that the 'set figures' within a passage are part of the rhetoric of the music and are derived from the drawing together or diminution of the bar divisions (Marpurg 1763 p. 144).[8] Hiller, speaking to the less-informed readership of the late eighteenth century (1774 pp. 175-89), clearly follows traditional methods of devising and performing passages. The singer compiles them from melodic figures and delineates the principal note of each figure.

Printz and Hiller – writing one hundred years apart – both stress the singer's awareness of the figures making up a melisma. The former 'composer' of the *Decoratio* – the singer – must perform with the correct *Elocutio*.

The articulation suggested by these comments concerning musical figuration is achieved by delineating the first note of a figure. The most common figures in Bach's music seem to be those implying particular rhythmic patterns. They are also particularly adaptable, harmonically and melodically. Printz describes three 'mixed' figures which 'partly remain [on the same note], partly move neatly, partly spring' ('Vermengte Figuren sind / so theils bleiben / theils ordentlich gehen / theils springen', Printz 1673 pp. 53–5). The *corta* consists of two short notes followed by one long (or vice versa):

Example C

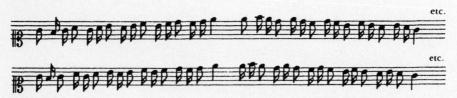

Printz also introduces a syncopated version which he considers rare.

The *messanza* according to Printz is a four-note figure consisting of notes which are both conjunct and disjunct. Although the examples contain several patterns, the predominant form – with a three-note conjunct figure followed or preceded by a leap – is distinctive in Bach's music (and is particularly suited to violin and keyboard styles) and will generally be termed *messanza* in this survey:

Example D

The *suspirans* is characterized by its upbeat quality with a rest for the first of four quarter divisions of the beat:

Example E

The *corta* and *suspirans* are specified by J. G. Walther in his article on *figura* in the *Lexicon* (1732 p. 244). Although they are not necessarily articulated consistently, a performer's knowledge of them might be important in the dividing and delineation of runs.

No mention has been made so far of the length of notes or the relationship between notes constituting a figure. A 'slurred' style seems to be associated with specific harmonic features, especially dissonance. Bernhard defines *figura* in general as a method of employing dissonances (Hilse 1973 p. 77). Printz and Walther make the *affective* role of dissonance particularly clear by relating dissonances to night, winter or black, the consonances to day, summer or white; one is not appreciated without the balance of its opposite (Printz 1696 p. 92; Walther 1708 p. 140).[9] The slurred style associated with harmonic accents, resolutions and passing notes seems mirrored by comments – particularly concerned with the *accentus* – in practical singing tutors. Praetorius may well imply a legato style with his description of the *accentus*: 'Accentus ist: Wenn die Noten folgender Gestalt im Halse gezogen werden.' ('*Accentus* is the drawing in the throat of notes of the following type', Praetorius 1619 p. 232).

The example abounds with notes at very close intervals (although no slurs are marked). Beyer likewise uses the term 'gezogen' in the definition and realization of the *accentus*, which he describes as notes moving from a line to a space or from a space to a line (Beyer 1703 p. 54).[10] In these cases some sort of slurring of close intervals may be implied.

Bernhard adopts the *accentus* as the first of his *Figurae Superficiales*, describing it according to its harmonic function. Walther copies him word for word:

Superjectio.
Insgemein *Accentus* genennet, ist eine Auf- oder Abschleifung von einer
Consonanz in eine *Dissonanz*; oder von einer *Dissonanz* in eine *Consonanz*
per secundam.

Example F

(*Superjectio* – generally termed *accentus*, is a sliding up or down from a consonance to a dissonance, or from a dissonance to a consonance, in seconds.)

(Walther 1708 p. 152)

Bernhard and Walther also relate the *accentus* to dotted rhythms
articulated by particular forms of syllabic underlay. Beyer also gives
clear examples of these devices:

[*Accentus*]. . .ist fast nichts anders als bey denen Weltschen *Anticipatione*
oder *Retardatione della Nota e della Syllaba?*
Was ist *Anticipatione della Syllaba?*
Wenn die *Syllaba* zu einer andern Noten / da sie doch eigentlich nicht
hingehöret / durch *secund*en und *Terti*en gezogen wird:

Example G

Con · fi · te · bor__ Ti · bi__ Do · mi · ne in . . .

Was ist *Anticipatione della nota?*
Wenn man einen Theil der vorhergehenden *Note* zur folgenden ziehet:

Example H

In Te Do · mi · ne spe · ra · vi, spe · ra · vi, spe · ra · vi

(*Accentus.* . .isn't that none other than those Italian anticipations or retardations of notes or syllables? *Anticipatione della syllaba* is the slurring of
syllables through seconds and thirds to other notes, to which, in fact, they do
not belong.
Anticipatione della nota is the drawing of a part of the preceding note to the
following.)   (Beyer 1703 pp. 54-6)[11]

It should be noticed that actual slurs are used in these examples
which, although primarily added to indicate underlay, clearly reflect
the grouping of the figure and its smooth articulation. Doles unequivocally relates appoggiaturas both to slurring and to accentuation
(Schneiderheinze 1985 p. 62).[12]

The association of dissonance with slurring may have led composers
and singers to slur noticeably conjunct figures. The relationship between chromaticism, close intervals and 'pathetic' *Affekts* is substantiated by Walther's description of false relations (1708 p. 157).[13] Bernhard further suggests that articulation might be influenced by the
Affekt: strong passions such as Joy and Anger would not be especially
slurred, but sorrowful and gentle words require a milder, slurred style.
He recommends that such a *cantar d'affetto* be emulated by instrumentalists, despite the absence of text (Hilse 1973 pp. 20-1).[14]
Sharper articulation, for certain figures, was recommended from
the time of Praetorius. *Gruppi* (cadential turns) need to be 'scherffer
als die Tremoli angeschlagen werden' ('more sharply attacked than
tremoli') and a clear, sharp performance is required of *tiratas* (fast runs
up and down) (Praetorius 1619 p. 236).

Later writers introduce slurs in their examples of passage-work.
Kürzinger (1763 pp. 34-48), like Beyer, demonstrates the dotted form
of the *anticipatione della nota* with a slur, but he also slurs simple
four-note patterns, such as the *groppo* (group of conjunct notes, the
first and third being usually of the same pitch) and *tirata* (shooting
run of conjunct notes). Many examples show first a version in plain
notes, then one with added figures and slurs. Here again, harmonic
implications might be evident, since such figures often constitute the
ornamentation of a single note. Slurs might warn against accenting
the inessential within the figure.

Vocal articulation, then, may have been influenced by a number
of factors. Longer note values were obviously related to the strength
and length of syllables and their position in the musical metre. Faster
values - constituting the *Decoratio* - were lightly articulated, accentuation within passages being influenced by bar acccents. If the singer

had been brought up in the Italian/Lutheran tradition he would have delineated the standard figures within the passage according to his knowledge of ornamentation and musical rhetoric. Certain figures of a dissonant or 'pathetic' nature might well have been sung in a specifically 'slurred' style, the 'gliding passage or Grace' which writers of the Tosi tradition considered as ornamental.

We have no source relating directly to Bach's performance practice. His pupil, Kirnberger, suggests that the music of Bach and its performance be regarded as a special case (at least in the musical scene some twenty years after Bach's death). In a study of dissonant passing notes, he states that, for the prospective composer,

Es ist beßer, daß man hierin den Capallmeister *Graun*, den wohlklingendsten und nachdenklichsten Setzer für den schönen Gesang, als *Händel* oder *J. S. Bach* zum Muster nehme. Der letztere wagte hierin am meisten, daher erfordern seine Sachen einen ganz besondern Vortrag, der seiner Schreibart genau angepaßt ist; denn sonst sind viele von seinen Sachen kaum anzuhören.

(It is better to take Kapellmeister Graun, the most euphonious and thoughtful composer of beautiful melody, than Handel or J. S. Bach as a model. The latter was most adventurous in this respect, and his works thus require a very special execution that is exactly suited to his style; for, otherwise, many of his works would sound hardly bearable.)   (Kirnberger 1771 p. 216)

Could this 'special' style be related to the 'rhetorical' method of performing, delineating the components of the *Decoratio*? Later styles of singing, with their greater emphasis on legato, may well have obscured such figures in the name of melody, thus destroying the shape of the music and causing each contrapuntal part to be too overbearing.

SLURS AND UNDERLAY

By far the most common use of slurs in notated music is as an indication of textual underlay. Slurs were first used as a substitute for ligatures, which had been rendered redundant by the introduction of progressively smaller note values in notation. Praetorius (1619 p. 29) was one of the first writers to recommend such a substitution.

J. G. Walther, writing nearly a century later (1708 p. 35), likewise relates ligatures and slurs to notes performed to one syllable only. His observation that slurs are often omitted in longer melismas reflects well the general inconsistency of use at this time. He also notes that slurs have a different function in string music, indicating notes to be played in one stroke. This suggests that, while slurs had some bearing on articulation in instrumental music, their role in vocal music was purely to denote underlay. Moreover, the fact that many melismas were sung with some degree of articulation suggests that slurs in vocal music cannot necessarily be interpreted as indications of legato.

The most obvious instances in Bach's vocal works where slurs merely indicate underlay is when text is omitted. Here the slurs show, in the autograph score at least, the position of syllables to be reproduced by the copyist of the parts. Many chorales from the Leipzig cantatas fall into this category; not only was the chorale itself often added after the rest of the cantata had been composed (apart from those cantatas based on chorales themselves) but the verse to be sung was sometimes chosen later (Marshall 1972 vol. 1 pp. 66–7). Slurs indicate the placing of text in such cases, and indeed these are quite often adopted by the doubling instrumental parts.

Sometimes text is omitted (when it is to be repeated) in the course of a more complex movement. In the opening chorus of BWV 245, bb. 50–5, the text 'dessen Ruhm in allen Landen' is repeated successively in all the vocal parts. In the autograph P 28, the text is often omitted: in such instances the melisma 'Lan' receives a long slur and the repeated quavers (sung to separate syllables) are all individually flagged. Both these measures are clearly a shorthand for text underlay (see Plate 1).

The most striking example of slurs being added to clarify underlay is in the printed parts of BWV 71, produced by the Mühlhausen town council in 1708. The use of movable type precludes the beaming of notes into separate groups. Since each note is individually flagged, the grouping and underlay of notes are difficult to discern without the slurs.

SLURS AND ARTICULATION

Yet some vocal slurring may indicate a particular style of articulation. One of the earliest uses of slurs is in Monteverdi's *Il quarto libro de madrigali* (1603). 'Piagne e sospira' opens with four conjunct chromatic semibreves in all voices. These are clearly slurred in pairs (as are later instances of this material). The chromaticism and text both suggest a pathetic *Affekt* which seems appropriate in view of the later writings on the *accentus* and its association with the 'night/winter' of dis-

1 St John Passion, BWV 245/1, bb. 51-61. Mus. MS P 28

sonance. Slurs are used very sporadically for two-note chromatic figures elsewhere.

Praetorius uses slurs at matching places in the two cantus parts of 'Siehe wie fein und lieblich ist' from *Polyhymnia Caduceatrix* (1618–19) (Example 1). Given the number of unslurred melismas elsewhere, these

Example 1

slurs are hardly necessary as indications of underlay. Evidently they relate to the stylish performance of one of the *accentus* figures, the *anticipatione della nota* (slurs were indicated for this figure by Beyer in his treatise of 1703; see p. 22 above). Praetorius gives the unornamented version in plain minims; thus slurs are associated with the ornamental *Decoratio*.

A similar selective use of slurs for dotted figures is evident in the works of J. R. Ahle, a predecessor of Bach at Mühlhausen: for example in the first motet of *Erster Theil Geistlicher Dialogen* (1648).

In Bach's music the slurring of longer four-note *circolo/groppo* figures undoubtedly reflects the momentum of the music, linking all the notes within one harmony and implying an accent only on the first note of the slur. In BWV 133/2, b. 11, the slurred pattern preserves the accentual outline of the previous bar (Example 2).

Example 2

The rhetorical power of the *corta* rhythm can be quite pronounced, especially in the *anapaestic* version. In BWV 245/23a (St 111) the slurred *corta* throws the accent on to the weak 'bad' part of the beat; this syncopation creates an unusual accent on 'diesen', which is particularly appropriate in this context. Here the rhythm, underlay and accentual slur are chosen to evoke the taunting of Pilate (Example 3).

Example 3

Lä·ssest du die · sen los.   so bist du des . . .

The rare *anticipatione della syllaba* is slurred in BWV 211/8 (P 141, parts Wien SA.67.B.32), b. 20 etc., presumably to underline the comedy of the piece, since in each case the slur implies the accentuation of the weak syllables (Example 4).

Example 4

Heu · te _ noch.   heu · te _ noch.   lie · ber_   Va · ter, thut es _ doch

One further possible function of slurs has not been covered so far. Robinson (1715 p. 22) seems one of the first writers to link slurs with breathing: 'Sometimes several Notes are to be sung in one Syllabe, and by consequence in one Breath, which then are generally limitted with a Tye.' Jablonsky's general encyclopaedia and Walther's *Lexicon* suggest that a similar use prevailed in eighteenth-century Germany (Jablonsky 1717 p. 145; Walther 1732 p. 94).

Such references to breathing imply some shaping of the musical line. Certainly an increasing interest in phrasing during the eighteenth century is suggested by Mattheson's comments on the 'flowing' of singing and J. J. Rousseau's emphasis on phrasing in singing (Mattheson 1739 pp. 150-2; Rousseau 1768 pp. 376-7). Perhaps some of the longer and apparently redundant slurs added to Bach voice parts (e.g. BWV 97/1 in St 64) dictate a style of performance like that implied by modern phrase marks.

DOTS

The use of dots and information relating to their use is far sparser than that for slurs. One of the first general definitions of the dot is Walther's *Punctus Percutiens* (Walther 1708 p. 34). Marked notes are 'dergleichen gestoßen' ('equally detached'). In Walther's *Lexicon* (1732 p. 204) the *Détaché* (*abgezuckt*) defines notes lasting for half their value.

Both dots and strokes are used in music of this period, Doles and Marpurg both implying that dots and strokes mean the same thing (Schneiderheinze 1985 p. 57; Marpurg 1763 p. 142). Quite often the choice of dots or strokes may have been in the hands of the printer.

Sometimes dots or strokes might have accentual implications. Agricola uses small wedge-like strokes in one example (see p. 14 above) to indicate a small accent ('kleinen Nachdruck'). However, it is noticeable that Agricola adds 'I will indicate with strokes. . .', as if their meaning might not be fixed and thus not obvious to the reader.

An accentual use of strokes might sometimes be inferred from the context in which they appear. In the autograph score of Telemann's 'Ich gläube an Jesum Christum', movement 1, bb. 74-5, the vocal parts contain strokes virtually every other crotchet beat. These coincide exactly with double-stopped chords in the string parts (GB Lbm Add. MS 32389). Thus the strokes 'translate' the natural accents in the string parts into stresses in the vocal parts (Example 5).

Example 5

Walther (1708 p. 35) introduces the slur covering dots as a specific string device, the notes played in one bow-stroke, but detached. Doles describes this in vocal technique as 'Tragen der Töne' ('carrying the notes') - one should draw the first notes into the others without completely separating them (Schneiderheinze 1985 p. 58).

ARTICULATION MARKS WITHIN MELISMAS

Since singers trained in improvised coloratura, or at least in performing notated passages, would have delineated figures naturally within melismas, slurs were not generally required to indicate the component figuration. Slurs in any case were particularly useful in indicating underlay, which was often unclear in manuscripts or publications with movable type.

However Couperin's church music shows some slurs within melismas. These might imply some shaping or 'phrasing' of the line. The slurs are so inaccurately placed in the editions as to suggest no strict figural articulation (e.g. *Sept Versets du motet*, 1705 'Qui Regis Israel'). French composers were perhaps the first to show a tendency towards legato style in some keyboard idioms, so these slurs may allude to a general legato (Lohmann 1982 pp. 187–211).

Instances of slurs within melismas are rare in Bach's music. Some may suggest a style of articulation contrary to that expected by the singer, an articulation, for example, that went across the natural 'good' and 'bad' implications of the beat. The first 'Kyrie' of BWV 232 (P 180) is a good example. The predominant instrumental slurring from b. 5 is the pattern: ♪♪♪♪ The slur defines the semitone between beats 1 and 2 and 3 and 4 (but never 2 and 3 or 4 and 1). This slurring is reproduced in the vocal melismas to 'le' from b. 30, both in the autograph score, P 180, and in some of the Dresden presentation parts.

However, more often than not slurs confirm an articulation that could be inferred from other considerations. The most common slurring connected with basic figural patterns is that of paired notes. In the alto part (St 104) of BWV 47/1, b. 69, the slurring reflects an underlay which is common elsewhere (e.g. b. 72, soprano and alto) (Example 6).

Example 6

|er| · hö   het

Although this might have been a mistake on the part of the copyist[15] (confusing the pattern with that of b. 72, for instance), several slurs in this part show signs of revision or extension; the revisions to the slur-

ring may well be in Bach's hand since this is evident in some of the trills
(e.g. b. 210).

Furthermore, paired slurring is sometimes found in autograph
scores. BWV 108/1, P 82 bb. 15–16, shows figuration which clearly falls
into stepwise pairs. In BWV 88/1, P 145, dotted pairs are slurred in
quite a number of vocal melismas (e.g. b. 111) and also in the instrumental parts.

Triple divisions of the beat may also be slurred: slurs at the end of
a melisma in the tenor part (St 56) to BWV 109/3 (parts heavily edited
by Bach) might demand an accent on the first of each group, before
the cadence in b. 11 (Example 7). Here the direction of the melodic

Example 7

line might be relevant: the melisma from b. 9 has descended to *g* by
b. 10, the first slurs coinciding with a return to the tessitura at the
beginning of the run; the three slurs imply accentuation of the first
note in the group in the only ascending part of the line.

A similar slurring in the vocal part (St 13b) of BWV 76/5, bb. 6/7,
likewise stresses the first note of each group, describing the arpeggio of
C major.

The most striking examples of articulation marks within melismas
are those which resemble violin bowings. In the alto part of BWV 109/5
(St 56) the slurs and dots, bb. 102–5, are probably added in Bach's
hand since his flat dots are particularly distinctive (Example 8). The

Example 8

implications of this are complex: the dot at the beginning of each group seems to signify that each first note is somehow isolated and consequently accented. The parallel oboe part is slurred consistently in fours, which would also imply an accent on the first note of each group. The two versions are thus presumably designed to coordinate, the voice having a more detailed articulation which gives it prominence. This cantata was first prepared for 17 October 1723, near the beginning of Bach's Leipzig career. Perhaps these markings were added to demonstrate to the singer, new to Bach's music, how a melisma *might* be articulated.

This example introduces the question of dots in vocal lines. Sometimes dots are added to notes which already have separate syllables: in BWV 42/4, St 3, the dot found in the tenor part for 'nicht' presumably implies a light end to the phrase and a quick execution of the strong consonant 'cht' (Example 9).

Example 9

Dots are sometimes found within melismas, presumably dictating a shorter articulation than is standard. They may also assist in the small-scale phrasing: in the autograph score of BWV 243 (D major version, P 39), the *corta* figure is defined as an *anapaest*, with the accent on the shorter notes (Example 10). Dots in the autograph

Example 10

soprano part (St 15) of BWV 36b/7 and in the copyist's part (St 82) for BWV 36/7 demand both a lightening of the quaver figure, defined by a leap of a fourth, and a light termination of the ascending *tiratas* in b. 38 (Example 11).

Example 11

The slurs and dots in BWV 47/4, in the bass part of St 104, are quite remarkable (Example 12). The dots suggest that the first note of each

Example 12

und   den   Hoch   ·   ·   ·   muth

of the *messanza* figures is isolated, the slur acting in the manner of a modern 'phrase mark' or merely as an indication of underlay.

The same separation of the first note of the *messanza* is evident in the instrumental parts, from b. 1, in quaver note values: ♪♪♪♪ The markings in bb. 36-7 may also allude to the upbeat syncopated figures in the instrumental parts from b. 9: ♪♫♫♫ The markings in b. 45 are even more unusual (Example 13). These

Example 13

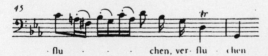

· flu   ·   ·   · chen, ver· flu · chen

imply a shortening of the first note in each pair with a slurring to the second. If these marks are accurately placed, they are unique in Bach's music, perhaps suggesting some form of Lombard rhythm: ♫ .

Larger rhythmic patterns within the music might be implied by slurs. In BWV 248/54 the pattern: ♫♫♫ / ♫♫♫ is evident in the vocal lines of both score and parts (P 32, St 112). This is established from the beginning in the instrumental parts and seems to dictate a specific rhythmic style, dividing each bar into a long downbeat followed by a short upbeat (or vice versa). This regularity of rhythm derives from the dance patterns which so often influence the structure and metre of Bach's music. Moreover the slurring reveals the rhythm opening the main subject of the movement, further evidence for the relationship between slurs and the diminution of the *Decoratio* (Example 14).

Example 14

Other vocal slurs within melismas may be of expressive rather than rhythmic importance. In BWV 98/3, P 160 b. 31, the slur coincides with a particularly *affective* chromatic passage to the word 'weinen' (Example 15). Here the repeated steps in b. 31 demand some form of

Example 15

articulation within the slur. The latter must function then as an 'affective' device, a mnemonic which might influence both the singer's tone and rhythm.

These examples of articulation marks used to delineate figures or rhythmic patterns within Bach's music can be interpreted in two ways: the comparative rarity of such markings may suggest that the singers were normally aware of this style of articulation, these examples being included to assist an inexperienced performer. Conversely, they might indicate *exceptions* to an otherwise standard style of articulation, perhaps totally legato, or based purely on metrical accent. If it is assumed that the normal role of slurs in vocal music is to indicate underlay it is unlikely that they should be used systematically in any other way. Since all the examples cited conform to the type of articulation we would expect with regard to the *figurae* concerned, it seems likely that Bach's markings represent a clarification of the norm. Furthermore, a control example from BWV 71/6 (St 377) shows that melismas were not automatically sung legato. The ripieno soprano part of b. 29 sings a simplified version of the run, which delineates a *suspirans* rhythm (Example 16).

Example 16

2

Articulation marks in string playing

BACKGROUND: STRING PLAYING IN MUSICAL EDUCATION

A study of the background to performance conventions is particularly desirable in string music: slurring relates closely to playing technique and may be notated merely for the convenience of the player and not for specific interpretative reasons. A glance at any of Bach's sources shows that instrumental parts contain substantially more articulation marks than the vocal parts. Did he include such detailed directions because he could not rely on his performers' technique, or because he deemed the performance practice to be fundamental to the musical style of each piece? Although we shall never know the details of Bach's performances, it is hoped that a detailed study of contemporary conventions will give us more insight into the relationships between performer, composer and notation.

Professional performers of Bach's time were presumably educated in an oral tradition, current in church, town and court circles. String playing was still relatively new in Lutheran music and school education, and not until secular music came more to the forefront of German musical taste in the eighteenth century were string tutors published in any quantity. This was the period of greatest expansion in non-specialist music-making; more players required clear instruction from books.

The versatility required in church institutions is well demonstrated by Bach's testimonials for his pupils:

Ihnen aber doch einen kleinen *proegustum* zu geben, so ist er *in compositione* wohl bewandert, hat auch verschiedene *specimina* alhier mit gutem *applausu* abgeleget; fernerhin spielet Er eine gute Orgel und *Clavier*, ist fertig auf

35

der *Violin*, *Violoncello*, v. andern *Instrumenten*, singet einen wo nicht alzu starcken doch artigen *Bass*, und ist überhaupt so / beschaffen, daß glaube, er werde zu der *vacanten* Stelle gar wohl können *embloiret* werden.

(To give you a slight foretaste, he is thoroughly expert as a composer and has given various samples of his work here with good acclaim. Furthermore he plays a good organ and clavier, is accomplished on the violin, violoncello, and other instruments, sings a bass that is, though not too strong, quite stylish, and his qualities in general are such that I believe he could well be employed for the vacant post.)   (*Dok* vol. 1 p. 48)

According to Bach's Leipzig memorandum of 1730, his singers were proficient instrumentalists and vice versa:

Fernerhin zu gedencken, daß da die 2de *Violin* meistens, die *Viola*, *Violoncello* und *Violon* aber allezeit (in Ermangelung tüchtigerer *subjectorum*) mit Schülern habe bestellen müßen: So ist leicht zu erachten was dadurch dem *Vocal Chore* ist entgangen.

(Be it furthermore remembered that, since the 2nd violin usually, but the viola, violoncello, and violone always (in the absence of more capable subjects) have had to be played by pupils, it is easy to estimate how much the chorus has been depleted in consequence.)   (*ibid*. p. 62)

That the versatility of church musicians and the constant cross-fertilization of singing and playing techniques was common in the Lutheran tradition is suggested by such treatises as the second edition of Herbst's *Musica Moderna Prattica* (1653). A small section giving ornamented cadences for violins (with directions for up- and down-bows), cornetts and flutes is added at the end (Herbst 1653 pp. 51-62). This is conspicuously absent from the first edition (1642) and from Herbst's model, Praetorius' *Syntagmatis Musici* vol. 3 (1619 - Allerup 1931 p. 7). More detailed instructions in string playing are offered in G. Falck's *Idea Boni Cantoris* (1688), another treatise inspired by Praetorius. Significantly, the first German tutor for string instruments alone comes from someone working within the *Kantorei* tradition (Merck, 1695). D. Speer's *Vierfaches musicalisches Kleeblatt* (1697) covers perhaps the widest field of *Musica Practica*: singing, clavier and thoroughbass, tuition in several instruments, and composition. A reference in J. Kuhnau's contract as cantor in 1702 shows that instrumental tuition had become an indispensable part of life in the Thomas-schule, Leipzig (Schering 1926 p. 60).

Herbst makes no essential difference between voice and instruments in his examples of ornamental figuration. Likewise, the preface to G. Muffat's *Florilegium Secundum* - primarily designed to explain the

Lullian style to a south German readership – gives examples of diminution similar to those encountered in German vocal treatises (Muffat
1698 pp. 27, 56) (Example 17). The examples marked * are particularly

Example 17

familiar, showing two-note *accentus* and *superjectio* figures. Furthermore, the cadential examples given just before this section make frequent use of the slurred pairs:　　These figures were common
currency in France, Italy and Germany, in both instrumental and vocal
music. We might expect, then, that string players possessed much the
same musical knowledge as singers and that they interpreted the music
in a similar fashion.

Leopold Mozart, writing outside the Lutheran tradition (1756),
clearly aims his words both at the amateur – giving initial instruction in the rudiments of music – and at rather more advanced players.
Nevertheless, he still demands a deep musical knowledge from the
player: '. . .ein guter Orchestergeiger aber muß viele Einsicht in
die ganze Musik, in die Setzkunst und in die Verschiedenheit der
Charakters. . .haben. . .'. ('. . .a good orchestral violinist must have
great insight into the whole art of musical composition and into the
variety of characters', Mozart 1756 p. 254).

Mozart implies that the performer's knowledge of the *Affekt* and
style of composition is of supreme importance, a view which shows
traces of the rhetorical-musical relationship emphasized by Baroque
theorists. As in singing, an awareness of the figural-rhetorical content of a passage would have influenced the player's approach to
articulation:

Man muß vorher alle Veränderungen des Bogenstriches genau zu machen wissen; man muß das Schwache und Starke am rechten Orte und mit rechtem Masse anzubringen verstehen; man muß lernen die Charakters der Stücke unterscheiden, und alle Passagen nach ihrem erforderlichen eigenen Geschmacke vortragen. . .

(One must first know how to make all variants of bowing; one must understand how to introduce weakness and strength in the right place and in the right quantity; one must learn to distinguish between the characteristics of pieces and to execute all passages according to their own particular flavour.)
(ibid. pp. 254–5)

Predictably, many of the figures introduced in the ornaments section are similar to those found in vocal writings: the *groppo* and *Cirkel*; the *tirata* (any shooting run – *ibid.* pp. 247–51). In comparison with his predecessors, Mozart uses far more slurs in conjunction with such figures, reflecting both the growing use of the 'ornament' of slurring and the increasing level of notated performance directions required by performers. As Geminiani remarked: 'Let none be startled at seeing so many different Marks over the Notes, since without the help of such Marks, no One can give Directions either to Sing or Play well' (Geminiani 1742 *preface*).

STRING-PLAYING TECHNIQUES

The drawing of the bow results in a natural articulation between each stroke. The nearest equivalents in singing are the limitation of the breath and stronger consonants. Given the length of the bow, the violin must necessarily be articulated far more frequently than the singer must breathe; the technique of producing the sound thus results in a regular mandatory articulation.

Tartini's remarks (1760 p. 11), relating bowing to breathing, are perhaps of special significance in the present study since they recall the associations commonly made between vocal and instrumental style: 'Your first study. . .should be the true manner of holding, balancing and pressing the bow lightly, but steadily, upon the strings; in such a manner as that it shall seem to breathe the first tone it gives. . .' Grüß (1988 pp. 331–2), in a study of remarks made around Bach's era (Muffat, Corrette, Eisel, Schütz), infers that bow-strokes were long and sustained unless notated with directions for staccato.

Much has been written on the 'Rule of the Down-Bow'.[1] Muffat observed that Italians disregarded the rule and generally played with alternate up- and down-bows. Indeed, Ganassi (writing about the viol, 1542 p. 10) considered it expedient that the player be able to perform with both up- and down-bows on 'good' notes, just as a swordsman must be able to use both hands in battle. Tartini, writing over two centuries later (1760 p. 17), offered similar advice: Allegros should be performed beginning with both up- and down-bows. However, the practice was clearly well known to the Italian Geminiani since his advice (1751 *preface* p. 4) in connection with one example was to ignore it.

The introduction of the rule of the down-bow by Herbst (1653 pp. 51-62) suggests that it was also known in Germany. That this treatise was primarily directed towards singers and that the bowing instructions were necessarily brief shows how fundamental the rule was. The examples themselves use 'T' (down-bow) and 'P' (up-bow). These are generally placed at the beginning of each example, allowing the remainder to be played 'as it comes', with a down-bow on most beats.

Corrette's examples of Italian bowing generally display the same continuous alternation of up- and down-bows, regardless of bar-line, as is demonstrated by Muffat's renowned Italian bowing of a minuet (Corrette 1738 pp. 27-8; Muffat 1698 p. 53). However, Corrette's Italian Andante (p. 27) contains a striking application of the rule, with two notes *unslurred* in the same bow-stroke (Example 18). This *corta*

Example 18

figure: ♪♫ * so often found in Bach's music (see p. 20 above) is one of the rhythmic features most likely to 'upset' the natural bowing-scheme in Baroque music.

The player's insertion of 'stopped' up-bow slurs ('craquer d'archet') was fundamental to French accounts of the down-bow rule. A stronger articulation was made with the replaced down-bow ('reprise d'archet'). Muffat's application of these rules to the minuet has often been observed. Such dance patterns, particularly in triple-time, may have been linked with patterns of dance steps, the stronger articulations (replaced down-bow) occurring at important synchronizations with the steps (Seagrave 1959 pp. 116-21).

The extent to which Bach's players adjusted their bowing to the metrical stresses of the music must remain a matter of speculation. Certainly some of the most common figures in Bach's music, *suspirans* and *messanza*, seem suited to, if not derived from, the natural stresses of up- and down-bows: Players may have adjusted their bowing of the *corta* figure according to the character of the rhythm:

dactyl   'craquer d'archet'

anapaest   'reprise d'archet'

Dadelsen conjectures that Bach would have used the replaced down-bow as a rule, because Riepel (1757) described it as the 'alte Art' (Dadelsen 1978 p. 109). This seems unfounded since the 'neue Art' (i.e. 'craquer d'archet') was used far more by Muffat in the *Florilegium Secundum* (1698) and long, apparently up-bow slurs covering notes with staccato dots were common in seventeenth-century German virtuoso violin music.[2]

Any player capable of performing Bach's works for solo violin would surely have had a bowing facility far more adaptable than any described in rules for the most basic applications. While much of Corelli's string music can be played straight through with few alterations to the natural succession of bow-strokes, the virtuoso music of Biber, J. J. Walther, Westhoff and Bach – particularly passages with double-stopping – requires adaptation of the bowing-scheme which is not indicated by the slurring alone. Thus slurs were not notated merely as technical instructions since in this sense they are incomplete; they must have specific musical significance.

ORNAMENTAL ARTICULATION

Virtuoso violinists of Bach's time (like those of today) learned multifarious slurred bowings as the basis of a fluent technique. Perhaps the very nature of his instrument and the bow itself were fundamental to this interest. The pre-Tourte bow was less evenly balanced, with more weight toward the heel. This resulted in a greater difference in the up- and down-stroke and a change of pressure within the stroke. Furthermore, the action of such bows with their thinner ribbon of hair on the lower-tension gut strings meant that the start of each stroke was more noticeable than on modern instruments, the first note of a slur thus resulting in a form of accent (Boyden 1965 pp. 324–30).

According to L. Mozart (1756 p. 122), slurred bowing gives life to the notes, rousing various emotions – modest, impertinent, serious or playful – in the hearer.[3] Quantz (1752 p. 108) also relates the alternation of passions to articulation, 'slurred and close intervals' being associated with melancholy, 'brief articulated notes or those comprising distant leaps' with gaiety and boldness.[4] Some of the first notated slurs in Mozart's tutor (1756 pp. 41–2) coincide with chromatic passages; the slur has not even been verbally defined at this stage. Although comparatively late authorities, these comments accord remarkably well with those of Bernhard and Walther (see p. 23 above).

Quite often Mozart implies that slurring is part of the music itself and ought to be understood by the composer:

Es giebt leider solche Halbcomponisten genug, die selbst die Art eines guten Vortrags entweder nicht anzuzeigen wissen, oder den Fleck neben das Loch setzen. Von solchen Stümpern ist die Rede nicht: in solchem Falle kömmt es auf die gute Beurtheilungskraft eines Violinisten an.

(There exist, unfortunately, enough of such half-composers, who themselves either will not indicate the style of a good performance, or put a patch by the side of the hole. We are not talking of these bunglers; in such cases everything would depend on the good judgement of the violinist.)   (Mozart 1756 p. 136)

Riepel, in a contemporary compositional treatise (1757 p. 151), suggests unequivocally that a knowledge of bow-strokes is as necessary for the composer as for the violinist: a poor composition can be completely transformed by ingenious slurring, and a composer can likewise ruin a piece through incorrect indications.[5]

Thus, in the same way as composers began to use compositional figures which originated as improvised ornamentation, the placing of slurs in the notation is the direct result of experience in performance style. The relation of slurs to the *Decoratio* of the music seems evident in Muffat's introducing the (notated) slur in the section on ornaments, where he also recommended the 'more useful' diminutions which could be added by the player (see Example 17). Simpson, Rousseau and Prelleur likewise describe the slur as if it were an ornament.[6]

Mozart affirms that slurring should be added if the composer has forgotten to mark the slurs or does not understand how to do so ('. . .wenn es der Componiste anzumerken vergessen, oder selbst nicht verstanden hat', Mozart 1756 p. 83). How are we to gauge when in fact the composer *expected* the player to add slurring, regardless of whether there was any marked in the notation or not? Are certain figures associated with specific slurrings? Is slurring related to particular metrical groupings?

Certainly the accentual implications of slurs seem particularly important:

Wenn nun dergleichen mehrere Noten nacheinander folgen, über deren zwo und zwo ein Bogen stehet: so fällt auf die erste der zwoen der Accent, und sie wird nicht nur etwas stärker angespielet, sondern auch etwas länger angehalten; die zwote aber wird ganz gelind, und still, auch etwas später daran geschliffen.

(If several notes of this type follow each other over which slurs are placed two by two, then the accent falls on the first of the two and is not only played somewhat louder, but also sustained rather longer; while the second is slurred on to it quite smoothly and quietly, and somewhat later.)   (*ibid*. p. 258)

Many of Vivaldi's slurs (far more adventurous than any found in French music) imply an automatic imposition of down-bow accents (despite the Italian boast of equal facility with up- and down-bows). Here the rhythm created by the slur is of prime importance, consistently linked to a particular component of the sequential *messanza* figuration (Example 19). Such patterns 'challenge' the natural succes-

Example 19 Vivaldi: Op. III no. 12 '1

sion of subsidiary bar accents, but, by their emphasis of the more important beats, contribute greatly to the momentum of the movement.

'Grammatical' or 'pathetic' accents caused by an appoggiatura and its resolution, or by a harmony note followed by stepwise passing notes (*accentus*), were those specifically designated as 'geschleiffen' or 'gezogen' in the vocal and compositional treatises studied in chapter 1. Paired bowing slurs are common in all European music of the late Baroque. J. J. Walther made frequent use of the slurred *corta* in his *Scherzi* of 1676:   Walther's Sonata 7 contains what is essentially the *superjectio* of Bernhard and J. G. Walther (Example 20).

Example 20

Some paired slurs in Sonata 1 even cross the beat or bar-line, linking notes which are usually conjunct and isolated from their neighbours by their unity of direction (Example 21). Such passages could well be

Example 21 J. J. Walther: Sonata 1, Allemande

compared with the *anticipatione della syllaba* of Beyer (see pp. 22–3 above).

Vivaldi's Op. III no. 11, Allegro, shows paired slurs for oscillating trill figures (in semiquavers) and for patterns in quavers, where the first note under the slur is alternately a harmony note and an appoggiatura. That paired slurrings were perhaps even more fashionable in the middle of the eighteenth century is shown by their use as a fundamental of the *galant* style. Bach's prime example of this genre, the Andante from the trio-sonata of BWV 1079, is typically based on paired 'sighing' figures.

The dotted pairs  have already been observed as common slurred figures in vocal music. An example was noted in Muffat's specification of cadential formulae (see Example 17). Vivaldi used them frequently, particularly in slow movements (Example 22).

Example 22 Vivaldi: Op. III no. 8/2

Many ornaments which could both be added by the performer and notated – *tremolo, groppo, circolo mezzo* and *tirata* – became delineated by slurs in the later treatises (e.g. Kürzinger, see p. 23 above). In cases where the figure (especially the *groppo* and *circolo*) is essentially the embellishment of a single note, slurs have the function of binding the notes together as if they were the one note (Examples 23 and 24).

Example 23 Vivaldi: Op. III no. 9. 2

Example 24 J. J. Walther: Sonata 1, Allemande

Many paired slurs seem more related to violin technique than to figuration, where they can render the music less difficult to play (e.g. in string-crossing passages). Geminiani (1751 p. 27) implies that paired slurring can be applied wholesale to notes of a particular value as a general playing style.

Some of Vivaldi's slurs – particularly in later works – seem designed to create a more or less continuous legato, dividing the music into manageable bow lengths. However, the placing of such slurs usually coincides with the metrical accents (Example 25).

Example 25 Vivaldi: Sonata in D, RF 755 Preludio - Andante

DOTS AND STROKES

Marais describes dots under slurs in his gamba music as indicating notes to be articulated as if they were played with separate bows (Marais 1701 *Avertissement*).[7] Piani gives a very similar definition in the preface to his violin sonatas (1712), as does Corrette in his tutor of 1738 (p. 35). J. G. Walther asserts that such notes are to be equally detached, implying negation of the standard 'good' and 'bad' pairing (1708 p. 35). General dictionary definitions of 'spiccato' or 'staccato' are often applied specifically to string playing. All these references call for a shortening and not an accenting of the notes.[8] The entry in Chambers (1783 vol. 4) relates spiccato specifically to Italian music, and this might accord with Tartini's comment that Allegros in Corelli's music were to be played with notes of half length (Tartini 1760 p. 15). It is hardly wise to apply such late comments to Corelli's own performance practice, let alone to that of Bach, but it may be that with the changing tastes towards a legato style in the late eighteenth century, Tartini was attempting to preserve a dying style of playing. Certainly, Baroque bows do produce a naturally articulated line in fast music, so this might be the type of staccato to which the later writers (using 'transitional' bows?) refer.

Muffat introduces staccato, like the slur, in the ornaments section. He implies that staccato can be linked to a lively mood:

Es kan die *Disjunction* letzlich die Dantz-Bewegung lebhaffter zuerwecken, wenigsten in den Noten mittern *valors* oder gantzen Trippel Noten oder essentialn Theilen in denen *Proportionibus* zu weilen gebraucht werden, doch daß es ohne *Affectation*, oder Reissung der Saiten, sondern allzeit nachdrücklich moderirt und sauber geschehe.

(The *Disjunction* can lastly bring out the dance movement more vivaciously, at least when used with notes of moderate value, measures composed entirely of three-beat notes, or proportionate subdivisions of the same, but always expressly moderately and cleanly, without affectation and undue pressure on the strings.)   (Muffat 1698 p. 27)

Riepel suggests a special function for dots, giving less rather than more prominence to the notes affected: only 'half a knife-edge' of bow-hair is used, specifically for accompaniment, so that the principal voices are well distinguished (1757 p. 19).[9] J. G. Walther made little distinction between dots and strokes, since both his definitions – 'zugleich gestoßen' for dots (1708 p. 35) and 'von einander abgesondert' for strokes (1732 p. 575) – are basically the same.

Strokes seem to be more common as the eighteenth century progresses, but Quantz's comments that a single note with a stroke is
accented if followed by notes of lesser value can hardly be applied to all
earlier music (1752 p. 201).[10] Geminiani (1751 *preface* p. 8), Mozart
(1756 p. 43) and Riepel (1757 pp. 16-17) suggest that strokes imply a
lifting of the bow. Clearly the practice was not fixed and each case
should be dealt with separately. Only in examples where a difference is
specified or where both are used should dots and strokes be interpreted
differently.

SUMMARY

A study of J. S. Bach's string slurrings should take several factors into
account. First, Bach's own comments suggest that his school students
were educated in the traditional Kantorei tradition, where versatility
in all the aspects of *Musica Practica* was commonplace. As in singing,
certain ornamental figurations deriving from improvisation may have
been associated with particular delineation or articulation patterns.
Secondly, slurring often has the technical task of making the music
manageable, and here the player had to be aware of the accentual
implications of the metre and slurring. Such is the rhythmic power of
slurring on contemporary instruments that bowing is fundamental to
the interpretation of the music, to the rhetorical-affective message
which the composer intended. The initial distinction between the
instructive (technical) and interpretative (musical) functions of slurs is
obviously not clear cut.

3

Articulation marks in wind playing

TONGUING AND SLURS

The background to wind playing in Lutheran education is identical to that for string playing: Bach's testimonials show the tremendous versatility of players at his disposal. The university student, F. G. Wild, plays the flute and harpsichord in church services and is also an accomplished composer (*Dok* vol. 1 p. 127). Bach gives a good report for an apprentice to the Stadtpfeiffer, the official town musicians: C. F. Pfaffe is proficient on 'each instrument used by the Stadtpfeiffer, violin, oboe, flute, trumpet, waldhorn and other bass instruments' ('jedem *Instrumen*te, so von denen Stadtpfeiffern pfleget gebrauchet zu werden. . .' - *Dok* vol. 1 p. 147).

The wind player, like the singer, need break the musical line only when taking a breath. There is no feature such as the bow on the violin which results in a regular, mandatory articulation. However, since long before the time of Bach, commentators had been aware of this and recommended means of synthesizing articulation. Ganassi (1535 pp. 12, 87) specified three pairs of articulation syllables - te-ke, te-re, le-re - related to the variety of consonances in speech, and associated the flow of breath with that expressively used in singing. The advice of Mersenne that the wind player specifically imitate the voice through the articulation and movement of the tongue has already been mentioned (see p. 12 above). Several later writers also used the example of bow-strokes in descriptions of wind tonguing.[1]

The woodwind instruments of Bach's time were fully developed only in the last decades of the seventeenth century. Many of the important makers and pioneers - in particular the Hotteterre family in France - were experienced players and teachers, aware of the growing demands

47

of Baroque figuration. This response to the music of the age is also evident in the variety of tonguing syllables recommended by writers of the early eighteenth century. The detail may well be related to the 'rhetorical' qualities of music; the subtleties of musical 'speech' must be reflected in the performance. Furthermore, the greater agility of the instruments and the detail of tonguing may have been developed to complement the sophistication of string bowing, evident in the virtuoso schools of Italy and Germany.

The standard pairing of notes within the metrical hierarchy is not surprisingly just as fundamental to wind as to string technique. Italian sources tend to favour a strong-weak pairing, such as in Ganassi's 'te-re', according to the usual connotations of 'good' and 'bad' notes. French sources (and the francophile Quantz) tend more towards iambic pairing: after the initial syllable *tu*, 'good' and 'bad' notes are articulated *ru-tu*. This was undoubtedly related to the mannered style of performance using *notes inégales* (Mather 1973 pp. 32-8).

Some advice on tonguing seems remarkably similar to that given for bowing patterns. Hotteterre (1707 p. 25) recommends a standard tonguing for the *corta* pattern, which corresponds exactly with the retaken down-bow of string techniques ('alte Art', see p. 40 above):

The conclusions here seem much the same as are reached in other parts of this survey: the player must be aware of the metrical and figural qualities of the music if he is to choose a suitable articulation from a wide choice of possibilities.

Mersenne's comments suggested that a 'slurred' style is all too easy to achieve in wind playing. Most writers seem to agree that a notated slur indicates that only the first note of the group is tongued, some making the obvious observation that slurred notes are to be performed in one breath.

Notes within slurs were sometimes articulated with chest (i.e. breath) accents rather than tonguings. Quantz (1752 p. 65) recommends this for slurred repeated notes of the same pitch ('mit Bewegung der Brust'). Corrette (1735 p. 21) specifies the same technique for slurred notes which also have staccato dots or strokes.

Dots and strokes seem to be the most obvious means of designating a more pronounced articulation, using breath control in addition to tonguing. Schickhardt (1710 p. 1) uses strokes to designate 'staccato', no advice on playing technique being offered. Granom (1766 p. 115) describes 'staccato' as 'to strike every Note distinctly'.

Writers imply no standard distinction between strokes and dots; indeed Corrette (1735 p. 21) and Wragg (c. 1790 p. 12), speaking over fifty years apart, indicate that they mean one and the same thing. The variety of use seems to be just that observed in vocal and string notation.

ARTICULATION MARKS IN THE WIND REPERTORY

Although some aspects of style, such as disjunct motion, are more suited to the violin than to the oboe or flute, much of the actual figuration of Baroque music is the same for all instrumental media. Furthermore, according to the evidence of numerous title-pages, many composers published collections allowing for interchange of media. It is very likely that commercial considerations influenced this policy; music that could be played on a wide range of instruments would lead to greater sales. The optimum instrumental medium might depend on the background of the composer and his music.

M. de La Barre, for instance, was one of the foremost flautists of his time and was anxious to bring his instrument to perfection. Thus his *Premier Livre des trio pour les violons, flutes et hautbois* (1694/1707) might have been composed with the flute most in mind. Mattheson's *Der brauchbare Virtuoso* (1720), however, provides demanding music for flute or violin, with little distinction between the two instrumental media.

Although Mattheson (1739 p. 82) comments that 'Auf Violinen, z.E. setzet man gantz anders, als auf Flöten' ('one composes completely differently for violins than for flutes'), he gives few clues as to how the two styles might be differentiated. Perhaps he is considering the implications of range, tessitura and orchestral colour rather than the essential figuration.

A distinction between the instruments of any particular family is even more difficult to determine. Wragg's elementary tutors for flute and oboe (c. 1790), written at the very end of the eighteenth century – at a time when instruments were generally more sharply distinguished – are, in their general advice, virtually identical.

Slurred figures for wind reveal exactly the same features that are found in other media. That slurs are primarily related to the *Decoratio* of the music is shown by the predominance of slurs in Quantz's chapters on ornamentation, extempore variations on intervals and cadenzas (1752 chapters 8, 13, 15). Here standard paired intervals, *groppos* and isolated groups of conjunct notes are frequently delineated by slurs. Hotteterre's *L'Art de preluder* (1719) is likewise addressed to flute improvisation, and the copious slurring indications relate both to the delineation of figures and the application of a specific slurring style to extended passages.

In the woodwind repertory and tutors, paired and appoggiatura figures are, predictably, the most common. Examples in *The Compleat Flute-Master* (1695) show predominantly paired patterns. The sources in Germany, France and Italy likewise display extensive paired slurs. In France the slurring of notes in pairs (*lourer*) was a fashionable device derived from drone instruments and sometimes connected with *notes inégales* (Mather 1973 p. 39). Mahaut's flute tutor (1759) shows a whole repertory of slurring patterns within exercises, complementing well the examples by L. Mozart for violin.

In general, slurs are more common in string writing than in wind. Bowing influences the accentual scheme of the music, enforcing an up- or down-bow at a particular point. In wind playing slurs are not so fundamental to the technique; tonguing and slurring are employed in accordance with the style and figuration of the music. They are thus related more to interpretation than to the control of playing technique.

4

Articulation marks in keyboard playing

Bis zum späten 17. Jahrhundert erfolgte die Verbreitung von Kompositionen besonders für Tasteninstrumente vorwiegend durch handschriftliche Überlieferung, der persönliche Kontakt von Lehrer und Schülern machte eine Notation aufführungspraktischer Details überflüssig. Mit der späteren Ausweitung des Notendruckes und dem aufkommenden musikalischen Dilettantentum ergab sich die Notwendigkeit, die mündliche Tradition durch Hinweise im Notentext zu ersetzen. So sind beispielsweise gedruckte Klavierwerke Bachs meist sorgfältiger bezeichnet als handschriftlich überlieferte.

(Until the late seventeenth century the dissemination of compositions, especially for keyboard instruments, was predominantly a transmission through manuscripts: the personal contact between teachers and pupils rendered a notation of details of performance practice superfluous. With the later expansion of printed music and the rise of musical amateurs, it became necessary to replace the oral tradition with indications in the notation. So, for example, the printed keyboard works of Bach are usually more carefully marked than those that are transmitted in manuscripts.) (Lohmann 1982 p. 185)[1]

Lohmann's comments about notated articulation in manuscript sources of keyboard music seem to substantiate observations already made in the study of vocal, string and wind techniques: performers were clearly educated in all conventions of performance practice and, as composition was so often taught in conjunction with performance, their understanding of the music itself might have been deeper than is usual today. This latter point seems particularly relevant to keyboard performance, for thoroughbass – learned at the keyboard – was perhaps the most universal means of compositional instruction (see the testimonial for F. G. Wild, pp. 16–17 above). Furthermore, improvisation was a considerable element of the player's technique, if the severity of tests given to prospective organists of Bach's time is reliable evidence (Williams 1984 pp. 43–7). The vagueness of notation in the seventeenth century (particularly in tablatures) might be a tacit reflection on the skill of performers. It need hardly be stressed that skilful keyboard performers were proficient on several instruments (Bach himself is testimony to this): most major composers worked in courts, opera houses or churches, and would have had much experience of instrumentalists and singers.

Conventions in keyboard articulation have been thoroughly studied in recent years (Lohmann 1982; Fuchs 1985; Jenkins 1976). Conclusions seem much the same as those for other instrumental media: articulation according to the natural metrical hierarchy ('good' and 'bad' notes) was reflected in the systems of paired fingerings, modified by the style of the piece, speed of notes and the distance between them, a knowledge of harmonic accents and specific figures. The standard scalic fingerings often begin with three consecutive fingers until the 'good' finger is reached (Example 26). This shows parallels with the

Example 26 J. S. Bach: 'Applicatio' BWV 994 from Wilhelm Friedermann Bach book
     Library of the School of Music, Yale University

rule of the down-bow and the application of the stronger tonguing syllable to initial notes of passages.

A general trend toward the standard legato style of the nineteenth century is also observed: the invention of the fortepiano, the advice given on posture and finger action and, above all, the evolution of a smooth system of fingering with the thumb passed under the other fingers. This is reflected in the compositions themselves, with longer phrases and slower harmonic pulse. Couperin was one of the first composers to indicate phrase-ends by commas within the actual notation (*Pieces de Clavecin* III, 1722), and references to 'phrase' in music are increasingly apparent in dictionaries.[2]

THE DEFINITION OF SLURS IN KEYBOARD SOURCES

Slurs in keyboard music might have demonstrated a manner of performance that had been known for many years within an oral tradition. Another function may have been to imply an unusual articulation, one not expected by the player well versed in the conventions (Schwarz 1972 p. 318; Fuchs 1985 pp. 44-5).

It seems that slurs were first used in keyboard music to define something that was, at the time, 'extraordinary'. Scheidt introduced four-note slurs for passages of continuous semiquavers - i.e. at the *Decoratio* level - in his *Tabulatura Nova* (1624). These he termed 'imitatio violistica', observing that they were commonly used by contemporary viol players and sounded 'charming and agreeable' on keyboard instruments. Here, then, a small-scale legato - or at least a grouping delineated by a single initial accent - is introduced which Scheidt recommends be applied in keyboard performance. In scalic passages such slurs may well imply the cessation of paired fingering, all notes within the span being played by adjacent fingers.

More definite legato implications of slurs seem evident by the time of C. P. E. Bach (1753 p. 111), whose description matches well that of L. Mozart (see p. 42 above). Slurred notes are held for their full length, only the first note receiving a slight stress (although the third note in a group of four may receive a 'scarcely noticeable' pressure).[3] Marpurg (1755 p. 28) gives similar advice: a slurred note is not released until the next is struck.[4]

Many earlier writers, particularly in France, describe superlegato appoggiatura figures (generally termed 'port de voix') which complement the observations made of legato *accentus* figures (see pp. 21-3 above). Nivers (1665) declares that with such figures '. . .il ne faut pas lever les doits si promptement' ('it is not necessary to lift the fingers so promptly'; i.e. before the next note is struck). That the legato style was becoming more established is suggested by Saint-Lambert's advice (1702 p. 49) that the two notes of a 'port de voix' should overlap. Rameau (1724 'ornaments table') further demonstrates this with the written values of the notation.

A similar trend can be observed in Germany: Kuhnau (1689) directs that the second note of an *accentus* figure should be 'fein sachte' ('refinedly soft'), and C. P. E. Bach (1787 p. 94), over fifty years later, is insistent that 'Figuren, wobey die zum Basse anschlagende Noten durchgehende Noten oder Vorschläge sind, werden in allerley Zeit-Maaße ohne Andeutung geschleift' ('passages in which passing notes or appoggiaturas are sounded above a bass are slurred in all tempos, even in the absence of a slur'). This latter advice should make us wary of regarding all slurs as indicating 'exceptional' instances: dissonances require a legato resolution and these, most common of occurrences, may or may not receive slurs (earlier composers, such as Nivers, do not use slurs).

A further function of slurs, relevant only to keyboard music, is the sustaining of slurred notes until the end of the slur. This seems to have originated in France. Saint-Lambert (1702 pp. 12-14) defines this 'liaison' in detail, outlining exceptions to the rule that all notes are sustained. Rameau (1724 ornaments table) demonstrates that the slur is really a shorthand for a sustained arpeggiated chord.

Couperin's *Pieces de Clavecin* quite often show a cautionary longer note value for the first (and sometimes the second) note under the slur:

 This style of performance seems evident, to a lesser extent, in

D. Vetter's *Musicalische Kirch- und Hauss-Ergötzlichkeit* (1709 '13). which consists of chorale-settings in a consistent 'style brisé'. Here sustained arpeggios are written in the full notation with ties. In a few cases a slur is also marked. Marpurg, who made a thorough study of French music, notes that slurs are used both for their normal, quasi-bowing, function and also to indicate which notes 'harmonize together' and are held within the duration of the slur. He stresses that it is better, though, to write in the correct note values, with the notes sustained (1755 p. 28).[5] C. P. E. Bach's description (1753 p. 112) is much the same; according to him, the full notation is common in France. Here he may be referring to the type of notation employed by Couperin (above). Certainly J. S. Bach used accurate sustained notation in the Presto of the Italian Concerto BWV 971 (Example 27). The sustaining

Example 27

function of slurs seems peculiar to harpsichord music and might be designed to counteract the lack of a real legato on the harpsichord (since the action of the plectra can cause a percussive effect). J. J. Rousseau (1768 p. 135) describes the 'coulé' as practically impossible on the harpsichord, requiring a gentle and sustained touch 'very difficult to describe'.[6]

DOTS

No descriptions of dots are given in seventeenth-century keyboard tutors. C. P. E. Bach (1753 p. 111) explains that dots and strokes are synonymous and uses dots in his examples since '. . .bey der erstern leicht eine Zweydeutigkeit wegen der Ziffern hätte vorgehen können' ('with [strokes] a confusion with fingering numerals can easily arise'). However, in his own *Sechs Sonaten. . .mit veränderten Reprisen* (1760), dots and strokes are sometimes used within the same movement. The strokes are engraved in a wedge-like form which, visually, would suggest a sharper detachment than the dots. Marpurg (1755 p. 28) refers only to dots and, like C. P. E. Bach, indicates that such notes be held for '. . .nur etwann bis zur Hälfte' ('only somewhat up to half') their written value. In a later publication (1762 vol. 1 p. 20) he notes that both dots and small strokes indicate detached notes.

The use of dots in published music increases during the eighteenth century. In his *Pieces de Clavecin*, Couperin uses dots with slurs to specify the 'Lombard' rhythm, and strokes to define staccato. Virtually all the latter relate to weak divisions of the beat ('bad' notes) and merely emphasize the dance-like rhythms (by lightening the upbeats) (Example 28). Kauffmann uses strokes to specify a continuous staccato

Example 28 Couperin: Pieces de Clavecin II, 'Les Moissonneurs'

in his fughetta on 'Wir glauben all an einen Gott' (*Harmonische Seelen Lust*, 1733-6). Handel's practice, in his organ concertos Op. 4 and 7, is to use strokes in the organ part for crotchet motion (generally disjunct intervals) in important tutti sections. Dots are sometimes used in the string parts (never in the organ) and appear with faster note values (e.g. Op. 4/2: Allegro, ma non presto, b. 1, triplets). The use of strokes with longer note values may suggest that they are associated with a heavier style of performance: that appropriate for the metrical beat rather than the 'ornamental' figuration.

SLURRED FIGURES

'Eine Setzmanier. . .ist. . .nicht anders als eine Verbindung einer

oder mehrer Nebennoten mit einer Hauptnote aus der Melodie. . .'
('A set-mannerism is nothing other than a combination of one or more
adjoining notes with a main note from the melody') (Marpurg 1755
p. 37)

Marpurg's description accords well with observations made for
vocal, string and wind performance: certain patterns are connected
with the ornamentation of a single note, each group being delineated
in performance. Scheidt, describing slurs in relation to string techniques, slurs four-note figures (of the *groppo* or *circolo mezzo* type)
which are already inherently grouped.

Kauffmann uses four-note slurs for descending *tirata* figures in
ornamental interludes between lines of the chorale, e.g. 'Herr Jesu
Christ mein's Lebens Licht' (which opens *Harmonische Seelen Lust*,
1733-6). The general slurred style may well be linked with the direction 'con affetto'. J. L. Krebs also uses slurs for descending groups of
four notes in 'Allein Gott' b. 5 (*Clavierübung c.* 1750).

Predictably, paired slurrings feature as regularly in keyboard music
as in other instrumental media. They appear quite often in the second
volume of Scheidt's *Tabulatura Nova* for much the same type of figuration as was slurred in fours in the first volume (similarly termed
'imitatio violistica'). Kuhnau's use of paired slurrings is generally
matched more to a specific pairing in the intervals (e.g. *Clavierübung*,
1689 Partita 2, Allemande, b. 17). Couperin often uses paired slurrings
with the type of sustained notation mentioned above (p. 54). Here the
slur presumably implies a slight shortening of the second note in
each pair.

Handel's use of keyboard slurs is usually minimal. The paired slurs,
when they do appear, may well suggest a sustaining much in the same
manner as Couperin's (Example 29). Kauffmann's use of paired slurs is

Example 29 Handel: Op. IV no. 2, Allegro ma non presto, autograph, British
        Library, King's 317

far less selective; he applies them to entire sequences of notes, regardless of the inherent figuration (Kauffmann, *Harmonische Seelen Lust*,
'Ach Gott von Himmel', although these slurs are initially and appro-
priately associated with stepwise motion). This resembles the wholesale

slurring often found in string sources, where a regular accentuation is implied by the first note of each slur. Krebs' setting of 'Vater Unser' (*Clavierübung*, *c.* 1750) is a similar case: here the continuous paired slurs for rising disjunct intervals seem linked to the prevailing chromaticism, the 'pathetic' *Affekt* of penitence.

Both Kuhnau and Kauffmann slur dotted pairs. C. P. E. Bach's insistence that the second note of a dotted group is always shortened implies that the main function of a slur covering such a figure is to cut the second note short rather than merely to sustain the first (1753 p. 113).[7] This would prevent the short note from sounding slurred into the next beat.

The *suspirans* pattern occurs with surprising frequency in keyboard music. It is, in fact, one of the most common slurrings to appear in Froberger's *Suittes de clavessin* (*c.* 1697). In the Allemande from Kuhnau's Partita 2 (*Clavierübung*, 1689) the slurring first appears when the unslurred note is tied (b. 9). Later on in the piece, bb. 12-13, the same slurring is applied to continuous semiquavers. The Praeludium to Partita 1 (bb. 28-30) shows a similar upbeat slurring with hand designations (Example 30).

Example 30

Such is the detail of slurring in this publication that Kuhnau may well have intended it to serve as instruction to students (as its title suggests). Quite often the figuration for a particular level of diminution is slurred for an entire movement (e.g. Partita 4, Gigue), and, as in the above example, most markings delineate the component figures of passages. Certainly far fewer slurrings are marked in Kuhnau's *Frische Clavier Früchte* (1696).

SUMMARY

In general slurs are rare in keyboard music. When they do occur, they are very similar to those found in other media. Their implications are presumably the same, although the technical means to their realization vary. The player's judgement in choosing a suitable slurring or grouping of notes is not conditioned by the methods through which sounds are produced, such as is the case in string playing.[8] The keyboard player, as a composer, understood both the notated and performing arts of music; articulation is the midway point between the two.

5

Articulation marks and rhythmic inequality

'If they [notes] are notated slurred in pairs, and are otherwise eligible, this is virtually an indication of inequality. They must in any case be slurred by pairs in performance if taken unequally.' (Donington 1974 p. 452)

Donington's statement makes two assumptions: notated paired slurs might indicate inequality and unequal notes are slurred in pairs, by convention. Given the preponderance of paired slurs in Baroque sources and indeed in Bach's oeuvre, it is clearly worth investigating this claim.

Since *notes inégales* in their most systematized and comprehensive form are a specific feature of French writings, these should be given priority. Most French instrumental treatises introduce the slur under a variety of descriptions - *coulez, liaison, tenue* - as an ornament or grace, the notes being played in a single bow-stroke or tonguing. *Notes inégales*, on the other hand, are usually described in the sections dealing with metre. This immediately suggests a distinction between the two: slurs are related to the superficial graces, applied by the performer to the notes as they stand; *notes inégales* are, on the other hand, part of the rhythmic drive of the music and constitute an alteration of the written note values.

Demoz (1728 p. 178) seems alone in describing paired slurs in relation to metre: such notes in simple duple or triple time are slurred together in a 'touching manner' ('d'une maniere patétique & touchante'). Although Demoz's terminology (e.g. 'deux en deux' and specification of metre) has much in common with descriptions of *notes inégales*, at no point does he categorically call for a rhythmic alteration, more for a mannered style with an emphasis on the first note of each pair:

LOURER, C'est éxprimer les Notes qui sont liées de deux en deux par cette figure ⌢ en les coulant, caressant & roulant de telle sorte que les sons soient continus, liez & conjoins, comme ceux des Airs du jeu des Instrumens appellez *Musette, Cornemuse, Viélle*, & en marquant sensiblement la premiere Note de deux en deux. . .'

(LOURER is to express the notes which are joined two by two by this figure ⌢ slurring them, caressing and rolling them in such a way that the sounds seem continuous, bound and united like those in 'Airs du jeu' for instruments, called *musettes, cornemuses, vielles*, marking tenderly the first of each pair.)

(*ibid*. pp. 181-2)

A mannered interpretation of slurred pairs might well lead to un-equal notes in performance but not one French writer refers specifically to this. Quantz (1752 p. 106) perhaps comes closest to saying this when he excludes *notes inégales* from fast vocal passages 'if they are not otherwise supposed to be slurred' ('wenn sie anders nicht geschleifet werden sollen').

Much evidence supports the notion that *notes inégales* are related to a slurred style, *notes égales* to a more detached style. Saint-Lambert's comment (1702 p. 25) that the former give 'plus de grace' may imply a slurred style. Loulié (1696 p. 29) also suggests this by stating that music of a disjunct or detached style is unsuitable for unequal performance. Choquel (1762 p. 106) states that unequal quavers in 3-time render the melody 'joined' and 'more fluent', terms more often applied to the effect of slurs.[1] Loulié (1696 pp. 29-30) introduces the verb 'lourer' in connection with the mild application of *notes inégales*, a verb which is usually associated with a legato style.

Other writers imply, however, that there is no direct link between *notes inégales* and a slurred style. Some even give examples of fast or animated music in their description of the rhythmic convention. Hotteterre (1719 p. 58) states that in 2-time ('On ne la connoît point dans les Musiques Italiennes' / 'unknown in Italian music') the quavers are dotted and played in a lively and staccato manner. Bacilly (1668 p. 343) remarks that dots of addition are not indicated in music that is to be performed unequally in order to avoid an old-fashioned jerky style.

Although this could be read to imply that such music is to be per-formed legato, when the context of Bacilly's remark is examined it is clear that he intends all notes sung in passages to be given separate throat-accents. Only certain notes are exempted from this style and these bear no relation to the *notes inégales* conventions (see p. 13 above).

Many string treatises introduce *notes inégales* with reference to bowing. Muffat's examples (1698 pp. 24, 53-4 examples QQ-RR) are clearly given separate bows, the long note being played down-bow, according to the bowing rules he outlines in the preceding examples. Corrette (1738 p. 34) shows 'coups d'Archet détaché', with no reference to the cancellation of *notes inégales*.[2] Later treatises echo Muffat's association of unwritten inequality with down- and up-bows (Brijon 1763 pp. 21-2; Tarade 1774 p. 9). Hotteterre's specification (1707 p. 22) of the standard double-tonguing 'ru-tu' for unequal quavers also precludes a true legato.

The automatic coupling of *notes inégales* with legato style seems, then, to be an over-simplification. The variety of convention in France, the centre of the most regular practice of rhythmic inequality, should make us wary of associating slurs with *notes inégales* elsewhere.

If paired slurs were ever to indicate *notes inégales* in Bach's music, the most likely instances of their use would be where a player of the French tradition might automatically apply the convention (determined primarily by the metre) and the German player would be less sure and require some indication. The Ouverture, BWV 831, of *Clavierübung* II is a particularly important example since Bach obviously had a definite contrast of national style with the 'Italian Concerto' in mind. In the Courante (3/2 metre) crotchets would normally be the values subjected to inequality. Neither crotchets nor quavers are slurred in pairs. Some crotchets, conjunct and disjunct, are notated in dotted rhythm, which could represent a notated inequality. In the Gavottes, no paired slurs appear and all slurs that are present cover three or more notes. Passepied 2 employs appoggiatura symbols. This type of notation does suggest a mannered interpretation perhaps not unlike *notes inégales*, but such *accentus* figures are common currency throughout Europe. The only paired slurs to occur in the remainder of the work are the two pairs in b. 23 of Bourrée 2. These are separated by a leap (thus not in a sequence of conjunct notes), the slurs seeming to stress the affective quality of the semitone of the first pair and the striking leap to the second pair. It would be unlikely that these were the only two pairs played unequally if *notes inégales* were to be applied to this movement.

Much has been made by certain scholars of Bach's use of dots to cancel *notes inégales*. The most obvious example is b. 8 of Variation 16 of *Clavierübung* IV. Both Collins (1967 pp. 482-3) and O'Donnell (1979 pp. 343-4) suggest that the dots here cancel inequality, and that the first dot in the LH of b. 8 is erroneous and redundant, since the leap cancels inequality. It is quite true that the dot is 'correctly' omitted from the RH part of the same bar, but the first note in b. 9 LH, separated by a third, is also marked with a dot. A further discrepancy is evident in the fact that these are semiquaver values in ¢ metre, not normally eligible for inequality.

The *agogic* implications of the first notes under slurs have already been mentioned in relation to L. Mozart's comments (see p. 42 above). It can hardly be denied that, in certain circumstances, slurs might encourage the player to hold the first note under a slur longer than its exact written value, especially when dissonance is involved. However, there is no conclusive evidence that slurs are used to imply *notes inégales* in the highly organized manner advocated by French writers. Nor are dots used consistently enough to imply a negation of the unwritten convention.

SUMMARY OF PART I

Several points must underpin any detailed study of Bach's notated articulation. First he was living and working in an environment where there was no clear division between the role of composer and performer; both, in a sense, were *practical* musicians. Such musicians were aware of the grammatical hierarchy of the Baroque metrical system, as they were of the oratorical quality of specific devices such as dissonance. The musical style itself derived from the ornamentation of an underlying network grounded in the conventions of strict counterpoint. Much of the *rhetorical* interest of the music lay in this ornamentation, the *Decoratio*, which could be improvised by the performer or notated by the composer. The recognition and delineation of such figures was one of the fundamentals of articulation in performance.

Articulation marks have a variety of meanings according to the instrumental medium involved. In all media slurs can indicate the component figuration, acting as the clarification of the notation rather than as indication of exceptions. They can also dictate a specific slurred *Affekt*, which is also often concerned with a specific type of figuration or level of diminution. In string performance, where slurs relate to the method by which the sound is produced, the accentual function of slurs is particularly significant, complementing or adjusting the grammatical hierarchy. What is striking is that the resulting articulation required from all instruments is basically the same. This is substantiated by the remarkable versatility of both composers and performers.

Part II

THE PRINCIPLES OF BACH'S NOTATED ARTICULATION; A STUDY OF THE SCORES AND PARTS OF THE CONCERTED VOCAL WORKS

6

Articulation marks within the compositional and notational procedure

The role of slurs and dots within the compositional process is a crucial factor in establishing the musical significance and norms of Bach's notated articulation. Here the question of authenticity is of considerable importance, particularly in the case of performance parts prepared by copyists and edited by Bach himself. The concerted vocal works provide the most suitable material for study since these survive in a large corpus of primary sources which follow a consistent format: the autograph score and a set of performance parts. As many autograph scores are hurriedly prepared composing drafts, articulation markings in such sources may reasonably be regarded as those that Bach considered fundamental to the composition. Most of the original sets of performance parts clarify and greatly amplify these markings and give a view of how Bach interpreted his own music from the viewpoint of performer.

AUTOGRAPH SCORES

Robert Marshall (1972) has examined Bach's compositional procedure in great detail, showing that Bach, like most of his contemporaries, was a remarkably fluent composer. Only in exceptional cases did he experience difficulties in determining the basic content and figuration of a movement. Indeed, Bach may well have spent more time on the editing and perfecting of his music, an activity in which he especially indulged during the last two decades of his life. Although the composer's first notation of a piece hardly represents his initial conception or 'idea' of the work, it is the closest distinct record we have of the compositional process.

Sketches

A small proportion of the sketches transcribed by Marshall (*ibid.* vol. 2) contain slurs. Nearly half of these relate to vocal lines and presumably outline the underlay to be adopted. This is particularly necessary when the text is not included (sketch 2,[1] BWV 2/3) or when the syllables are poorly placed (sketch 64, BWV 88/4). Significantly, both these examples are written in tablature, where the clarity offered by slurs is particularly important.

More interesting is the slurring which is related to alterations made to the notes themselves. This is especially common in vocal lines where a single note is later embellished. Here the added slur not only clarifies an unclear grouping (often rendered untidy by the alteration) but confirms the original underlay (sketches 14, BWV 24/5; 113, BWV 179/3). A similar function might be observed in the non-vocal sketches. In sketch 166 ('Orgelbüchlein') the motion of the chorale was originally notated in minims and later embellished with dotted crotchets and quavers, each minim group covered by a slur (Plate 2; Example 31). This suggests that Bach thought of slurring as part of the

Example 31

originally:

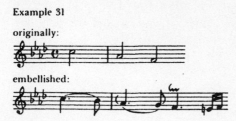

embellished:

2 Orgelbüchlein. chorale prelude. 'O Traurigkeit, o Herzeleid', unfinished sketch.
Mus. MS P 283

Decoratio, uniting the notes which embellish each note of the cantus firmus.

A deleted draft from BWV 115/1 (sketch 84) shows even more clearly the relationship between slurring and the ornamental figuration added to a plainer frame (Plate 3; Example 32). The slurring here has

3 BWV 115/1. bb. 1-6. deleted sketch. Mus. MS 631

Example 32

originally: embellished:

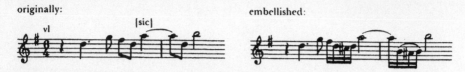

implications not only for bowing (foregrounding the minims by uniting the semiquavers in a 'weak' up-bow) but also for the character of the music. While the original version with two quavers preserves the natural binary division of the beat, the new figure and slur crosses the quaver division and provides a new rhythmic element.

Slurs in sketch 135, BWV 206/7, clarify the performance of the syncopation (Example 33). Since many of these slurs are omitted in the

Example 33

final version Bach may have used the slur in the sketch to remind himself of the dissonance. Once this had been realized in the notated harmony, the slurs would have served their purpose within the compositional process. A similar example is BWV 179/5 (sketch 114) where a slur appears for the first oboe figure (Example 34). This slur prob-

Example 34

ably served to remind Bach that the quavers belong together, as an ornamentation of one note and harmony. By the time he came to write the score this function of the slur would have become redundant since the harmonic rhythm and regularity of figuration were now established (the continuo line with its repeated notes was almost certainly added after the top voice in the sketch). The slur was restored in the parts (St 348) – possibly by Bach himself, since his dynamics are evident in these copies by J. A. Kuhnau – as a performance direction to the oboists.

Many of these longer instrumental drafts show Bach's tendency to notate the melody line first, in surprising detail and often continuing several bars beyond the accompanying parts. Bach thus notates the *Decoratio* at the outset of the compositional process, automatically associating slurs with a dynamic solo line. The high proportion of woodwind solos with slurs suggests that Bach did not view them merely as a technical aid to the bowing-scheme.

Completed scores

While it is almost certain that slurs in sketches were written at the same time as the notes or, in the case of alterations, slightly later, it is often difficult to determine the chronology of articulation marks in longer, completed drafts.

Chorales are the most obvious instances where slurs were added simultaneously with the notes. The chorale was often chosen late and added at the end of the completed score (Marshall 1972 vol. 1 pp. 66-8). Quite often the verse of the text is not given with the music, so that the slurs indicate the underlay of the eventual text. When the verse is chosen it is invariably written after the music or placed against one vocal line only, so that the other three parts would still require indication of underlay.

Slurs in sketches were sometimes associated with the later addition of smaller note values, notated ornamentation. This feature is also evident in completed scores. In BWV 175/1 (P 75) the recorder-lines (bb. 1-2) first consisted of tied semibreves, the semiquavers being added later. This regular *circolo mezzo* figure is typically associated with a four-note slur and the slurs (recorder 1, b. 1) were undoubtedly added at the time the *Decoratio* was devised.

The chronology of articulation markings can often be determined by examining instances of slurs obscured by the line of, or additions to, another part. In BWV 12/4 (P 44/7) b. 13, for instance, the first two slurs in the alto part are obscured by the beaming of the obbligato oboe above. Here, then, the vocal slurs were definitely present before all the musical lines were complete. A similar example is found in the composing score of BWV 134a/4 (Paris MS 2) b. 48. Here the first slur in violin 1 is obscured by the bass-line from the system above. These examples substantiate some of the evidence found in the longer sketches: principal lines with some slurring were included before the bass-line.

The ink colour can also reveal which slurs were added later. In BWV 76/1 (P 67) the ink colour is inconsistent throughout, reflecting many changes and the later addition of inner parts (although the ink itself is inconsistent). However, the slurs that do appear are invariably in the same shade of ink as the notes to which they belong (and indeed the ties which are necessarily contemporaneous with the notes). The last line of f4v demonstrates this well: the tenor bb. 104-8, alto bb. 103-4, are all written in a pale brown ink. The remainder of the system has been written in a blacker ink. However, the tenor slurs in b. 107 are in the original paler colour, which implies that they were drawn at the time of the notes.

Ink gives a sure guide to slur chronology in BWV 84/3 (P 108). The violin part at bb. 184-5 was originally written erroneously (with slurs) in the oboe stave. This has been blotted out (with sand?), which suggests that both notes and slurs were wet when the alteration was made.

The evolution of a slur pattern in the course of a movement may also suggest that the markings were included at the time of the notes. The autograph score of BWV 151/3 (Veste Coburg) (Plate 4) opens with the oboe line slurred in pairs (in anticipation of the vocal underlay in b. 17?) (Example 35). However, the notes are grouped with a leap

Example 35

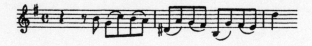

between the first and second followed by three conjunct notes; a derivative of this figure (b. 5) receives a slur for the conjunct notes (Example 36). The obvious derivative with a rest (bb. 9-10) is unslur-

Example 36

red. However, when the three quavers are extended upward or follow a tie, the three-note slurring is sometimes introduced (bb. 11, 24). The first three-note slur to be found with a figure equivalent to that of the opening is a single instance in b. 39 (in an instrumental interlude without the influence of a vocal underlay). The lure of the paired vocal underlay returns in b. 87 where ·the oboe and violin are slurred simultaneously with the vocal underlay. However, as if to show that he had finally decided on the rhythmically more interesting three-note pattern, Bach slurs the entire passage bb. 90-3 with the three-note slur (simultaneously with paired vocal underlay). The fact that this final slurring (that adopted by the partly autograph instrumental parts) is found in its complete form only towards the end of the movement suggests that it evolved as Bach actually composed and was certainly not a later addition. Such a later addition or alteration would surely have been placed against the first bars of the piece.

Similarly in the autograph of BWV 57/3 (P 144) Bach initially established paired slurring as the ruling articulation (Example 37).

Example 37

But the first slurs in the violin 2, b. 10, and the first in the violin 1, b. 15, are rather longer than they should be, impinging on the territory of the second (for notes 3 and 4). Here Bach apparently recognized the three-note slurring implicit in the note-grouping (three conjunct notes followed by a leap) but then reminded himself that he had established paired slurrings at the beginning. The same graphological feature is evident later in the movement: b. 34 (violin 2) where there are three slurs, the first rather too long; 49-55 (violin 1, 2) where the slurs are very hurriedly placed with the first two frequently running into each other. By b. 109, both violin 1 and 2 are regularly slurred with a single three-note slur at the beginning of each bar. Relapses to the original paired slurring are evident in bb. 114-15, 126; here the first two slurs are frequently joined. Thus in this movement the more rhythmically

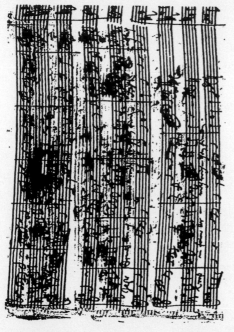

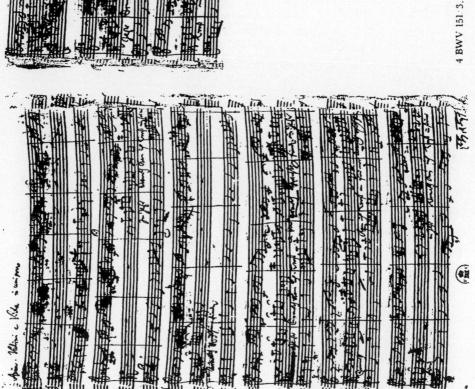

4 BWV 151: 3. autograph score

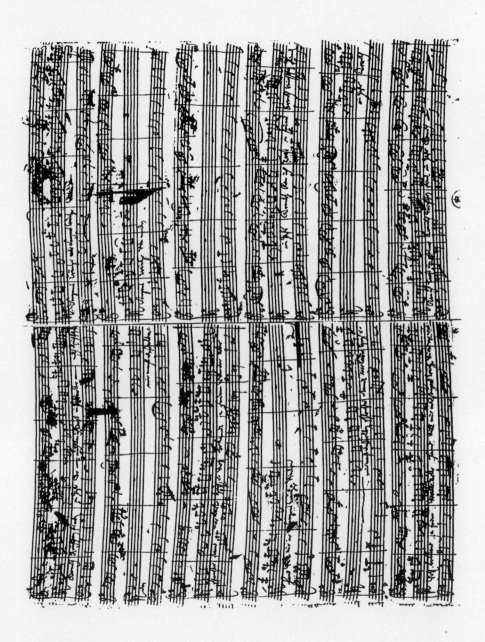

interesting slurring for conjunct note-groups is developed out of the
initial paired slurring (Example 38). Bach clearly first considered the

Example 38

paired slurring to be applied regularly as a paired *Affekt*, regardless of
note-groups, but soon discovered that a secondary figuration – that
introduced in b. 9 – was emerging with its own slurring.

   The ink colours suggest that all these slurs were exactly contemporary with the notes.

Problems of authenticity

Few problems are as insurmountable as the question of authenticity.
Marshall (1983) has recently demonstrated that certain markings in the
score of BWV 102 may have been included by the nineteenth-century
editor Wilhelm Rust. His arguments are based both on the atypical
appearance and detail of the markings and on the existence of later
'control' sources which omit them. The discussion is disturbingly convincing and Marshall surmises that many more markings in Bach's
primary sources may indeed be of doubtful origin.

   The characteristics of Bach's hand have been fully discussed by
Dadelsen (1958 p. 66; 1978 p. 104); slurs above the notes are placed too
high and slurs below too late, curving tightly at the left, thickening and
tailing off to the right. However, despite the characteristic curve of
Bach's slurs there is no particular factor that unequivocally distin-
guishes them. Dadelsen's observation of slurs below notes starting too
far to the right is of utmost significance in the interpretation of markings in this survey. The opening *circolo mezzo* figure of BWV 245/1,
for instance, seems on diplomatic evidence to be slurred from the
second note; only with the slurs *above* the groups (e.g. in the viola,
b. 7) is the first note covered, and now the fourth note is frequently
omitted (see Plate 5).

   Dots are more easy to recognize as Bach's. Emery (1957 p. 54) has
pointed out that Bach's dots are typically flat, almost like the modern
'marcato' mark. This does not exclude the possibility, of course, that

5 St John Passion, BWV 245.1, bb. 1-10. Mus. MS P 28

other scribes could have drawn dots in the same way, by holding the pen in a similar fashion.[2]

The observations of the appearance of Bach's articulation marks by Dadelsen and Marshall do not account for the fact that Bach's additions to instrumental parts are often written in a finer nib than is characteristic in many scores. Consequently they do not always betray striking graphological features. The surest grounds for the authenticity of articulation marks may be summarized as: (1) their appearance, (2) their appropriateness, (3) the type of source concerned (i.e. less detailed markings are usual in a composing score), (4) their transmission in later sources. These points are variously demonstrated by the following examples.

1. Slur extensions in BWV 110/1 (P 153; St 92):

The extension of slurs has been observed and fully recorded by Dürr (*NBA* 1/2 *KB* pp. 79-95): ♩♩♩ ♩♩♩ to ♩♩♩ ♩♩♩ Alterations are evident both in the autograph score P 153 and in the original parts St 92. The style of extension is one frequently adopted by Bach: the pen passes through the two original slurs, joining them into one and rendering their original appearance as concealed as possible (see, for instance, BWV 1004 Ciaccona, b. 245 in P 967: each slur is extended to the right; BWV 1002 Borea, b. 18-19: two [?] slurs made into one). However, exactly the same style of extension is shown in the examples given by Marshall (1983), some of which are definitely inauthentic since they are in sources written after Bach's death.

The ink colour of the addition to P 153 is striking. In the autograph P 153 the slurs are a curious dark blue-black colour quite unlike any other markings in the score. Those in the parts St 92 are more grey and are usually distinguished from Bach's editorial additions (trill-signs and the unmistakable lettering of dynamics) which are browner and thicker. However, in some places the ink colours of Bach's hand and the slur alterations match: in the part for oboe 1 the autograph 'piano' compares well with subsequent slurs, b. 48. This does not rule out the possibility of a second editing by Bach at a later date (Dürr 1976 p. 105 notes a second performance between 1728 and 1731).

The second criterion for authenticity - the appropriateness of the markings - is satisfied: the new slurring not only produces a comfortable bowing but also follows the sequence of conjunct notes. This also creates a long accent at the beginning of each bar followed by more 'upbeat' articulation at the end.

The final considerations - type and relationship of sources - are more problematic. The altered markings in the score, P 153, were clearly not designed as a model for those in the parts St 92 since the first extensions in the score occur in the oboe lines in b. 49 while those in the parts begin in b. 25. The authenticity of those in the score could thus be doubted since Bach did not need to add them for the benefit of the copyist of the parts. The only circumstances in which Bach might have added new slurs to an existing composition were when he was preparing a new fair (or presentation) copy such as P 25 for BWV 244 or P 226 for BWV 1027.

The ink colours of score and parts do not match: it may be that the scribe was using a poorly mixed ink which had turned from dark blue to grey by the time he came to alter the parts. However, it is more likely that the revisions of score and parts were made at different times (particularly as they do not exactly match). In practical circumstances then, the parts may have been altered first, the score later (by the same scribe? by a later possessor?). Dürr's examination suggests that the alterations in the score are inauthentic since an early-nineteenth-century copy of the work (P 1159) shows no sign of the alteration (*NBA* 1. 2 *KB* p. 65). The score bears signs of Zelter's possession (*ibid.* p. 56),[3] pointing towards a performance of this work during the 1820s. Given Zelter's frequent additions to Bach autographs for the purposes of his own performances, he is the probable author of the slurs in the score.

Nevertheless we must not rule out the possibility that Bach made or instigated the alterations to the parts. Certainly they should not be ignored on stylistic grounds since a similar change is made in the oboe parts of BWV 249/11 (St 355), sources which show signs of much autograph revision (and copying). Brainard considers these alterations to be authentic (*NBA* 2/7 *KB* p. 27).

2. Markings in autograph scores which do not appear in the parts:

Most instances in this category can be explained by a peculiarity in the original parts rather than the score. In several cases Bach apparently did not edit the non-autograph parts and many slurs may have been omitted by the copyist. This kind of problem will be examined at length in the next section. However, two cases deserve special attention. The extensive slurring in BWV 245/7 (for the quaver figure b. 3f) appears only in the autograph score P 28. This situation is easily explained by the fact that the score is of later origin than most of the extant parts St 111, so the markings reflect Bach's later thoughts (*NBA* 2/4 *KB* pp. 76, 196). BWV 56/1 contains the paired 'sighing' motif which is so often associated with a slur. However, only at three points in the violin 2 and violin 1 do these slurs appear in the parts (St 58). This is well explained by the fact that Bach's hand is never evident in the editing of the parts for this movement; although the score P 118 is extensively marked it is never certain that the copyist would have reproduced all the slurrings. However, what is extra-ordinary about this case is the fact that the slurs in the score are marked comprehensively only as far as b. 33, which corresponds exactly with the end of the first page. The second page shows a marked change in Bach's hand. The script is more hurried, mistakes are common, and the notes lean to the left. Bach clearly worked slowly and carefully on the first page, perhaps copying from an existing draft and including extensive articulation marks. After this point the slurrings seem only incidental to the compositional process (see Plate 6).

Although the most comprehensive articulation marks are found in scores of a calligraphic nature, we must be wary of regarding all such slurrings as authentic. Some of the slurs in the 'Et in Spiritum Sanc-tum' from BWV 232 (P 180), for instance, were probably included for C. P. E. Bach's later performances (*NBA* 2/1 *KB* pp. 347-8). They implement the standard three-note pattern on the tied figures (e.g. bb. 31-5) which Bach purposely left unslurred.

PERFORMANCE PARTS

Although many articulation markings are present in the first written record of composition - the autograph score - many more are found in the original performance parts, prepared directly from the autograph (or, in the case of dublettes, from existing parts - Dürr 1976 pp. 8-10). Sometimes the markings merely complete those suggested in the score and no previously unmarked figuration is slurred or marked with dots. However, many marks are new and these may be significant in re-flecting Bach's own interpretation of the music. As has already been observed, the graphic evidence for the authorship of articulation marks is often slim. Only by assessing the characteristics of a wide range of sources can conclusions be reached.

Authenticity of markings added to parts

Bach usually left the bulk of the copying process to a chief copyist

6 BWV 56 1 bb. 1 62. Mus. MS P 118

6 *(cont.)*

(Hauptkopist). Less experienced scribes were given the task of preparing doubling parts (dublettes) from the principal copies. Nevertheless Bach himself often added the final chorale to cantatas, this being chosen after the remainder of the score was complete (see pp. 25, 69 above). Sometimes he finished parts begun by copyists or even, particularly in the 1730s, copied out entire sets of parts himself.

However, caution is needed even in the case of autograph parts: in the autograph part for ripieno soprano (St 92) of BWV 110/1 two non-autograph trills are discernible, bb. 45, 125. Although there are few slurs that are worthy of interest in this part, this occurrence should make us wary of regarding an autograph part – and, as has been shown already, an autograph score – as entirely authentic.

Although the level of Bach's editing of non-autograph parts can vary widely, regular instances of continuo figuring, dynamics and trills suggest that Bach usually attempted a systematic review of his copyists' work. A note made on the folder to the parts St 8 (BWV 39) originally read 'NB ist nicht durchgesehen'. The 'nicht' has been covered by 'völlig' in what could well be Bach's hand (*NBA* 1/15 *KB* p. 196). This suggests that copyists made a practice of showing their work to the composer. The fact that Bach had not checked the parts (when they were first prepared) seems particularly significant, since the date of the first performance of this cantata is 23 June 1726, exactly in the period when Bach's revision of parts seems to have been little more than cursory (see pp. 86–7 below).

If parts containing autograph dynamics and ornaments also show rather more slurs than the autograph score, it is likely, though not certain, that these are also in Bach's hand. Examination of a large number of parts in the original shows that the ink colour and thickness of added articulation marks often matches that of the dynamics and ornaments. However, consistency of ink colour and thickness can vary within a short space of time; some form of corroborative evidence is usually required.

Added slurs are most definitely authentic when they are connected with an autograph trill symbol or appear to be drawn in the same stroke. Bach had several ways of combining the two markings: *tr⁀*   is perhaps the most common.

The flat form of dots has been observed as a characteristic of Bach's hand (see pp. 74–6 above). Attribution is even more certain if Bach has also added 'staccato' in the same ink at the head of the movement. This is evident in the viola part (St 15) of BWV 36b/1.

Sometimes the copyist of a part omitted bars or notes; Bach's hand is often evident in the necessary insert. This is the case for bb. 39–43 in the violin 1 part of St 389 for BWV 58/5. The notes and slurs here are much lighter and browner than those of the copyist. The slur in b. 41 is so faint and scratchy that it has been redrawn. Although by no means all the other slurs in the movement are of the same quality, many do match the autograph material (e.g. the second slur in b. 8, incidentally omitted from the autograph score, P 866; slurs in bb. 24–6).

Another clue to Bach's authorship of slurs is his insertion of appoggiaturas connected with slurs. In the soprano part (St 52) to BWV 84/1 an appoggiatura and slur are added at the beginning of b. 36. The conspicuous light-brown ink of this addition almost certainly matches the autograph trills (e.g. bb. 32, 40).

In general Bach's copyists followed the markings in the sources they were using without obvious augmentation. However, in many cases it is difficult to discern which slurs were included at the moment the notes were copied. A control is provided by passages which have been erroneously copied and subsequently deleted or marked 'tacet'; here, then, Bach is unlikely to have added further markings. In the violin 1 part of St 52 for BWV 84/3, bb. 161–81 have been deleted to facilitate an easier page-turn for the player. There are no slurs whatever in this passage (the rest of the part has been heavily augmented with slurs which may be Bach's; see pp. 182–3 below). A particularly interesting case is the tenor 2 part for St 77 (BWV 215/2 and 3). Here the recitative and aria were erroneously copied out (they are to be sung only by tenor 1). In the aria the slurring generally accords with that of the score (with a few omissions); however, the text is not yet included. Thus the practice of this copyist ('Hauptkopist E' in Dürr 1976 p. 108; *NBA* 1/37 *KB* pp. 49, 56–7) was to copy the musical notation more or less exactly and add text at a later stage.

Some deleted passages suggest that copyists continued patterns for which Bach provided only a few opening bars in the score. This is evident in the oboe part (St 33a) – marked 'tacet' – for BWV 201/7. b. 9 (3rd slur) and b. 10. Never, however, do deleted passages reveal that copyists actually devised new slurring patterns.

Sometimes a striking unevenness of markings in a copyist's part might be significant in reflecting the copyist's 'normal' level of slurring. In J. H. Bach's violin part for BWV 98 (St 98) the first page is well marked with slurs, but after this the slurs abruptly cease. This suggests that most of the slurs were added in a revision after the part was completed, the editor marking only the first page.

Although there seems to be very little evidence that copyists consistently devised their own slurring schemes there are a few instances where slurs added to parts are of an unusual shape or result in an unusual articulation.

Dürr notes three different stages in the addition of slurs in St 28 for BWV 108 (*NBA* 1/12 *KB* pp. 49-51): those in the hand of the copyist; those added by Bach himself; those in a grey-black ink of unknown origin. However, Dürr admits that the last two inks are scarcely distinguishable. He further differentiates between the styles of articulation implied by the two inks: the unknown (grey-black) ink is, according to his observations, associated with a more cross-beat slurring, which, he suspects, is contrary to Bach's intended on-beat style (and could further imply a general legato rather than a specific articulation).

Examination of St 28 suggests to the present author that Dürr's distinguishing of two different inks is influenced by his suspicion of the musical style of the 'upbeat' slurs rather than by the actual colours of the ink, which are not obviously distinguishable. Several features imply that the cross-beat alterations and additions are part of Bach's general revision. In movement 1 the first slur in question is the third in the first bar (oboe). An extension to the right in 'blacker' ink is hardly noticeable; the stroke could as well have been retaken half-way through owing to a fluctuation in the ink-supply. The autograph score, P 82, in any case shows the slur covering the fourth note at this point. A more noticeable extension in the part has been made at the equivalent place in b. 26; here, however, there is certainly no change in the ink colour. Dürr also places some of the longer slurs in the third category of 'grey-black' slurs. However, that of b. 32 (oboe) shows no unequivocal sign of extension; indeed, it becomes slightly browner rather than blacker (as Dürr describes 'Tinte b') towards the right. In any case, surrounding longer slurs (e.g. b. 33) are also brown and definitely show no signs of extension.

The autograph score, P 82, shows fewer upbeat slurs in movement 2 (in bb. 5-7 the first three notes are slurred rather than the last three:

♪♪♪♪). However, the last slur in b. 9 crosses the bar-line itself.

Most of the 'upbeat' slurs in the obbligato violin part for this movement (St 28) are in the brown ink characteristic of Bach's markings:

bb. 3-4, 8, 33, 37 (extension in brown: Dürr singles this out as a *blacker* alteration), 41, 46, 51, 55, 56, 58, 60-1, 64. All these markings are identical in colour and width to the autograph dynamic markings.

Movement 5 shows the greatest use of cross-beat slurs. However, some of these are implied in the autograph score itself (e.g. b. 1, slurs 2-3) although the placing is often haphazard. The two violin 1 parts also contain slurs which are fairly poorly placed. Most extensions in the main part are in the browner ink of the autograph dynamic markings. In the violin 1 dublette extensions are, admittedly, slightly blacker. However, this is exactly the same colour as the autograph chorale added at the end of the part. Furthermore, the first half of b. 39 was omitted by the copyist. Bach's insert is very clearly marked with the cross-beat slurring. These slurs show no sign of later addition and surely reflect Bach's intentions throughout (see Plate 7).

BWV 13/5 provides another problematical example of extended slurs. The violin part in St 69 is marked in great detail. However, many of the upbeat slurs show signs of extension from: 𝄞 to:

𝄞 It is the appearance of these extensions which is most atypical of Bach: many (e.g. bb. 6-7) have been extended with a curious wavy line. Some (e.g. b. 28) seem also to be too steep and angular for Bach. However, many of the markings denoting a similar style of slurring have the curve more typical of Bach: bb. 37-8, 44, 46, 49, 65 onwards. The dots which clarify many of these upbeat slurrings are slightly flat, as is often observed for dots in Bach's hand.

Helms' arguments (*NBA* 1/5 *KB* p. 218) that these markings might be doubted on the grounds that Bach seldom marked parts in such detail, seem, in the light of many of the observations made in the present study, to be unfounded. Admittedly the autograph recorder part for the same melodic line shows far fewer markings (the second recorder part is a direct copy of Bach's by J. H. Bach). However, some markings such as the second slur in b. 5 and most of those in b. 6 show the upbeat style.

It has often been suggested that Bach added more markings, the longer he worked on the editing process (Kilian 1983 pp. 27-9). Here it is quite possible that he edited the violin part after writing the recorder part (which seems a logical course of events: the basic notes were surely of primary importance in the process of copying). Only the appearance of the markings counts against Bach's authorship, but, as has been shown, by no means all the 'upbeat' slurs are drawn in this way. As

7 BWV 108, 5, 6, violin 1 dublette part; autograph insertion b. 39 (line 11) and chorale. Mus. MS St 28

most of these are found in the first half of the movement, Bach may
well have been working with an uneven nib which he replaced during
his editing of the movement.

Although it is not always possible to prove that the slurs and dots
added to parts are in Bach's hand, it is quite striking that many parts
which show little or no sign of his revision in other respects contain
few articulation marks. The parts of the following movements barely
augment the slurrings implied by the score or even contain fewer markings altogether:

BWV	date	
94/4	6/8/24	flute parts poorly edited (JSB evidence in continuo though)
170/1	28/7/26	
45/1	11/8/26	
45/3		
45/4		
35/1	8/9/26	fewer markings in parts
56/1	27/10/26	slurs in score for first page; very few in parts (see pp. 77-8 above)
56/3		fewer markings in parts
56/4		fewer markings in parts
49/1	3/11/26	slightly fewer markings in parts
49/3		
55/1	17/11/26	fewer markings in parts
55/3		
51/4	17/9/30	fewer markings in parts
213/11	5/9/33	violas virtually unmarked in parts
234	1735-50	score generally more accurate/complete

The bias of this list towards the late months of 1726 is very striking.
Clearly Bach was short of time during this period or he trusted his
copyists and/or players to devise their own articulation.

Some sets of parts show marked fluctuations in the detail of indicated articulation and these usually reflect partial editing by Bach.
In BWV 164 (26/8/25) only the viola part (St 60) shows evidence of
Bach's editing. It contains a greater number of slurs than the other
parts (particularly in the first movement) reflecting just how much
should be added to the other parts. The autograph parts for BWV 11/11
(St 356) are most conspicuous since they contain slurs and dots which
are totally absent in the other parts (notably the string parts) and score.
The part for flute 2 is in Bach's hand and comprehensively marked,
while the copyist's part for flute 1 (with matching figuration) remains
unmarked. Detailed markings begin to appear after Bach takes over
the copying in b. 7. Nevertheless the predominance of autograph parts

does not necessarily guarantee complete markings. The slurs in the oboe parts (St Thom) for BWV 14/4, for instance, are very sketchy, as are those in BWV 30a/1 (St 31).

Sometimes Bach as editor had time only to check the notes, so an autograph insert shows a slurring which is totally absent elsewhere. In BWV 85/5 the continuo parts throughout are poorly marked; only Bach's insert in the transposed continuo part, b. 25, contains the slurring. Similar examples are BWV 194/5, b. 46 (violin 1 dublette) and BWV 40/7 bb. 43-6 (oboe 1).

While the presence of Bach's hand in a set of parts, either as scribe or as editor, does not mean that the articulation is included in its most complete form, those movements which *are* comprehensively marked invariably show definite evidence of Bach's hand.

Virtually all well-marked movements comprise a fairly ornate instrumental obbligato (e.g. BWV 97/4). Presumably Bach would have spent considerable time in devising the articulation schemes for these. Furthermore, since a large ensemble is not normally involved, there is far less chance of disagreement between parts or incompleteness in subsidiary lines.

Some large ensembles are, however, marked in more detail than is the norm. BWV 57/1 (St 83) shows clear evidence of an extraordinarily thorough revision by Bach. The ink colour of his trills matches well the slurs, which are, in turn, easily distinguished from the later markings by Zelter. The latter show a pronounced difference in articulation style: an accent mark is added to the violin 1 dublette at b. 6, and throughout the same part crotchet rhythms are frequently slurred (Appendix 2 shows that in 3/4 the crotchet pulse is seldom slurred; see also p. 113 below).

The chronology of Bach's revisions

Bach's revision of scores and parts was not always a single process, but one which could have been undertaken in several stages and at different times. In BWV 108 (St 28) Bach's hand is evident in the dynamics (and slurs and dots?) of the principal violin 1 and 2 parts (J. A. Kuhnau). However, most dynamics in the two dublette parts are in the hand of the copyist, which suggests that Bach edited the main parts before the dublettes were prepared. Nevertheless, some markings in the latter are autograph: several trills, some dynamics and an insert in the violin 1 dublette, some dynamics in the violin 2 dublette (e.g.

movement 5, bb. 16, 20, 31). Furthermore Bach wrote out the heading 'staccato sempre' in all four parts. Clearly, then, Bach did not examine the parts in a single process.

At other times Bach subjected sets of parts to revision only after all the parts and dublettes had been copied. Thus the secondary copyists used the uncorrected part of the 'Hauptkopist' before the parts were checked by Bach. A typical example of Bach's editing of an entire set of parts is St 59 for BWV 81. In movement 3, b. 6 (violin I) has been omitted by the copyist and subsequently added below by Bach. Exactly the same omission and correction is evident in the dublette. Furthermore, many of the slurs in this movement are added in the same thick brown ink of Bach's inserted b. 6:

bar	main part: (slur no.)	dublette: (slur no.)	present in autograph score. P 120:
1		1	yes
6	1-3	1-3	yes
8	1	1	no
9	1	1	no
10		2	yes
11	1-2	2	no
12-14 (2)	all	all	no
24	2-3	3	no
36		2	no
38-9	all	all	no
40		1	no
41		2-3	no
45		3	no
46		3	no
49	3	3	no
50	1-2	1-2	no
52		1	no
57		1	yes
58		3	no
59		1-2	yes
62	1-3	1-3	no
66	2-3		no
67-73	all	all	no
75		1	yes
76-	(ink colour less distinct) most?		no

This table shows that the browner slurs (Bach's?) correspond well with those that were absent from the autograph score and thus not included by the copyist of the first part (J. A. Kuhnau); the second copyist then apparently omitted some which were in the first part (e.g. b. 10 (2); b. 57 (1)). Although comparison of ink colours is never the most reliable method of proving that a revision has been made, some passages are very clear indeed, in both parts: in the passage bb. 12-14 only the third slur of b. 14 is in the autograph score; this one is noticeably lighter than the surrounding slurs matching the colour of the notes.

Many slurs in the two violin 2 parts might be (by comparison with the autograph dynamics) in Bach's hand. However, in b. 26 of movement 1, the main part has paired slurs, the dublette a single four-note slur. Could it be that this discrepancy (and indeed the many more that are often observed in sets of original parts) results from the fact that Bach edited these parts from the score with no reference to each other?

The autograph and semi-autograph parts, St 89 (and a Coburg violin part), for BWV 151/3 contain several discrepancies. The autograph oboe and violin 1 parts have virtually identical articulation markings (as printed in *BG* 32); this suggests that they were prepared with reference to each other. The autograph violin 2 part, however, contains fewer dots and some slurs which cross the central beat of the bar (e.g. bb. 4, 14) and the bar-line itself (bb. 51-2). An even greater extension of the cross-beat slurring is shown in Kuhnau's violin 1 (Coburg), which contains autograph dynamics. Here, in passages such as bb. 4-5, the *superjectio* figure is slurred in cross-beat pairs (from the fourth note) (Example 39). That Kuhnau was probably copying from the score

Example 39

(Coburg) rather than from Bach's autograph parts is suggested by the fact that the slurs for bb. 2-3 seem to have been originally pairs (as in the autograph score) and subsequently enlarged. The incorrect *e"* note-head in b. 29 might also derive from the alteration in the autograph score at this point. The viola part shows an articulation scheme roughly compatible with the fully autograph violin 1 part (although many dots are missing and slurs are imprecise). Anna Magdalena's dublette (Coburg) for the violin 2 follows the autograph violin 2 part (which, incidentally, contains more cross-beat slurring than the autograph violin 1 and oboe parts, bb. 51-2, but marginally less than that of Kuhnau's dublette (violin 1), e.g. bb. 4-5, edited by Bach).

The probable sequence of copying is: (1) autograph score with original paired slurring in bb. 1-2; (2) autograph oboe and violin 1 parts prepared together or from each other; (3) autograph violin 2 part, with some later thoughts on cross-beat slurring; (4) Anna's direct copy of violin 2; Kuhnau's violin 1 copied from score (the chorale at the end in Kuhnau's hand suggests that this part was written later than the alto, tenor and bass parts at least, since in these the chorale is added in Bach's hand); (5) Kuhnau's violin 1 edited (by Bach?) with complete cross-beat slurring. Inconsistency here, then, might be due to Bach's changing conception of the articulation from paired to cross-beat slurring, evident in the score itself (see pp. 70-1 above). His copyists seem to have reproduced directly the slurring in whichever version they happened to be copying.

SUMMARY

This survey suggests that Bach gave articulation marks in scores rather more attention than is often thought. Slurs seem to be associated with the addition of 'passages' (*Decoratio*) to slower note values. They may also indicate how motifs within a movement have similar origins but evolve with completely different rhythmic characteristics.

Bach usually edited and revised the performance parts prepared by copyists and notated much of the articulation at this stage. Generally he amplified the markings notated in the score, although some sources show a development and refinement of the articulation scheme (see pp. 133-4 below).

7

Principal articulation patterns in the instrumental parts of vocal works

Having observed the role of articulation markings within Bach's compositional process, in this chapter we turn to the nature of the markings themselves and the specific figuration with which they are associated. The survey concentrates on a large group of sources - those vocal works for which both an autograph score and an original complete set of parts survive (Appendix 1) - with the assumption that an observation of general trends will outweigh individual problems of accuracy and interpretation (great though many of these are). Each slurring is discussed with regard to the metre, figuration, instrumentation, bowing and tessitura concerned. The stage at which it is included (in the score or parts) will also be considered, as well as the regularity of use within the movements involved.

The following commentary should be read in conjunction with Appendix 2. Each pattern is, for convenience, specified in quaver values. However, the exact note values depend on the relationship between 'Metre' and 'Division of pulse': e.g. the quarter pulse in C-time is the semiquaver.

SLURS RELATING TO FOUR (OR TWO)-NOTE GROUPINGS IN DUPLE DIVISIONS OF THE PULSE

1A

The association of 1A with string playing is reflected in Scheidt's *Tabulatura Nova* (1624) for organ, where it is named 'imitatio violistica' (see p. 53 above). With continuous passage-work it allows a traditional

91

hierarchy of bow accents with the 'strong' down-bow on the first and third beats of the bar. However, 1A is just as common in wind parts.

Bach's use of 1A seems evenly spread throughout his career although, considering how few works were written during the 1730s, the high proportion of examples in this period is striking. This is, however, the case with most slur patterns and reflects more the greater care and time spent in preparation of sources than a definite change in articulation style. Most of the autograph scores for the Leipzig cantata cycles 1723–7 are composing scores, whereas the major works of the 1730s – BWV 232, 244, 248 – survive in revision copies.

In nearly three-quarters of the cases of 1A the slurs are found in the autograph score. The composing sources of 1723–7 show that Bach introduced this slurring relatively early on in the process of composition.

Pulse

The majority of examples use 1A for the quarter division of the pulse (e.g. semiquavers in C-time). Striking cases of the eighth division are found in the virtuosic obbligati of BWV 97/4 (violin), and BWV 94/4 (flute). BWV 20/8 shows the pattern interspersed with staccato quavers (see Example 46).

The half division is used regularly only four times in C-time or 2/4 (quavers). Slurs covering the quarter pulse in 3/8 (five examples), and the single wind examples for the twelfth pulse in 6/8 and 12/8 (demisemiquavers) concern regular figuration (the fastest note values) and imply three pulses in a 3/8 bar or compound group, rather than one.

Tessitura and instruments

1A is used both by obbligato instruments and ensembles. Although there are twelve instances for basso continuo alone, most examples relate to the higher instruments. This is not surprising if it is considered that the quarter pulse occurs most frequently in the upper voices, responsible for much of the *Decoratio*. Most of the examples for wind are for oboes: this reflects more the preponderance of oboe parts than a neglect of slurs for flute. Horns have two regular instances of 1A, trumpets one regular use (BWV 11/11).

Figuration

Few cases show 1A used for exclusively disjunct figuration (B), especially in wind parts. Six string cases are evident, mainly of arpeggio figuration. Most instances of the *messanza* figure do not have sufficiently large leaps to be registered as disjunct; only BWV 97/4 comes into this category. The *messanza* is often found in those instances where a variety of figures is involved (category C).

Single conjunct figures constitute a substantial proportion of the uses of the 1A slur: these involve either four-note figures (i.e. *groppo, circolo mezzo*, turn, etc.) or four descending notes, many of which begin with an appoggiatura (the fourth note being the harmony-note). The slur is used far less frequently for groups of four ascending notes (*tirata mezzo* – see Fuchs 1985 p. 102).

Most mixed uses of 1A (category C) concern oscillating, trill-like figures in addition to the figures already discussed. 1A is seldom applied indiscriminately to continuous passages (without some recurring figuration).

1B

1B is rather less common than 1A (particularly in wind parts) but it appears in the autograph scores in over half the cases. It is especially suited to string bowing, with a long down-bow followed by a short up-bow. Dots for the unslurred note feature in a third of the examples; this last note can often be quite disjunct (BWV 232/2) or closer (at the same pitch as the last note under the slur, BWV 211/2). These last two examples show the dots written into the autograph score; the score P 180 of BWV 232 is a revision copy; however, that for BWV 211 (P 141) has the appearance of a composing score. The dramatic increase in the use of dots for the unslurred note of 1B during the 1730s reflects a general trend towards clarification and greater detail in the notation.

Pulse division
Like 1A the majority of uses of 1B are for the quarter division of the beat. There is one string example of the eighth division for ¢ (semiquaver motion); in musical effect this is similar to semiquaver motion in C-time. Rather more surprising is the greater number of uses of 1B for the half division of C-time or 2/4 (quaver pulse), particularly in string parts. Half of these are only sporadic appearances.

Tessitura and instruments
The usual bias towards the higher instruments is evident, although

1B is used by a large range of obbligato instruments (including two instances for viola da gamba; two for violoncello piccolo; one for viola). Oboes and flutes use 1B to a more equal extent than 1A. Two examples show regular figuration for bassoon but no brass instruments whatever are featured. 1B is particularly appropriate for solo lines since it brings out more detail in the figuration than the more standard 1A pattern.

Figuration

Only seven string examples and one for wind show 1B used exclusively for regular disjunct figuration (B); these generally relate to ascending arpeggio figuration in solo lines. In the other categories, 1B is used equally for conjunct ascending and descending notes (1A was more suitable for resolutions and the natural falling of lines). Few appoggiaturas are evident with 1B; its function is more to impart a dynamic energy to the lines.

Many examples of the 1B slur cover the standard four-note figures. The four-note figure with a leap between the third and fourth notes (returning to the pitch of the first) is particularly appropriate for 1B. Here, as with the *messanza* figure, the slurring mirrors exactly the conjunct component of the figuration.

1C

By far the most common slurring of all is the paired pattern 1C; this can be applied to groups of two, four, or more notes. The majority of Bach's recorded uses of 1C for both strings and wind is found in the autograph score, which suggests that paired slurs might often be fundamental to the composition itself, particularly when associated with the resolution of dissonance (e.g. 'sigh' figures).

Pulse division

Over half the instances of the 1C slur are for the half divisions of the pulse, which is unique among the slurrings so far discussed. The half pulse is most likely to be slurred when some form of harmonic accent is evident. The 1C slurring is, however, never applied to dissonances covering the whole beat. In compound times it is used for the sixth division of the pulse.

In a few cases 1C is used both for the half and for the quarter divisions. Generally the two divisions are distinguished by different figuration. Usually the half-pulse use of 1C corresponds to specific figures (such as 'sighs' – which are invariably harmonic accents – and dotted patterns); the quarter-pulse version can cover more varied patterns.

Tessitura and instruments

Although 1C is used considerably more than the other patterns discussed, the bias towards the higher instruments is still evident since the higher parts have faster-moving lines. Nevertheless there is a small group of examples in which only the continuo has 1C slurs. Here there is usually a definite pattern to the bass figuration which is not evident in the higher parts: dotted rhythm in BWV 124/3 (slurs for even rhythms appear elsewhere); stepwise and arpeggio movement in BWV 175/4; oscillating semitones in BWV 17/5; *superjectio* in BWV 14/2. The bass-line in BWV 52/3 moves in continuous semiquavers, whilst the violin parts do not. In BWV 17/5 the lower voices move in half divisions of the pulse while the other parts move in quarter divisions. The horn and trumpet appear in a very small number of examples.

Figuration

A small number of instances of 1C cover exclusively disjunct figuration (category B) in string music and even fewer do so in wind examples. This slight difference might relate to the instrumental idiom: 1C can be used as a standard bowing technique when string crossings are necessary, such as in cases where one note is constant (often an open string). Here the slur might have a purely accentual function reducing the number of separate bows by a half. In woodwind playing, leaps are less practicable and slurring implies more a definite legato. 1C is used for exclusively disjunct figuration when specific patterns are involved: the dotted version in BWV 244/52, 44/3, 232/III; stepwise patterns (i.e. with the last note of the slur at the same pitch as the first note of the next slur) in BWV 195/2 and 177/2; paired thirds (BWV 248/61); oscillating intervals in BWV 245/1. The use of 1C exclusively with disjunct figuration that has no inherent pairing is very rare. The slurring in BWV 244/35 is exceptional here, and is clearly designed for a special *Affekt*, on the viola da gamba.

Most disjunct figuration is found in the C category, in movements where the paired slurring is the dominant *Affekt* throughout (e.g. BWV 244/29). J. G. Walther (1708 p. 35) uses the 1C slurring in his description of ligatures, where he relates it specifically to bowed music.

It is impossible to note all the other uses of 1C: paired stepwise figuration and single 'sigh' patterns (i.e. suspensions or appoggiaturas) virtually demand slurring (practically all occurrences in the music studied are slurred); oscillating intervals and the *superjectio* also imply a natural pairing (as suggested by J. G. Walther's discussion of the *accentus*: see pp. 21–3 above). Another common *accentus* pattern is the dotted rhythm (*anticipatione della nota*). The notes might sometimes be disjunct but conjunct successions of dotted pairs are those most usually slurred.

Conjunct four-note figures (i.e. *groppo*, *circolo mezzo*) are quite commonly slurred with 1C in string music, although not as frequently as with 1A. Another 1A pattern is the four-note appoggiatura, resolving downwards to the harmony-note. Several examples show this slurred with 1C, but it is significant that there is often a discrepancy between the sources (e.g. BWV 248/57: most parts 1A).

1D ♩♩♩♩

1D is the exact complement of 1B: the first note rather than the last is unslurred. It produces the rhythm of the *suspirans* figure, which, as the earliest example (BWV 71) suggests, is characterized by a rest or tie on the beat, followed by three quavers or semiquavers. The bowing implications might also be important: if each beat is to begin at the same point in the bow, the down-bow on the first note must be three times as fast as the up-bow for the three slurred notes. This would give an accentual quality to the unslurred note.

From the beginning of the Leipzig period, the pattern of four notes with the first separated (often by a leap) and the other three slurred is common. As with 1B the unslurred note is increasingly likely to receive a dot, although only in the 1730s is the dot found in the scores. Most such scores are revision copies, but the autographs of BWV 248/31 and 30/8 have the appearance of composing scores. The bias towards 1D in string lines approaching the 1730s is made even clearer by the fact that many apparent uses of it before that time are in later performance material added to the original sets of parts. The relevant parts for BWV 103/3 (Krebs' part for 'Violino con: ou Trav') and 47/2 (autograph part) date from the 1730s. In the case of BWV 10/2 the dots are found in an original part, but the slurs above them are of the 1A type (i.e. covering the first note); this suggests that the choice of 1D (i.e. the dots) was a later thought.

Pulse division

Unlike both 1A and 1B, nearly a third of the uses of 1D cover the half division of the beat.

Tessitura and instruments

Used generally in the higher obbligato parts, 1D is consistent with other slurring patterns discussed. One (virtuoso) instance for trumpet, with a dot for the unslurred note, occurs in BWV 248/64. In some movements it appears in the continuo and not in the upper string parts, e.g. BWV 91/5. Here the figuration of the continuo is not found in the upper parts. The predominant note value is also different: dotted semiquavers and demisemiquavers for upper parts and quavers for continuo.

Figuration

1D is obviously suited to any figuration showing characteristics of the *suspirans,* or the *messanza* (with the first note separated). Four-note figures with a leap between the first and second notes are also common. Several instances show the slurred group or the first (unslurred) note at constant pitch throughout a sequence. One example (BWV 211/2) shows the first note of the slur at the same pitch as the preceding unslurred note. Like 1A, descending conjunct figures are slightly more common than ascending.

Only two string examples show 1D used exclusively for detached figuration; in these cases (both from BWV 248) the pattern is emphasized by the rest for the first note. Surprisingly, five instances of exclusively disjunct figuration are evident in wind music.

1E

The use of 1E, evenly spread chronologically, is quite rare, especially in wind music. Clearly, the bowing implications (reversing the succession of 'strong' down-bows) preclude its general use.

Pulse division

Two thirds of the string instances of 1E cover the half pulse. Nearly all instances for wind music relate to the half pulse.

Tessitura and instruments
Upper parts, one example for bassoon.

Figuration

The implied pattern of notes – leap followed by two conjunct notes,
followed by a leap – is rare in Bach's music. Frequently the fourth
note and the first note of the next group are conjunct (here the slurring
4L is common). In BWV 232/1 the second and third notes are often
constant within the sequence so 1E is particularly appropriate. 1E gives
an 'upbeat' nature to the line and, when combined with 4L, a completely syncopated articulation is achieved (BWV 58/3).

SLURS RELATING TO THREE-NOTE GROUPINGS IN TRIPLE DIVISIONS OF THE PULSE

2A

2A is the complement to 1A, for triple divisions of the pulse; all three
notes are covered. Its use is evenly spread throughout the examples and
the majority of cases are found in the autograph score.

Pulse division

All instances of the sixth division of the beat for 2A relate to simple
time signatures with semiquaver triplet motion (the fastest note values
concerned). In the majority of compound times, 2A covers the third
division of the pulse; only in 3/8 is the whole division (i.e. quavers)
covered. Such cases suggest one beat per bar (the slur creating a single
accent). Instances of the third pulse in 3/8 (e.g. BWV 32/3) demand
a slower tempo with more accents per bar.

Tessitura

Upper strings, oboes; flutes become more common after 1725. Trumpets and horns are significantly more common than in the list of four-
and two-note patterns, and most cases are for quavers (semiquavers
in the virtuoso trumpet part of BWV 5/5). Some cases show 2A only
for the continuo line, e.g. BWV 211/8. Here the continuo slurs are
found only in the piano sections (when the voice is present). However,
similar figuration without slurs is found in the upper parts (which

are in Bach's own hand). A definite inconsistency of articulation is implied here, the slurs creating a softer sound for the background continuo accompaniment.

Figuration

Two string examples show 2A used exclusively for disjunct motion; none is found for wind. Arpeggiated figuration features frequently in the mixed category C. 2A is widely applied to mixed figuration (i.e. a general slurred style for a particular division of the pulse which is not necessarily related to specific motifs), particularly in wind writing. Three-quarters of the examples show 2A used for conjunct motion up or down; a stepwise relationship between successive groups is also common. Three-note figures (i.e. single trills or mordents) are frequently covered by 2A.

The distinction between 2A and 2B is the most difficult problem of legibility encountered in Bach's manuscripts. The only figuration which can be none other than 2A is the 'Pastorale' rhythm: ♩ ♪ A stepwise relationship between successive groups may also imply a 2A slurring.

2B ♫♪

2B could be compared with 1B (for duple divisions); the last note of each group is separate. In contrast to 2A, the change of bow on the last note allows each slur, in succession, to be played with a down-bow. This imparts a rather stronger definition to the line. The slurring would also suggest the underlying 'Pastorale' rhythm: ♩ ♪ These bowing implications might account for the comparative paucity of examples in wind music.

Instances are evenly spread, and most are evident in the autograph score. Two examples with a dot for the last note occur in the 1730s (BWV 244/1 is the only substantial example), and render the placing of the slur much more accurate.

Pulse division

As 2A. Most examples in C-time, though, show 2B covering the third division and not the sixth; this produces a down-bow on each beat.

Several examples from the early Leipzig years show the whole beats in 3/4 covered.

Tessitura

Upper strings and woodwind. Only three examples (two sporadic) for horns and two for trumpets.

Figuration

The only noticeable difference between the figuration associated with 2A and 2B is the greater instance - particularly in string examples - of category B (exclusively disjunct figures) for 2B. It enhances the momentum of disjunct motion, without creating too many technical difficulties. This is substantiated by BWV 9/3, where the continuo is slurred with 2A for conjunct motion, 2B for disjunct. A similar instance may be BWV 30/10 (violins), although here the legible distinction between the two is difficult to determine. All other features resemble those of 2A, with as many indistinguishable cases.

2C

This, the equivalent of 1D in duple divisions of the beat, is by far the rarest among the triple-division category. Although it allows a down-bow on each beat, it may be that too much accent is caused too early in the beat; this would be contrary to the inherent flow of compound metres. Three-quarters of the instances appear in the autograph score; 2C is not used in the Weimar examples.

Pulse division

As 2A and 2B; no simple triple (other than 3/8) or quadruple times. BWV 57/1 is the single sporadic instance of 2C for the beat of 3/4.

Tessitura and instruments

As 2A and 2B.

Figuration

The only instance of disjunct figuration under 2C, BWV 100/3, shows the unslurred note repeated as the first note of the slur. Otherwise 2C seems to relate exclusively to conjunct figuration, generally charac-terized by a leap between the unslurred note and the first of the slur.

Roughly half the instances show a rest or tie for the unslurred note. A recurring 'pedal' on the second and third notes of the group seems an obvious circumstance for the choice of 2C (BWV 32/3). The dotted rhythm under the slur in BWV 244/30 seems influenced by the style of a Passepied and imparts a dragging character to the movement, entirely appropriate to the mood of the text.

SLURS RELATING TO SIX-NOTE GROUPINGS

3A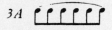

This six-note slur corresponds to 1A and 2A for four- and three-note patterns respectively. Spread throughout the chronology, over half the instances of 3A are found in the autograph score. It is slightly more common in string music.

Pulse division
3A is used most commonly for the half pulse of 3/8 and 3/4 (strings), often also for the sixth pulse of 6/8 (woodwind).

Tessitura and instruments
Upper strings and woodwind; one example for trumpets. Several examples show independent use of 3A in the continuo. Most of these are characterized by continuous semiquaver movement in the bass, not present in upper lines.

Figuration
BWV 147/3 is the only example of exclusively disjunct motion. In BWV 248/4 the arpeggiated section bb. 92-8 is subjected to a general slurred style which was originally associated with conjunct figuration. Over half the examples feature six-note figures (discrete conjunct figures with some form of circling turn); half of these contain a single leap.

Several examples show a discrepancy between the sources, the most common being the presence of 1C (paired) slurring. Quite often there might be inconsistencies within the same parts (e.g. BWV 23/3). Sometimes a chronological difference in the performance material might be evident: in BWV 194/1, 1C seems to be the later version (although it is found at certain points in both versions); in BWV 185/1, however, the 3A slurring of the semi-autograph score, P 59, and the Weimar parts, St 4, is only partially changed to 1C in the Leipzig parts.

A significant use of 3A is found in BWV 245/24. Here the upward-rising scalic figures of the opening are unslurred. However, whenever the vocal line is present, they are slurred with one slur per bar. The character of these runs is not altered rhythmically by the slurring; rather a dynamic contrast is implied, the slurs allowing less bow per note and consequently a softer tone. (See pp. 98–9, 153 for other examples of the 'softening' role of slurs.)

3B

Single, regular instance for flute, reflecting the exact layout of notes (leap after slur). Given the imprecision of the manuscript notation, this could equally be 3A.

3C

This slurring divides a compound-time group or a bar of triple time down the centre. Thus, although the first note of each group/bar receives a strong accent, beats two and three are obscured. This syncopated element of the slurring creates much momentum in fast triple metres. The most common version, with only the first group of three slurred, FO, is especially suited to bowing, with a long down-bow followed by an articulated upbeat. However, a substantial number of instances are also recorded in the wind survey. 3C is found throughout the chronology and is progressively evident in autograph (generally revision) scores.

In four string cases and two for wind, dots are found for the unslurred notes; only in BWV 249/1 and 3, however, is this a regular feature.

· *Pulse division*
Half pulse in 3/4 and 3/8; sixth pulse (i.e. semiquavers) in 6/8, 9/8 and 12/8.

Tessitura and instruments
Higher strings and oboes. The presence of 3C in several obbligati reflects Bach's preference for this slurring in solo lines.

Figuration

Only a few examples show 3C used exclusively for sporadic disjunct figuration. However, several instances in category C show arpeggiated figuration. 3C is generally closely linked with the figuration itself. The second group (when unslurred) is usually disjunct, the first conjunct, and quite often a repeated three-note figure (e.g. BWV 40/4). The quality of momentum peculiar to 3C is, then, usually inherent in the patterning of the notes.

3D

3D could well be compared with 1D (for four-note patterns). The bowing implications are even more pronounced since the initial down-bow needs to be five times the speed of the ensuing up-bow. This leads to a dynamic start to every beat, followed by a gentler run. Nevertheless 3D is equally common in wind music.

3D shows an even chronological spread within the Leipzig years; over half the instances are present in the autograph score.

Pulse division

Half pulse in 3/4 and 3/8; sixth pulse in 6/8 and 12/8.

Tessitura and instruments

Common in ensemble movements with several types of instruments playing, 3D shows the usual bias toward upper strings and oboes.

Figuration

One example shows 3D used exclusively for disjunct notes. The majority involve conjunct scalic figuration often separated by leap from the unslurred note (especially in the string examples); indeed many examples show the first note as a rest or tied note. The upbeat qualities are thus inherent in the music itself. Some examples show a specific five-note figure (i.e. a group of five notes turning in on itself).

3E

Follows conjunct notes isolated by leaps. Dots for unslurred notes in BWV 248/15.

3F

Similar in effect to 1D, 3F is a rare slurring occurring initially in the parts alone but, by 1726, also in the autograph scores. Several examples show a dot for the first note.

Pulse division
Half division of pulse in 3/4 and 3/8; sixth in C-time and 6/8.

Tessitura and instruments
Upper strings, oboes. Flutes more common in the later examples.

Figuration
Virtually all instances of 3F cover three-note groups, preceded or followed by a leap, which gives the pattern a similar rhythmic quality to that of the four-note *messanza*. Two instances show the slurred notes constant within a sequence. One example (BWV 39/3) features regular disjunct figuration.

3G

3G is progressively evident throughout the chronology, occurring in most autograph scores. Its character, with the four slurred notes at the end of each group, is very similar to that of 1A; in many instances there is one unslurred note of double length.

Pulse division
3G covers the half division of the pulse in 3/4 and 3/8; the sixth division in compound times.

Tessitura and instruments
Upper strings and woodwind, progressively more examples for flutes. Some examples for trumpets and horn (in BWV 248).

Figuration
A substantial proportion of the examples of 3G cover four-note appoggiaturas, of the type observed for 1A. Falling scales are far more common than rising. Many instances cover four-note figures.

3H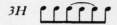

A rare slurring reflecting a three-note figure within six-note figuration. Its qualities thus reflect the *messanza* figure.

3I

3I emphasizes the first and third divisions of the beat and, in string examples, results in a long down-bow followed by a short up-bow. However, 3I is as common in wind writing.

Pulse division
Half division of the pulse in 3/8 and 3/4; sixth division in compound times.

Tessitura and instruments
Biassed towards upper lines. The exclusive use for continuo in BWV 248. 1 reflects the continuous semiquaver movement in the bass, not evident in upper parts. Most wind examples are for oboes. One substantial example for trumpets.

Figuration
As a relative of 3G with the four-note slur at the beginning (BWV 248, 54 uses both extensively), 3I assumes many of the characteristics of 1A. The dubious examples from BWV 36/7 and 100/3 show far more affinity with the figuration of 3C, so it is likely that the slurs are poorly placed.

3J

3J is used exclusively to highlight pairs of semitones within six-note patterns. The slurs reinforce the *accentus* nature of such figures.

CROSS-BEAT SLURRING: QUADRUPLE/DUPLE DIVISIONS OF THE BEAT

Simple time

4A

A very rare pattern, 4A is generally found in string obbligato lines. It could be regarded as a cross-beat extension of 1B and generally reflects the grouping of the notes. Although the examples from BWV 108/2 and 177/4 both contain small leaps underneath the slur, the identity of the slurred pattern is still evident. However, the example from BWV 98/1 shows less relation to the note pattern and seems to function more as an extended accentuation of the first beat of the bar. In BWV 108/2 the pattern often crosses the bar-line (bb. 9–10) and it is extended for an extra beat in b. 33.

4B

All examples (in semiquavers) except BWV 108/4 show 4B with a quaver for the last note under the slur and for the unslurred note.

    Pulse division
Quarter division of pulse for slurred notes in most simple metres; eighth division in ¢ (i.e. all concern semiquavers).

    Tessitura and instruments
Upper strings and woodwind.

    Figuration
4B is most suited to scalic passages of five notes (four semiquavers followed by a quaver). In such instances, then, the slurring is directly related to the note pattern. Five-note figures are found in some instances.

4C

Very rare extension of the 1B pattern to cover two beats. Although several two-beat slurs could be read as 4C, the example in BWV 47/2 is clarified by a dot for the last, disjunct note.

4D

4D reverses the bowing-scheme and, although the example from BWV 30a/1 covers a four-note figure, the handwriting suggests in some instances that 1D was intended. However, both autograph scores show 4D clearly in b. 5.

4F

One sporadic instance for flute.

4G

4G could be regarded as an extension of 1D: a short, fast first note followed by a long up-bow. However, rather more instances are found for wind. It is progressively evident in autograph scores.

Pulse division
Quarter pulse in most cases. Three examples of eighth division in C-time, one of twelfth division in 6/8.

Tessitura and instruments
Upper registers, particularly obbligati. Surprisingly, there are fewer rather than more instances for flute after 1725; no examples for brass.

Figuration
Many of the string instances concern seven-note figures (some of these are extended four-note figures). There are also examples of *messanzas*, four-note figures, scales and appoggiaturas. Several instances have a rest for the unslurred note.

4H

Rare three-note slur, found, in nearly all cases, in the autograph score.

Pulse division
Generally quarter division of pulse: two examples of the half division in C-time.

Tessitura and instruments
Mostly obbligati (with one for violoncello, one for viola) in the upper range. One notable virtuoso obbligato for trumpet in BWV 5/5.

Figuration
Mostly all conjunct, three-note figures. BWV 244/42 is a single, spectacular instance of 4H crossing three-note arpeggios (spanning up to an eleventh) within a string-crossing passage. Such cross-beat arpeggiation is common in the virtuoso string writing of BWV 1001-6.

41

Two instances with a four-note scale or figure placed in the centre of the bar. Absent in the earlier autograph score (P 43) of BWV 30(a)/1, in the later (P 44) the slur covers the final quaver. Dots cover at least one of the unslurred notes.

4J

One instance in continuous semiquavers (covering syncopations).

4K

Most examples have a single quaver or rest for the unslurred note. This means that the long slur can be played up-bow. 4K is increasingly found in the autograph scores. It is equally common in string and woodwind lines.

Pulse division
Quarter division of pulse; eighth division for three examples (i.e. all are semiquavers).

Tessitura and instruments

Most ranges covered. The proportion of examples for basso continuo alone is rather higher than usual. One example for horn.

Figuration

Usually descending scales and six-note figures for strings. *Messanzas*, four-note figures, ascending and descending scales for wind (as in the case of 4G).

4L

Only two string instances, one for woodwind. All feature cross-beat paired figuration and are used in conjunction with 1E.

4M

One string instance, reflecting a descending three-note motif crossing the beat and bar.

4O

The single example, for oboe, makes little sense of the rhythm or figuration. The marking is probably a reminder that a slurring (e.g. 1D, or 1A for the *messanza* figure) is to be applied.

SLURS CROSSING THE BEAT: TRIPLE DIVISIONS OF THE BEAT

Compound time

5B

Similar to the 2B slurring but covering five notes. The examples in BWV 96/1 shows extensions from 2A/2B in the continuo parts, BWV 249/11 extensions in the oboe parts. In BWV 110/1 all sources have been extended from 2B slurrings. There are grounds for doubting the authenticity of this alteration (see pp. 76-7 above).

5E ♩♩♩♩♩

An extension of the 2C slurring, 5E occurs in only three string and two wind parts (and is also present in the autograph score). Most feature conjunct motion and demand the use of a long up-bow. The dots under the slur in BWV 30/5 suggest the type of up-bow staccato observed in the virtuoso violin-writing of J. J. Walther (see p. 40, n. 2 above); this is also shared by flutes. In the autograph score of BWV 100/5 the 5E slurring for oboe d'amore is one of several longer slurrings with dots for the unslurred notes.

5F ♩♩♩♩♩♩

Single instance for oboe, part of a succession of two-note slurs (covering a sequence of semitones) of the 2B/2C type.

5G ♩♩♩♩♩♩

The single example from BWV 176/5 is essentially an extended upbeat *corta* rhythm.

SYNCOPATED PATTERNS

It is impossible to list all slurred syncopations. However, a study of the most regularly and consistently slurred examples shows that the majority of instances follow the syncopated accent: ♪ ♩ ♪ A few follow the metrical accent and, consequently, lessen the force of the syncopation: ♪♩ ♪

BWV 30/1	bar 1	vl. 2. obs, fls
215. 3	1	vl. vla, obsdm
248/31	1	v
244/8	1	vl. 2, vla, fls

BWV 248/51 is unique in having both types of syncopation in succession: bb. 1–2 ♪♩ ♪ | ♪♩ ♪ However, many instances later in the movement (e.g. b. 52) show the first bar slurred in the same way as the second.

CORTA RHYTHMS

The *corta* rhythm is one of the most fundamental rhythmic patterns in Bach's music. Most slurs covering patterns of irregular note values relate to some form of *corta* rhythm. The majority of these show the slur covering the *dactylic* rhythm, within the metrical unit. However, a few cover the *anapaestic* rhythm, within the metrical unit (e.g. BWV 29/3 b. 17). Rather more define the same rhythm (both in string and wind music) across the metrical unit: ♪♫♫♪ Of these, BWV 36/5 b. 19 even crosses the bar-line.

Virtually all the slurs relate to conjunct notes, exceptions being BWV 29/3 (v, b. 17); BWV 248/31 (v, b. 13); BWV 30/8 (vl, b. 18). Most of these more ornate slurrings are found in parts rather than scores.

REPEATED NOTES UNDER SLURS

Repeated notes of the same pitch under slurs fall into two categories: those in which slurs are added to a sequence of repeated notes in regular metrical groupings; those defining recurring patterns beginning off the beat, which can be identified as specific rhythmic figures within the music.

Instances in the first category are common throughout the Leipzig years, slurs covering three, four, or six notes, according to the metre. Such slurs are particularly common in arioso or recitative passages, or in the more meditative 'B' sections of arias. They provide a background which is both unobtrusive and coherent, causing a natural diminuendo within each group:

BWV 245 34	7 4. 24	continuo
32 4	13/1/26	strings
201. 7	c. 1729	continuo (B section)
51. 2	17/9/30	strings
248. 18	26/12/34	oboes
244. 12	30. 3/36	continuo
244/18		strings
244/19		continuo
244/64		violin 1

Rather more interesting are the cases in the second category where the repeated-note figure and its slurring have a regular identity within the music. The effect could well be compared with the standard slur-ring patterns outlined in Appendix 2:

1B:	BWV 26/4	19.11.24	continuo
1D:	114/5	1/10/24	continuo (with dot for unslurred note)
	42/3	8/4/25	bassoon (rest for unslurred note)
	108/2	29/4/25	continuo
	248/64	6/1/35	strings (rest for unslurred note)
	244/8	30/3/36	continuo
2A: (Pastorale)	87/6	6/5/25	continuo
	244/1	30/3/36	continuo
3D:	245/35	7/4/24	continuo
	29/1	27/8/31	strings
	232/12	21/4/33	strings
	213/11	5/9/33	continuo
	248/54	6/1/35	strings (some notes for unslurred)
5C:	97/2	1734	continuo (with dots)

These patterns emphasize the upbeat nature of the repeated notes (the down-beat is usually a rest in cases of 1D and 3D) and provide a constant rhythmic patterning throughout the movement concerned. Clearly the slur has the function of shaping and identifying each group – as in the case of standard slurs – but without any legato connotations. Notes of the same pitch before the slurs are sometimes marked with a dot, suggesting exactly the accentual shaping that would be applied to notes of differing pitches.

'Shaping' of groups of notes seems also implied by the following marking in the autograph timpani part (St 350) for BWV 11/11 b. 40. Here the slur obviously has little to do with actual playing technique (Example 40).

Example 40

8

Fundamentals of Bach's notated articulation

THE INCIDENCE OF SLURS

That Bach related articulation to the notated *Decoratio* of the music is reflected by the musical material in which articulation marks most often appear. Appendix 2 shows that extensive slurrings are most often applied to the quarter-pulse figuration in C-time (i.e. semiquavers), sometimes also to the half pulse. These are the levels at which the figuration is ornamentation of the basic harmonic and contrapuntal structure. In 3/4, where the figuration is often in quavers, slurs for the half pulse predominate. Similarly in compound times, it is the third and sixth divisions which are generally slurred.

Slurs are most often associated with the upper voices: this again reflects the greater amount of figuration, the highest level of 'diminution' which is found in the higher voices. Too much figuration in the bass could well obscure the harmonic rhythm and thus the fundamental structure of the piece. Another important observation is the comparative lack of slurs in ₵ time. This metre is often identified with works of the *stile antico*, where the level of ornamentation and diminution is far lower. Extensive slurring would blur the fundamental notes and detract from the grammatical accents of the metre which are so crucial in the preparation and resolution of dissonance. Grüß (1988 pp. 333-4), quoting C. P. E. Bach, notes that strict contrapuntal pieces are 'nur Musik' in which 'taste' plays but a small part. Slurs, then, are associated with the ornamentation and 'style' inherent in figural music.

The earliest examples, from the Weimar cantatas, show slurred 'legato' movements coupled with expressive *Affekts*: the majority are in minor or flat keys and are often marked with an expressive title such as

113

'Adagio'. However, throughout the Leipzig period slurs are found as frequently in fast movements, and in major keys. Here slurs are often related to playing techniques and, in performance, influence the rhythmic drive of the music.

The relation of slurs to specific figures is evident throughout this survey. Many slurred groups comprise conjunct notes which are inherently grouped (such as four-note groups of the *groppo* and *circolo* type). Small-scale harmonic accents are also frequently slurred. However, slurs appear in many other contexts and influence rhythmic or melodic accents. The more common, standard slurrings such as 1A, 1C, 2A and 2B seem to be those which are applied regularly to figuration of a particular division of the pulse, the standard metrical pulses delineated by the first notes of each slur. Most of the more colourful, cross-beat slurrings date from the Leipzig period and especially from after 1730. It may be that Bach's experience with chamber music at Köthen greatly developed his interest in notated articulation. The most common patterns such as 1A, 2C, 2A and 2B are often evident in the scores, although usually only for a few instances of the figures concerned. The more complex patterns are also occasionally found. In cases where the level of articulation marking in the score is the same as that in the parts, the score is usually a fair or revision copy. Thus such markings have been written in after the process of composition has been completed.

A complete slurring scheme might be found in the composing score when a recitative or chorale movement is based on a continuous and repetitive accompanying figure. Recurring figures such as pairs, four- or three-note figures are commonly associated with slurs from their conception:

BWV 24/6	20/6/23	P 44/4
147/8	2/7/23	P 102
40/5	26/12/23	P 63
10/6	2/7/24	Washington
175/1	22/5/25	P 75
175/5		
56/2	27/10/26	P 118
51/2	17/9/30	P 104
248/3	25/12/34	P 32
248/61	6/1/35	
30/7	1735-50	P 44/1

Slurs were sometimes included at an early stage to indicate exceptions to the standard metrical hierarchy: cross-beat slurs are evident in

BWV 10/1, bb. 8-9 (Washington); BWV 26/4, bb. 17-20 etc. (P 47). BWV 6/5, bb. 3-4, etc. (P 44/2) shows unusual slurring of *corta*. Slurs in Bach's early drafts can be used to underline the accentual quality of the music. In the opening ritornello of BWV 98/3 (P 160), virtually the only slurs present are those at the final cadence (Example 41).

Example 41

Although a similar slurring is applied in many other places in the parts (e.g. b. 14), Bach used these slurs in the score to define the cadence of the ritornello, where the harmonic rhythm quickens from one to three accents per bar.

The scores of the 1730s do, of course, show the most detailed markings in composing scores. Particular detail is evident, for instance, in the score P 141 for BWV 211. The violin obbligato for BWV 29/3 (P 166) might be a revision score, but perhaps Bach was composing slowly and carefully here, anticipating his use of the same 1D figuration (with a dot) in the movement for organ obbligato later in the work.

THE INCIDENCE OF DOTS

Substantial and regular passages with dots appear in sources of the Leipzig period. Dots often clarify rather than interpret qualities inherent in the music or give more precision to slurred passages. Many also imply a negation of the expected metrical accents, giving the notes concerned a background or accompanimental role. The increasing use of the term 'staccato' in sources of the Leipzig period seems to complement or replace dots of this kind. Grüß (1988 pp. 332-3) suggests that this is a notated exception to the standard imposition of long bow-strokes.

Sometimes dots may be applied to create a special 'staccato' *Affekt*. In BWV 147/8, b. 11, dots (in St 46) define a solitary arpeggio figure which stands out from mesmeric slurred figures. That Bach sometimes thought of the 'staccato' style as essential to the character of a movement is suggested by the presence of dots in the oboe d'amore part (St 87) for BWV 183/4. Here the opening two bars of the movement are copied in Bach's hand and subsequently deleted (presumably because this movement belongs to the oboe da caccia part). In this short extract, which must have been written quickly with all performance markings included at the same time as the notes, the dots and trill are present, but not the opening (obvious?) slur (Example 42).

Example 42

Grüß (1988 p. 333) considers a continuous staccato style to be a fashionable feature characteristic of the *galant* style evident, for instance, in the B Minor suite, BWV 1067 (for which performance material from the late 1730s survives).

Dots are used increasingly during the Leipzig period to clarify the extent of slurs. Here the dot might also have accentual qualities, since single notes marked with dots have to be snatched (particularly with the bow) in order to give slurred groups enough tone and delineation. The autograph solo violin part of the concerto BWV 1041 (St 145) suggests that this type of marking can be associated with the delineation of a solo part. In the opening ritornello the solo and ripieno violins have the 1D figure, (bb. 4-6), but when exactly the same figuration occurs in a solo episode (e.g. bb. 89-98) a dot is usually marked:

BWV 249/3, bb. 77-9, etc. (P 34) is an interesting case where a single dot is used to clarify the end of a hastily-drawn slur: In the parts (St 355) dots are generally given for all three unslurred notes.

Bach in his later years sometimes experimented with combinations of slurs and dots:

BWV 11/3	St 356	19/5/35
BWV 30a/5	P 43, St 31 (BWV 30)	28/9/37
BWV 195/3	P 65, St 12	1735-50

The two latter instances occur in movements of a noticeably melodic *galant* nature; indeed this style of notation seems a particular feature of mid-century music. It implies even pulses of sound during a single bow-stroke or breath (with breath accents or mild tonguing). This is thus contrary to the usual accented patterning inherent in both Bach's figuration and notated articulation. Nevertheless, this style of marking is not peculiar only to the 'modern' style: it has already been demonstrated in J. J. Walther's music (see p. 40 n. 2 above) and is an important example in J. G. Walther's (1708 p. 35) description of articulation marks (where the notes are 'zugleich gestoßen'). Bach himself used it early on in his career as an extraordinarily pictorial device in BWV 61/4 (P 45/6) (Example 43). Dots and slurs are also used in com-

Example 43

bass   und   klo · pfe an

bination as a refinement of Bach's more usual articulation style (Example 44). Here the common ID *messanza* articulation seems stipulated,

Example 44 BWV 170 5 (St 94), late autograph flute part

but clearly there is a difference between the dot covered by a slur and that without (tonguing only on the latter?). Although it is impossible, or even undesirable, to establish a literal meaning for this notation, its function is surely to encourage the flautist to give particular attention and delicacy to the articulation; his eye is drawn to the fact that recurring figures (e.g. *messanza*) in Bach's music are articulated slightly differently according to where they fall in the musical sentence. Exactly the same type of figuration receives a similar marking in a string part (Example 45). Here the dot at the end of the slur functions

Example 45 BWV 98. 1 (St 98)

both as the end of the first figure ♪♪♪♪ and the start of the next:
♪♪♪♪ Furthermore the resulting difference of the two dots (the first cut
short at the weak end of the bow, the second receiving a fast, separate
stroke) underlines the metrical difference between the second and
third beats of the bar.

The use of dots and slurs in the composing score of BWV 20/8
(Sacher Stiftung) b. 3 reflects Bach's attitude to notated ornamentation (Example 46). Here the demisemiquavers are clearly an elabora-

Example 46

oboe 1/violin 1

violin 2
oboes 2-3
viola

basso continuo

tion of a quaver *e″*, the slur ensuring that the *groppo* figure is heard
as a single quaver pulse, the dot for the quaver ensuring that this
note is isolated as if it were preceded by a single quaver (as in the bass).
For the performer these marks ensure coordination of the first violins
and oboe with the lower parts.

Bach rarely used strokes, and when he did it is often impossible
to distinguish their meaning from that implied by dots. An accentuation may be implied when both dots and strokes are used in the same
movement. Bach may have added the articulation markings to Krebs'
violin concertante part (St 63) of BWV 103/3 (see Example 63); here
dots are used to clarify a typical 1D slurring pattern in demisemiquavers (b. 2) while a sharply syncopated pattern in quavers is marked
with strokes (b. 5). Similarly, in BWV 248/1 both score and parts (P 32,
St 112) have strokes for the semiquaver arpeggio motif (e.g. flutes b. 25)
but much of the non-motivic quaver movement is marked with dots.
These last two examples suggest, then, that strokes may sometimes be
used to distinguish rhythmic staccato figures from lighter accompanimental devices of a different division of the pulse. Dreyfus (1987 p. 90)
notes the use of strokes in the continuo parts of BWV 18 and 185 to
indicate the shortening of chords in secco recitative.

Dots are most likely to be found in parts and in scores which show signs of being a revision or fair copy. However, a significant number of composing scores contain dots, in sporadic instances at least:

BWV 199 8	Royal Library Copenhagen	12/8/14
44. 6	P 148	21/5/24
62 2	P 877	3/12/24
108/1	P 82	29/4/25
175 5	P 75	22/5/25
57. 5	P 144	26/12/25
43. 1	P 44/6	30/5/26
49 4	P 111	3/11/26
201 1;5;13	P 175	c. 1729
213 1;3;9	P 125	5/9/33
211/2;4	P 141	c. 1734
215/5;7	P 139	5/10/34
97 2	New York Public Library	1734
30a 3;5	P 43, 1	28/9/37

The incidence of dots is similar to that observed for the more complex slur patterns: composing scores from 1729 onwards (i.e. after the period of weekly cantata composition) show the most detail.

THE RELATIONSHIP BETWEEN STRING AND WOODWIND SLURRING

Appendix 2 shows that, although wind instruments feature in as many movements as string instruments, they receive only about two thirds the quantity of articulation markings. This underlines the observations of Part 1 that slurs as bowing directions are fundamental to the basic technique. The wind markings that are included are likely to be of purely interpretative significance.

Several movements seem to be very poorly marked for woodwind. While some such pieces are clearly in a style that is basically unslurred, sometimes a single marking in the score for a regular figure, or the appearance of markings in a unison string part, suggests that slurs have been omitted from the relevant wind parts. In most cases Bach's hand is not evident in the latter. In a few instances Bach edited woodwind parts but still added few articulation indications: BWV 41/2 (St Thom); 82/1 (St 54; flute version of oboe obbligato); 201/1 (St 33a; particularly trumpets). In such cases the equivalent string parts are marked in more detail.

When wind obbligato parts are well marked (e.g. the late autograph flute part for BWV 170/5, St 94) the detail and style of slurring is very similar to that found in a string obbligato. Most of the arias of BWV 249 (P 34, St 355) are excellent examples of detailed wind obbligatos, BWV 249/5 being interchangeable for flute and violin.

In ideal circumstances, then, wind parts are marked in as much detail as string parts. However, Bach was likely to give more attention to the string parts, perhaps because injudicious bowing could destroy the character of the music (see, for instance, the remarkably detailed bowing for BWV 97/4 (21/11/34) where bow direction is carefully regulated).

Most differences between articulation markings in wind and string parts are due to omission rather than to an intended contrast in articulation style. The overwhelming evidence is that the two media are articulated in the same manner. This is clearest in the cases where a string instrument is used as an alternative to the wind obbligato (for a later performance). Good examples are shown in BWV 96/3, 6/2, 16/5. Many more examples show string and woodwind instruments sharing the same lines. Usually the quality of the figuration defines the articulation rather than the medium used. This is demonstrated particularly by brass parts. Although the limitations of range mean that such instruments seldom play the continuous passage-work of the *Decoratio*, when they do receive figuration, the type of slurring is much the same as in other media (see, for example, the virtuoso trumpet parts of BWV 5/5 and 248/64, and the horn part of BWV 136/1, where slurred conjunct groups are interspersed with partly disjunct groups marked with dots).

However, in a small number of cases there does seem to be a contrast of wind and string slurring. One noticeable example is the descending four-note appoggiatura. 1A is by far the most common slurring for this pattern in both string and wind music. However, in three cases where the strings have the alternative 1C slurring, the oboe parts have 1A: BWV 76/8, bb. 5, 9; BWV 94/1, b. 4 (oboe 1A; violin a mixture of 1A and 1C); BWV 62/2, b. 2. Sometimes longer patterns are slurred in pairs by the strings, but with longer slurs in the oboe part: in BWV 82/5 all parts are initially slurred in pairs 1C, but subsequently the autograph oboe part is marked 3A (even while playing simultaneously with the strings). A similar example is found in BWV 72/5, b. 94.

Fuchs (1985 p. 84) gives an outstanding example from a cantata not covered by the present survey (BWV 22/5, P 119) of a consistent

1A/1C difference between wind and strings. Perhaps Bach regarded the tonguing of the oboe to be too strong for regular pairing; the pairs in the strings may be designed to create more tone rather than a mannered pairing.

This slight tendency toward longer slurs in wind lines is reflected in Appendix 2: the 1A pattern is one of the only regular slurrings for which woodwind instruments have a number of examples comparable to that for strings. Other longer patterns are similarly more common than the norm for woodwind instruments: 3G, 4G and 4K. The paired pattern 1C, although common, is not represented in such a high proportion as in the string survey and is applied more strictly to inherently paired figuration.

In BWV 72/5, bb. 1, 17, another difference is evident (Example 47).

Example 47

Bach may have intended the same sounding articulation here since the first of the two quavers would be cut short at the end of the downbow (and by string crossing). The violin pattern then might be regarded as a bowing slurring which achieves the same articulation as is notated in the oboe part.

Likewise in BWV 42/1 the oboe slur and the violin 'highlighting' have the same accentual function: the delineation of the *suspirans* (Example 48). In BWV 249/11 (St 355) oboe 1 of b. 70 seems to reflect

Example 48

the syllabic underlay with 1C slurs (3 per bar) while violin 1 has 3C which creates rhythmic momentum and generates a downbow at every bar line (Example 49).

Example 49

These observations show that in most respects articulation marks for wind match those for strings. Discrepancies which are apparent either show equally viable articulations or relate to differences in playing technique which produce similar musical results.

THE RELATIONSHIP BETWEEN VOCAL UNDERLAY AND INSTRUMENTAL SLURRING

Werner Neumann (1981 pp. 72-85) warns against directly associating the articulation between syllables with instrumental articulation.[1] He gives a succinct example of a vocal line doubled by an instrumental part; the slurring of the latter contradicts the vocal underlay. A further example could be taken from BWV 215/7 where the soprano line is doubled by oboe d'amore (autograph part, St 77) (Example 50). Here,

Example 50

bb. 29-30, the oboe preserves a consistency of slurred figures which is broken by the underlay in b. 30. However, given the accentual implications of slurs, the resulting musical effect is similar. The first note of these bars is an appoggiatura, which, we may assume, resolves to a 'weaker' consonance. In the vocal part this resolution is implied by the slur in b. 29, by the stronger syllable moving to a weaker in b. 30. The oboe does not have the syllabic stress on the first note of b. 30, but a similar stress is implied by the slur. The singer would surely not make a break in the sound after 'Ei'. A similar argument could be made for the discrepancy in b. 26 (the slur is admittedly rather short in Bach's oboe d'amore part). The apparent inconsistencies in the vocal part derive from the necessity to fit in the syllables somehow, without destroying the metrical accents of the music. The intended musical articulation is more that which is reflected in the oboe part.

This example shows that, just as the articulation of a vocal melisma is not necessarily equivalent to instrumental legato, syllabic change does not always preclude an instrumental slur.

Sometimes there is a clear relationship between the textual underlay and the notated articulation in similar motivic material for instruments. A specific underlay might be chosen and doubled by instrumental slurring in order to reinforce the sense or impact of the words. In BWV 248/51, b. 1, the slurring prepares for the vocal line at b. 21, which receives an accent on 'wann': Such an accent strengthens the questioning of the word 'when' and also coincides with a harmonic dissonance. The rhythmic force of a crowd scene might have encouraged Bach to slur the violin exactly according to the stresses of the vocal underlay in BWV 245/21b (St 111) (Example 51).

Example 51

Sometimes the implications of the text might evoke a specific slurring: BWV 199/2 centres on the words 'Stumme Seufzer, stille Klagen'
('sighs unspoken, silent grieving'): the word 'Seufzer' is set to a paired
figure of slurred semitones. The accented appoggiatura is an immediate evocation of a sigh; consequently the same slurring (1C)
is preserved throughout the obbligato oboe part.

Chromatic affective figures are also frequently unbroken, especially
when they indicate a pathetic *Affekt* (Example 52). Thus slurs can

Example 52 BWV 103.1 (St 63)

show how an emotive element in the text might be mirrored in the
music. Both a distinctive rhythm in the syllables and a sharp emotion
expressed by the words may be influential.

Agreement between textual underlay and instrumental slurring
might also depend on the figuration involved, regardless of the implications of the text. Paired slurrings are among the most common,
particularly those related to the resolution of dissonance.

Figures such as dotted pairs: 𝄐 are often consistently slurred in
both vocal and instrumental lines:

| BWV 67/1 | b. 99. etc. |
| 96/5 | 1. 9. etc. (first beat only) |

Some of these slurs over dotted pairs may relate to the harmonic stress
of the notes concerned. In BWV 245/13 the slurring occurs with the
descending figure (b. 3); other dotted rhythms (e.g. b. 5) are unslur-

red. This is exactly paralleled in the tenor underlay (unslurred) of bb. 19, 21, where the descending paired figures of b. 3 receive one syllable each while the rhythms of b. 5 have one syllable per note. In general the first note of the descending slurred groups (b. 3) sounds over a dissonance in the bass or is itself dissonant, that of the unslurred groups is consonant. The slurs then emphasize the harmonic accent and the legato of descending conjunct figures; a similar style is reflected in the vocal underlay.

Some small *tirata* figures are also consistently slurred and texted, especially where they stand out thematically from the surrounding texture:

BWV 67. 2	bb. 1, 7. etc.
122. 2	2, 16. etc. (but not in b. 10)

Groppo figures, which usually constitute the ornamentation of a single note, might also be ungainly if they were not to be consistently slurred and set to one syllable:

BWV 16 3	bb. 7, 24. etc.
28. 1	2, 14. etc.

Sometimes Bach initially associated instrumental slurring with underlay and subsequently adopted a less uniform scheme. In BWV 47/4 the opening bar of the violin follows the slurring and underlay of the bass in the autograph score, P 163 (Example 53). However, in the parts (St 104), a new version of the slurring is given (Example 54). Here

Example 53

Example 54

it seems Bach had second thoughts on the identity of the figuration, imparting an upbeat quality to the instrumental lines which is not preserved in the vocal underlay.

Exactly the same circumstances seem to surround the composition of BWV 151/3: the vocal underlay falls into regular pairs, represented as slurs in the autograph (Veste Coburg). This slurring appears only partially in the non-autograph viola part; in the other parts (largely autograph: Veste Coburg and St 89) a new slurring is adopted (see p. 70 above):  However, never is the paired vocal underlay for the same figuration changed. Bach evidently decided to ·relate the instrumental slurring to the structure of the figuration rather than to the syllabic stresses of the underlay.

Many more examples show a fundamental difference between vocal underlay and instrumental slurring. These seem to fall into two categories: those where the harmony and voice-leading suggest an instrumental slurring different from that of the vocal underlay; specific figures such as syncopation which might be accentually ambiguous.

The most common instance in the first category is the case of a group of four notes, descending, of which the first is an appoggiatura, the fourth the harmony note. Instrumental slurring may cover all four notes (1A), suggesting a consistency between the slurring and the harmonic function of the figure; the vocal underlay often demands a change of syllable on the third note (Example 55). This underlay is

Example 55 BWV 45 3

logical: if '-tes' were placed any earlier, it would receive an undue accent. Thus, while the instrumental parts are articulated according to harmonic concerns, the textual underlay is geared more towards syllabic stress.

The harmonic implications are more complex for the discrepancy in BWV 194/10 (Example 56). The underlay is straightforward: the

Example 56

O _____ wie   wohl   ist _____   uns   ge · scheh'n

accent is clearly on 'O' and not 'wie' and any other underlay would destroy the sense of the words. If this slurring were adopted for the oboes in b. 1, an accent would be thrown on to the third quaver (bb'). However, b. 2 begins with the same note as b. 1, so the quaver figure (b. 1) is merely an ornament to the first note of the piece, a four-note figure similar to a *groppo*. Such delineation of the figure creates an accent on the second beat throughout the piece. Sometimes paired slurs are used (e.g. continuo, b. 4) but usually the intervals are different and naturally paired.

Instrumental slurs seem often connected with conjunct notes approached by leap. Such slurring usually reflects the grouping of notes, but is totally unsuited to syllabic stress (Example 57). In BWV 96/3

Example 57 BWV 100 5

oboe

alto

Wohl _____ ge · than _____

the underlay is adapted to accommodate the two weak syllables: '-he die', b. 13 (Example 58). In at least one example of dotted rhythms a radically different slurring is adopted for voice and instruments. In BWV 84/1 (P 108) the instruments (oboe and strings) adopt the

Example 58

standard *anticipatione della nota* (see pp. 22-3 above): ♩♪ The soprano, however, has the *anticipatione della syllaba*: ♪ ♫ Although it has been suggested that syllabic articulation is by no means as powerful as instrumental articulation, the underlay here is clearly not fortuitous, as it is substantiated by the beaming; such regular cross-beat slurring of dotted rhythms is rare in Bach's music. Bach probably did not regard the slurring in Example 59 as a central issue – after all most

Example 59

of the slurred dotted figures are not accented appoggiaturas. The instrumental slurs perhaps contribute to the mood of the piece – three strong accents in each bar – the vocal underlay providing an incisive and rhythmic style. If the latter were adopted as slurring for the instruments, a break might occur before each group, which would disrupt the rhythmic stability. To a singer, concerned more with the articulation of syllables, the underlying bar-rhythm would be made clear by the quaver chord in the accompaniment.

Of all the regular figures, the rhythmic *corta* is subject to the most inconsistency. Perhaps it is its very rhythmic adaptability and ambivalent rhythm – *anapaestic*: ♫♪ and *dactylic*: ♪♫ – which accounts for its frequency in Bach's music.

BWV 103/1, P 122 bb. 42–3, oboe d'amore 2 and soprano, shows how
a slur clarifies the function of the *corta* in simultaneous voices (Example 60). The oboe uses the *corta* as the ornamental resolution of a

Example 60

suspension. The harmonic accent of the suspended $c\sharp''$ would suggest that this is a *dactylic corta*: ⌊♪♪♪ The 'a-' in the vocal part is
anapaestic: ♪♪♪ which represents, both harmonically and melodically,
the start of the next phrase. Here, then, the simultaneous *corta* rhythms
and the accompanying underlay act as a 'dovetail' of two phrases: one
begins as the other ends.

Another device with a characteristic rhythmic spring is syncopation.
The criteria of harmonic and rhythmic movement in the instrumental
part and verbal accent in the vocal line might account for most
discrepancies: BWV 39/4 (St 8) (Example 61). Here the slur in b. 1

Example 61

continuo acknowledges the rhythmic spring of the syncopation (with
an implied change of harmony on the half beat). Obviously a similar
accent on 'zu' would be textually inappropriate.

These examples of inconsistency between vocal underlay and instrumental slurring show that standard ornamental figures are usually
delineated in instrumental parts, while in vocal parts syllabic stress has

priority (articulation of figures being important in melismatic writing, see pp. 30–4 above).

CONTRADICTIONS BETWEEN SLURRING PATTERNS IN INSTRUMENTAL PARTS

It has already been shown that the completeness of markings in original parts varies widely. However, a considerable number of markings for matching or simultaneous musical material are contradictory. The overwhelming majority of these discrepancies involve paired slurrings (1C). Sometimes one individual part adopts a paired slurring, another a longer slurring: in BWV 248/57 b. 1 (St 112) the violin 1 part is generally marked with the 1A slur - albeit short - for the descending appoggiatura figure in b. 1 while the dublette is more usually slurred in pairs. The same figure is inconsistently slurred in BWV 213/3 b. 1 (St 65) and these discrepancies are still evident at certain points in the later version of the same movement, BWV 248/19 (St 112).

Clearly this apparent lack of care in the differentiation of 1C and longer slurs caused few problems to Bach's players since this trend is so often evident. In his *Praecepta* (1708 p. 35), Walther shows paired slurs as the standard mode of bowing. Perhaps Bach and his copyists wrote paired slurs when they required a general slurred style but had no particular slurring pattern in mind. Certainly Appendix 2 shows that the paired slurs 1C are by far the most common of all regular patterns.

Sometimes 1A slurs may have been used as a shorthand for continuous 1C patterns which have already been established (the longer slurs are, after all, quicker to draw). In the score P 34 of BWV 249/7 the oscillating seconds are slurred in pairs (1C) for the first four bars, but, after a page-turn in the score at this point, slurs of roughly twice the length are used for the next four bars and at several later points. The parts St 355 (partly autograph) show a similar trend (though the inconsistencies are not at the same points). Most of these parts predate the score and presumably reflect similar inconsistencies in the (lost) composing score.[2] A similar example of Bach adopting a longer slurring after a page-turn is in the partly autograph violoncello part (St 47) to BWV 182/6: from b. 69 the quavers are slurred with 1A rather than 1C, with no change of figuration or apparent change of hand.

The 1A slur itself might be interchangeable with a longer (often 2-beat) slur. In BWV 67/2 (St 40) 2-beat slurs are common (for the figure in b. 9) in the oboe and violin 1 parts. However, the violin 1 dublette usually has two 1A slurs. The oboe parts (St Thom) for BWV 3/1 show a similar discrepancy (e.g. b. 2 ob. 2, 2-beat slur; b. 3 ob. 1, two 1A slurs).

The most celebrated instance of contradictory markings for similar and unison lines is BWV 244/68. While Dürr (1974), the editor of the *NBA*, takes the attitude that there may have been a genuine 'imperfection' in the performance here which Bach did not have time to alleviate (despite the evident care spent in copying and editing parts), both he and Dadelsen (1980) observe that it is the non-autograph parts which deviate most. In preparation of his edition Dürr classes the causes of inconsistency as: lack of room; change of lines breaking slurs; thoughtless recopying of slurs in the first two categories; carelessness. He bases his edition on the autograph score and only those parts which are autograph, observing differences between instrumental families but rationalizing unison lines for similar instruments. All variants are listed in the commentary (*NBA* 2/5 *KB* pp. 222-30).

The largely autograph presentation parts for BWV 232 show similar discrepancies. Yet, as the present survey shows, and as both Dürr and Dadelsen have concluded, Bach did *aim* at consistency of markings. The consistencies vastly outweigh the inconsistencies. Editorial problems are usually concerned with incompleteness rather than inconsistency.

Most other types of slur discrepancy are concerned with the poor legibility of the markings. The problems distinguishing 2A/2B have already been noted. Sometimes the character of the figuration demands one of the two: the 'Pastorale' rhythm, consisting of only two notes, can clearly have no slurring other than 2A, covering the entire group. Similarly, a 2B slur is likely when the second and third notes are of the same pitch. Underlay slurs are also a clue to the level of accuracy with this type of slurring. In the autograph score (P 34) of BWV 249/11, bb. 11-12, one syllable is given to each triplet group, but the accompanying slurs frequently cover only the first two notes. Such evidence suggests that copyists (and indeed the composer) did not draw slurs of the 2A/2B type with particular care.

Some dots on third notes confirm a 2B pattern (e.g. BWV 201/9 bb. 1, 14 in oboe d'amore of St 33a). However, it is seldom clear whether the 2B with dot is to be applied throughout. Similarly the difference between the 1A slur and the 1D + dot in BWV 58/5, b. 5

onwards (St 389 and St Thom) is difficult to establish. The 1D pattern
is usually clear in the score (P 866; the opening of movement 5 dating
from the later version) although only the first dot is shown. One of the
violin 1 parts (St Thom – this part is of later origins, Anna Magdalena
and J. S. Bach) shows the complete pattern with dots; the part for
the earlier version (St 389) shows 1A slurs consistently (*NBA* 1/4 *KB*
pp. 133-5, 157). That the 1D pattern was probably Bach's choice in
the first version is reflected by his insert in this part, bb. 39-43.
However, here there are no dots as in the later part.

Throughout this survey it seems that inconsistency of slurring is
most likely with common patterns and, moreover, in movements where
several instruments participate. The obvious conclusion to draw from
this is that it simply does not matter exactly what articulation is used
when there is no single line consisting of a subtle interplay of con-
trasting and developing figuration. The main point seems to be that a
slurring is to be applied, to create resonance and underline metrical
accents (separate bows would render each note too important). A
movement such as the Allegro Assai from BWV 1041 is marked in the
autograph parts (St 145) with a horrifying variety of 2A and 2B slurs
(a similar example is the last movement of BWV 1050). What is consistent is the beginning of each slur, i.e. there are to be three accents
per bar. Bach presumably marked every bar in the piece to remind the
player of the essential style of the movement. What happens at the
'weak' end of every beat might vary according to the technical circumstances. Quite often Bach marks what appears to be an obvious

slurring throughout a piece (e.g. the rhythm: ♩♫ in BWV 67/6) as

a constant reminder to the player of the accentual style, not merely
as a performance direction. Schestakowa (1988) may be quite right to
suggest there is infinite variety in details of articulation in a movement
such as BWV 1050/3, and that countless permutations are implied by
Bach's markings. However, this does not mean that the markings are
to be followed blindly to reveal hidden depths within the music; they
show every sign of hurried if not unconscious activity by Bach which
might reflect or encourage the spontaneity of the performer.

Most of the myths of Bach's inconsistent and carefree articulation
hinge on these points. The musical style and structure of the piece
must be observed: just as 'ornamental' notes are of vastly differing
importance according to context and size of forces, so is articulation at
times crucial to the identity of the piece, at others, a more or less

routine system of accents. If the *accentual* quality of slurs is considered, and they are not merely regarded as legato 'ornaments' or even as 'exceptions' to a standard detached style, their role as clues to interpretation will so much better be understood.

AMPLIFICATION OF EXISTING MARKINGS FOR LATER PERFORMANCES OF CANTATAS

Kilian's excellent study (1983 pp. 27-9) of the growth of articulation markings in BWV 6/2 has shown that in repeated performances with new parts, Bach was inclined to augment markings until quite a comprehensive and logical system was developed. He may well have reached a closer 'understanding' of his own music, realizing the motivic structure of the line through detailed slurs and dots. Several other movements show a similar augmentation: BWV 151/1 was performed with a new autograph flute[?] part (Coburg, *c.* 1728-31; Dürr 1976 p. 105) in which virtually every note is covered by a slur or a dot (or even both) (Example 62). Such a comprehensive scheme is rare even

Example 62

for Bach and might provide a guide as to how similar movements would have been marked had Bach had more time for editing.

The new part 'Violino con: ou Trav' for BWV 103/3 (copyist: Krebs, 15 April 1731; Dürr 1976 p. 102) similarly shows much detail (and evidence of Bach's trills). Here both strokes and dots are employed (Example 63). Although no earlier oboe parts exist, the later auto-

Example 63

graph oboe part (St 54) to BWV 82 shows a level of detail that was almost certainly not found in its predecessors (this cantata was first performed in 1727; Dürr 1976 p. 94). If the flute part is a copy of an earlier oboe part, the first version contained very few markings indeed. However, as Dürr (*ibid*.) suggests, the flute may have been used for a single private performance in 1735; Bach certainly did not give it a thorough revision and many markings may have been omitted by the copyist.

One of the most striking examples of amplification of markings is shown by a comparison of BWV 79/2 with its parody BWV 234/5 (1735-50). Here the original obbligato for oboe or flute is given to strings (down an octave) with a full complement of slurs and dots; the melody is further embellished. Thus the slurs seem to be related to this process of ornamentation (Examples 64 and 65).

Example 64 BWV 79. 2, bb. 1 6

Example 65 BWV 234/5, bb. 1-6

EVIDENCE FOR A CHANGE OF ARTICULATION FOR
LATER PERFORMANCES
THE PARODIED 'WEIHNACHTSORATORIUM' (BWV 248)
AS A TEST CASE

BWV 248 (1734-5) provides a useful control by which to judge possible differences of articulation between different versions of other works (for which the same performance material was used). Here earlier versions of some of the music exist in independent sources, three cantatas written during the two preceding years: BWV 213-15.

In most cases the later version (BWV 248) shows an amplification of the existing articulation scheme, particularly in the addition of dots and strokes. Even when the instrumental medium is changed there is not necessarily a specific change of articulation, more a difference in the number of markings. Dots are added to the repeated-note figure in b. 13 of BWV 248/29 for oboes (the original BWV 213/11 is for violas, and no dots are present). Conversely, dots in the oboe part of BWV 213/7 at bb. 18-19 and 49-50 are not to be found in the violin part of BWV 248/41.

Most cases in which a considerable number of markings seem to have been added for the later versions in BWV 248 concern movements from BWV 214. For the latter work only the score (P 41) and six parts (St 91: vocal, viola and continuo) survive, so it is likely that many markings added to the lost parts survive only in BWV 248 (P 32 and St 112). Such movements include BWV 214/1 (BWV 248/1) where there are considerable additions of dots (for quavers) and strokes (for semiquavers) in the latter version. Dots are also the principal addition to BWV 248/8 (BWV 214/7).

The only striking evidence of a change in articulation style is shown in BWV 248/4 which first appeared as BWV 213/9. In the latter the partly autograph violin part is marked 'unisono e staccato' while BWV 248/4 has no staccato direction. An oboe d'amore is added to the violin and 2B slurring introduced for the quaver movement of bb. 1-2. Two principal slurs occur in the earlier version, b. 3: 𝄞 which become: 𝄞 Only the slurs in b. 5/6 are common to both: 𝄞 as are the paired slurs of b. 13, characteristically related to the alternating semitones. Many other features are similar: the passage bb. 38-42 and the slurring pattern in the bass for the second section (considerably amplified in BWV 248/4).

Several factors may have influenced the apparent change from a detached style to a more graceful, slurred style affecting much of the quaver figuration: the earlier text is petulant and defiant in character, the later, an exhortation to prepare for the beauteous Saviour. Similarly the decision to include an oboe d'amore (compatible with the words 'Schönsten!' 'Liebsten!') may have been part of the transformation of this movement.

Thus only an *affective* change in the text and nature of a piece seems to have influenced any changes of articulation in BWV 248.

EVIDENCE FOR BACH'S ALTERATION OF ARTICULATION

As the study of original parts has shown, changes or extensions to articulation markings are often evident. However, it is not always clear whether these were made during the initial editing or at the time of a later performance. Some examples show a change of articulation which was probably made between performances:

BWV 194. 1	longer slurs replaced by paired slurs. Movement 5 shows slightly more paired slurs in the earlier parts (St 346)
BWV 185 1	longer slurs replaced by paired slurs (St 4)
BWV 147 8	shorter slurs in autograph oboe d'amore part (St 46)
BWV 245/35	paired slurs replaced with dots

The first two instances concern an original Weimar version, the paired slurs being added for Leipzig performances. This change might reflect the desire for more tone (for a larger building?) achieved through the use of more bow per note. The change in the recitative BWV 147/8 (2 July 1723) is more curious. The oboes da caccia are marked with the 4G slurring: ♪♫♫♫♫ in the parts (St 46), which presumably reflect the (lost) composing score. However, an autograph part for oboe d'amore 1 is included in the set, which is on a spare sheet cut out of the violoncello part. This is consistently marked with the slurring: ♪♫♫♫ However, the autograph score P 102 dates from 1728–31 at this point and this reverts to the earlier slurring (Dürr 1976 p. 106). It is difficult to determine when and whether the oboe d'amore

part was used (there is no second part) and there seems to be no particular reason why Bach should have made such a change.

A specific change of articulation style seems to have been made in
BWV 245/35. The stepwise diminished seventh figure of b. 9 is slurred
with an inevitable paired 1C slur in most early sources (St 111). However, in the score P 28 (not autograph for this movement, but showing
signs of Bach's editing) these slurs are replaced by dots from b. 51
onwards. Slurs appear only in b. 11 of the previous material and these
clearly reproduce the markings of a previous (lost) score, unedited by
Bach at this point. The late violin part (doubling flute) is heavily
revised by Bach and here all instances of this figure appear with dots
(*NBA 2/4 KB* p. 274).

This change from an essentially legato style to staccato dots recalls
the change made in the opposite direction between BWV 213/9 and
BWV 248/4 (see p. 135 above). However, there is no change of textual
Affekt here. Perhaps the absence of this aria in the third version of
the work meant that Bach gave it special attention when it was revived
for the final extant version; the dots seem to imply a lightening of style.

Most instances of striking alterations in articulation style are far
more complex than is initially apparent. Examination of both *BG* and
NBA texts shows a striking difference between the slurring of 'Es
streiten, es pragen' from BWV 134a (1718) and its parody 'Wir danken,
wir preisen', BWV 134/4 (1724) (Example 66).

Example 66

BWV 134a. 4

BWV 134/4

Dürr, in the commentaries for both cantatas in the *NBA* (1/10 *KB*
p. 103 for BWV 134; 1/35 *KB* pp. 101-2 for BWV 134a) admits that
there is an ambiguity surrounding this change; it resulted from an
alteration during the course of composition of BWV 134a; the initial
grouping for the vocal underlay was altered from: ♪♪♪ to: ♪♪♪

Although he observes that the instrumental parts are more ambiguous and uncorrected, Dürr adopts the first version for the instrumentalists, the second for the singers. In BWV 134 the second version is used for both.

The problem is further complicated by the fact that some of the extant parts (St 18) were used for both cantatas: most instrumental parts, including the all-important violin parts, show evidence of adaptation for the later version. The existing vocal parts (for BWV 134 only) were copied directly from the originals by a copyist, and Bach himself inserted much of the new text. Furthermore, several indications in the score of BWV 134a (Paris MS 2) suggest that it was used for the second version initially. The score for BWV 134, P 44, was not, in fact, copied until c. 1731. Thus, if Dürr argues that the instrumentalists played the first version for BWV 134a, they should accordingly have played the same version for BWV 134, since the same parts were used.

A closer examination of all related sources shows us how complex Bach's compositional procedure was here. The version 𝄽♫ occurs three times only for violins in the first score (Paris): twice in b. 1, once in b. 21. The initial vocal entries (bb. 17, 18) were originally ♪ | ♫♪ then changed: ♪ | ♫♪ The first instance in the tenor part, alone, has the later slurring: ♪ | ♫♪ which immediately suggests an unusual time-sequence in the addition of these markings (although the slurs may have been misplaced from the start). The alteration is made again in bb. 23–4 but not in b. 28.

It is in b. 36 that the second version of the beaming first occurs unaltered: ♪ ♫ ♪ It was probably the tie here that gave Bach the idea of the syncopated version. However, the first version is given unaltered in b. 41, altered in b. 43 (tenor), unaltered again in b. 44 (alto).

Bach seems to have decided finally to opt for the second version at the return of the voices in b. 54 (no alteration); however, it is altered in b. 56 (tenor, second group), unaltered in b. 57 onwards, altered again in the central section, b. 101 (*NBA* 1/35 *KB* pp. 68–74 for a full list).

This score was used for several performances so many of the corrections could well have been included later. What is clear, however, is that the second version was decided upon for the vocal underlay before the work was in a performable state. As only three instrumental slurs for this figure were included, early on in the piece, any Köthen copyist would have been faced with a dilemma as to which slurring the composer actually intended (*ibid.* pp. 101-2).

The parts give no conclusive view of Bach's intention since no example shows one of the two versions consistently and accurately. The evidence suggests that Bach made the alteration of articulation during the composition stage, clarifying it in the later score.

A more convincing example of Bach's changing of articulation is evident in BWV 100/5. Here in both P 159 and St 97, 2A slurs are given for the oboe obbligato in b. 3 and many subsequent instances (Example 67). A second performance towards the end of the possible

Example 67

period for the first performance (after 1735; Dürr 1976 p. 111) is represented by a new set of parts, most in Bach's hand. The autograph oboe part shows considerably longer slurs throughout (Example 68).

Example 68

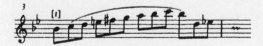

Although Bach seems to have changed an initial articulation of b. 3 by beat into a smoother melodic line, a long slur is suggested in both the score and original part for the shorter melisma of b. 2.

Considering the number of repeat performances and revisions of works undertaken during Bach's lifetime, changes made to the notated articulation are minimal. Slurs and particularly dots are quite often added to subsequent versions, but the markings evident from the earliest composing scores and parts are essentially unchanged. These observations suggest that it is quite in order to amplify markings found in poorly edited sources. However, major changes to the existing articulation seem to run against Bach's tendency to specify performance and ornament markings in as much detail and as didactically as possible.

SUMMARY

The last two chapters have revealed certain norms in Bach's notated articulation. The most common slurrings are those which reflect the typical figures of the compositional style, delineating the components of the musical line. They also have an important role in determining the regularity and rate of accentuation within the music, particularly when the implications of bowing technique are considered. Dots both clarify the extent of slurs and lighten particular note values within the texture.

Perhaps the most striking phenomenon is the virtual agreement of articulation styles in different media. Articulation according to the type of musical figuration usually overrides instrumental distinctions. Many elements of articulation are variable, but within fairly strict musical parameters. The frequent interchangeability of paired and longer slurrings suggests an indifference to the choice of slurring when it merely accords with the metrical stresses; quite often a 'slurred *Affekt*' is required which does not demand intricate articulation.

Bach's approach to articulation and its development within the compositional history of each piece is symptomatic of his attitude to composition itself: the details are often amplified and clarified with progressive unity and symmetry of material. However, the basic fabric and identity of each piece and its corresponding articulation are seldom altered after the initial stages of composition. As Grüß (1988 p. 334) observes, when a movement is carefully marked by Bach (particularly if solo lines are involved), articulation is no longer left to the whim of the performer, 'sondern formuliert eine zusätzliche Ebene von musikalischem Zusammenhang' ('but forms an additional level of musical coherence').

Part III

BACH'S REFINED ARTICULATION – THE INSTRUMENTAL WORKS

9

Bach's role in the preparation of printed sources

A study of Bach's involvement in the preparation of works for publica-tion is a useful introduction to notated articulation in instrumental works. Bach presumably devoted more time to the preparation of these than in the case of the concerted vocal works, so we would expect his indications of articulation to be the product of his most refined ideals. Corrections made (at Bach's instigation?) to the plates themselves, second impressions and autograph corrections made to finished engravings are all important evidence in assessing Bach's concern for the accuracy and presentation of his music.

BACH'S ROLE IN THE ENGRAVING PROCESS

Some writers have suggested that parts of *Clavierübung* III were en-graved by Bach himself (Kinsky 1937 pp. 42-3). However, Tessmer (*NBA* 4/4 *KB* pp. 8-14) and Butler (1980 p. 14) agree that it is likely that the similarity of the engraving to Bach's hand is the result of the work of an experienced engraver who reproduced exactly the graphic characteristics of an autograph *Stichvorlage*.

141

The sources of *Die Kunst der Fuge*, BWV 1080, contain by far the clearest example of Bach's role in the preparation of plates. Seaton (1975 pp. 54-9) notes that the autograph P 200 dates from well before the period of Bach's death, that it was originally designed as a fair copy (in preparation for printing?) and that it gradually became a revision copy, the changes being made over the course of several years. Moreover, Koprowski (1975 pp. 61-7) shows that the three sheets containing the 'Canon per Augmentationem in Contrario Motu' were the *Abklatschvorlagen* for the engraving. Thus, by studying the calligraphy of these sheets, which greatly resembles that of the printed version, Koprowski concludes that Bach himself prepared *Abklatschvorlagen* for nearly half the work. Other hands have been identified as those of Bach's sons, who were probably working in close cooperation with their father. Only the calligraphy in the style of the final chorale (to 'compensate' for the incompleteness of the work) dates from after Bach's death.

Differences of slurring between P 200 and the engraving suggest that – apart from the three *Abklatschvorlagen* – the two sources are not directly connected. Although most slurs in Contrapunctus 8 are found in both manuscript and engraving, those slurs in b. 4 of Contrapunctus 2, engraved in the style of Bach's hand, do not appear in P 200. Slurs in Contrapunctus 8 are, however, reproduced more consistently in the printed version; perhaps Bach included them in P 200 so that they could be added by whoever was preparing the *Abklatschvorlagen*.

By far the most interesting movements are the two keyboard canons, 'all' ottava' and 'per Augmentationem in contrario motu'. Three sources reflect some of the stages of Bach's thoughts on articulation. The canon at the octave appears in P 200 as a single-line version followed immediately by its resolution in two voices. In the single-line version of b. 3, the three notes are given as dotted quavers with staccato dots below: ♪. ♪. ♪. In the ensuing, two-part version, these are notated more precisely as quavers followed by semiquaver rests: ♪ 𝄿 ♪ 𝄿 ♪ 𝄿 This later notation is repeated in the printed version, with the addition of staccato markings: ♪ 𝄿 ♪ 𝄿 ♪ 𝄿

The final manuscript version of the 'Canon per Augmentationem' is on the three sheets (*Abklatschvorlagen*) marked '26, 27, 28', and this is basically identical to the printed version, with only minor differences. Small though these differences are, they are highly significant.

The RH slur, bb. 28-9 of P 200, covers all semiquavers after the tied note, while in the engraving this slur becomes two, the first covering the semiquavers of b. 28, the second, b. 29.

Immediate questions are posed by this difference: to what extent did Bach supervise the tracing process? Did he check that the finished engraving reproduced the tracing sheets exactly? Did he make or sanction alteration during the engraving process? The LH slurs in bb. 54 and 55 occur only in the printed version. This is clear evidence that additions were made by someone after the *Abklatschvorlagen* were prepared. However, some differences must derive directly from faults in the transfer process. The LH slurs in b. 82 stretch from notes 2 to 4 and from 5 to 9 in the manuscript, from notes 4 to 8 only in the engraving. This second version is nonsensical since the first two notes under the slur are at the same pitch.

The other late engravings - the Canonic Variations on 'Vom Himmel hoch', BWV 769 (*c.* 1747), *Musicalisches Opfer*, BWV 1079 (1747), and the six 'Schübler' Chorale Preludes, BWV 645-50 (*c.* 1748) - show no sign of Bach's involvement in the engraving process. An autograph copy exists for BWV 769 (P 271) but this is almost certainly a later 'private' manuscript, with the parts fully realized on three staves (the printed version generally shows only the single canonic voices). The *Musicalisches Opfer* likewise survives in no direct autograph model; the Ricercare 'a 6' exists in an autograph form (P 226/1) but this is written on two staves instead of six and was evidently not used as a *Stichvorlage*.

Wolff (1977 pp. 126-8) suggests that Bach may have employed a copyist to prepare the 'Schübler' Chorales from the original cantata autographs. However, comparison between the articulation markings in extant autographs of the cantatas and the organ version shows several important differences. BWV 648 is a transcription of BWV 10/5 (autograph score, Washington). With the exception of three instances, b. 2 (4-5), b. 7 (Alto, 4-5) and b. 12 (Tenor, 3-4), the cantata autograph contains no slurs.[1] In the organ version, there is but one slur, b. 2 (3-4), and this is clearly a misplacement of a slur for notes 4-5. Wolff suggests that Bach might have directed the copyist to transcribe the cantata version without slurs. The copyist may have seen the slur in b. 2 and mistaken it for a tie (Wolff 1977 pp. 126-7). However, the autograph score shows this particular slur accurately placed (despite Wolff's claim that it is 'so ungenau plaziert'), if a little high above the stave.

BWV 649 is an arrangement of BWV 6/3 (in autograph score, P 44/2). Here again the slurs show little evidence of a direct connection between the two sources: those of bb. 1 and 6 are omitted and those of bb. 7-9 cover one fewer note in the organ version.

BWV 645 is taken from BWV 140/4. Unfortunately the autograph score of this cantata does not survive. Original parts do exist, however (St Thom), and these show some variants in articulation.[2] The most significant differences are b. 2 (beat 1):

BWV 140/4:   ♪♫

BWV 645:   ♪♫

and b. 6 (beat 1):

BWV 140/4:   ♫♫

BWV 645:   ♫♫

Dürr (*NBA* 1/27 *KB* pp. 131-2) observes that one violin part of BWV 140/4 was revised at some later date to agree more with the version in BWV 645.

Many of these variants challenge Wolff's view that Bach might have employed a copyist to transcribe the chorales mechanically from the cantata originals. However, his scepticism of Bach's direct involvement in the preparation of the engraving is surely justified, since the edition is very inaccurate.

MANUSCRIPT EDITING OF FINISHED ENGRAVINGS

Jones has observed that four surviving engravings of the 1731 edition of *Clavierübung* I contain similar manuscript corrections. At least one of these (GB Lbm Hirsch III 37) appears to have been corrected by Bach himself (*NBA* 5/1 *KB* pp. 28-9). Jones infers that Bach and close members of his circle systematically corrected many copies after they had been printed. Such additions generally serve to clarify the notation: accidentals are frequently enlarged (e.g. BWV 827, Gigue, LH, b. 48 note 3). Bach's additions to GB Lbm Hirsch III 37 are conspicuous in their slightly brown ink and thin nib. Although Wolff (1979 pp. 65-74) has challenged the degree of systematic correction implied by Jones, he also notes significant additions by Bach in an example in the Library of Congress (many of which are in no other surviving example). Only one additional slurring is recorded in his table, introduced in BWV 826, Rondeau, for the figure beginning b. 99 RH.[3] Wolff identifies several layers of additions by Bach: in pencil, brown-black ink and red ink. This particular copy, then, was probably used over some period of time; the annotations seem more related to performance and teaching purposes than to a mass correction of engravings before distribution.

Clavierübung II· appeared in 1735, prepared by four different engravers; it contains many errors of notation. Emery (*NBA* 5/2 *KB* pp. 24-5) has shown that several surviving examples of the first impression have been corrected in a similar fashion. That many of these corrections are themselves inaccurate suggests to him that they were not undertaken under Bach's supervision but at the direction of the printer, Weigel, himself. However, one example - GB Lbm k.8.g.7 - is heavily corrected by Bach. Emery demonstrates that this is not the model for the corrected second impression (*c.* 1736) but a copy corrected for private use before the second impression was planned (*ibid.* pp. 28-9). In general this 'private' example contains more added articulation marks than the 'public' second edition. Perhaps this copy was used over a protracted period for teaching purposes, like the US Wcm example for *Clavierübung* I,. mentioned above.

Tessmer (*NBA* 4/4 *KB* pp. 14-16) observes that most of the surviving examples of *Clavierübung* III contain systematic manuscript correction: some corrections appear only in the first impression copies, others were made to the plates themselves in preparation for the second impression; further manuscript corrections were made to copies of the second impression itself. Although these probably all stemmed from the printing house, it is likely that they were based on a list prepared by Bach himself. The only articulation marks to have been added by hand are the slurs for all the paired quavers in BWV 678 b. 14. All seem to be in the same, rather hurried hand (thin, light-brown ink) in GB Lbm k.10.a.2 and GB Lbm k.10.a.42. Similar slurs were already engraved for bb. 5-6, so it does not seem that these slurs introduce any new pattern. However, it is curious that the similar and intervening passage, bb. 7-12, contains no slurs in any source. GB Lbm k.10.a.42 also includes some manuscript slurs for BWV 803. These likewise seem to be added for completeness and introduce no new articulation patterns: b. 38 LH, bb. 85-6 LH.

Bach's personal copies of the fourth part of the *Clavierübung* ('Goldberg' variations BWV 988, F Pn MS 17669) and the 'Schübler' chorales (W. H. Scheide collection) contain many additional articulation marks. Wolff (*NBA* 5/2 *KB* pp. 93-4) has observed that the additions to BWV 988 also appear in several other examples of the engraving, which suggests some degree of systematic revision. However, the 'Schübler' exemplar seems to have been more a copy for private use. Although slurs are carefully added to the ritornello for pedals in BWV 648, none of the ambiguous slurrings in BWV 645 has been clarified. Evidently the meaning of these slurs was obvious to Bach and not worthy of correction.

MODIFICATIONS TO LATER EDITIONS

The six partitas constituting *Clavierübung* I were first published individually between 1726 and 1730. The complete edition was published in 1731 using the same plates with various additions and corrections. Jones (*NBA* 5/1 *KB* pp. 18-23) conjectures that the first two partitas were subjected only to hasty revision (involving no articulation marks). The remaining four partitas were probably systematically corrected from a list supplied by the composer. Such additional slurs as there are seem to be associated with suspensions (e.g. BWV 827, Sarabande, b. 2); they thus do nothing to clarify the articulation of the more regular figurative patterns. More significant are the added dots, only one instance of their use being evident in the single editions (BWV 829, Courante, b. 23, RH 3,4). The additions occur in BWV 827, Burlesca, bb. 5-6, 21-2 (RH crotchets) and BWV 828, Menuet, bb. 1, 5 (last RH notes). The latter instance is visually striking, for in both cases the note-stem points upwards, above the stave, in the same direction as the dot: ⌡ This may prove that the addition was the product of Bach's later thoughts; for had this been merely a printer's omission, the tail (in both bb. 1 and 5) would surely have been engraved downwards to give room for the dot above the note-head.

Most changes of slurs in the second impression of the Ouverture BWV 831 from *Clavierübung* II are made in the Courante. The music from the Courante to Passepied 2 has been re-engraved and thus changes in this area are not made to the original plates but are the result of a more careful engraving.

SUMMARY

Only in certain circumstances, then, is it possible to discern Bach's role in the preparation of editions. In cases of copies annotated by Bach there is always the problem of the function of such sources. Some might well have been copies corrected for distribution; others might have been teaching copies used over several years. There is, however, evidence to suggest that Bach's conception of the articulation sometimes developed after the engravings were first made, although many additions rectify printers' omissions. This corresponds with Bach's tendency to add more slurs to later manuscript sources. One interesting but slightly negative conclusion is that Bach does not seem to have prepared or edited the printed sources with any more care or detail than the manuscripts of the concerted vocal works. Furthermore, he does not betray a different policy for 'private' and 'public' notation – such as giving more indications in the latter since it was addressed to the uninitiated (contrary to Lohmann's assertions, see p. 51 above). Indeed, the degree of additions to his personal copy of *Clavierübung* II suggests that he gave the closest attention to private, teaching copies. Articulation was used by Bach here as a notated instructional device.

10

/

Articulation marks in fair copies of works for instrumental ensemble

ACCURACY AND COMPREHENSIVENESS OF ARTICULATION IN BWV 1030 AND 1027

Fair copies of instrumental music provide the most favourable circumstances for viewing Bach's approach to notated articulation. Like the printed sources, they are the product of a far longer gestation period than the concerted vocal works, but as manuscript sources they reflect, or at least derive from, 'private' performance and teaching. However, even in sources such as these there are considerable differences in Bach's attitude to notating articulation: he included many slurs in the sonata for flute and obbligato harpsichord in B minor BWV 1030 (P 975), but generally only for the first appearance of new figuration; the players must infer the remainder. In the sonata for viola da gamba and harpsichord in G major, BWV 1027 (P 226), however, virtually every mark that seems to be needed is present.

This difference might reflect the instrumental media involved: the slurring and consequent bowing is of fundamental importance in the production of notes on the gamba while the articulation of the flute is synthesized through tonguing. Furthermore, the layout of the two manuscripts is different: in BWV 1030 flute and harpsichord share the same score while BWV 1027 is preserved in separate parts. Each player of BWV 1030 can see the other's music (presuming that this score was prepared specifically for performance) while in BWV 1027 each receives an individual part with matching articulation instructions. The latter autograph (c. 1740) seems designed specifically for performance:[1] the first two movements of the gamba part are on the inner pages of the bifolio; the player need only turn the copy over after

148

the second movement to play the remainder of the sonata without a break.

For a fair copy it is quite surprising how vague some of the markings in P 975 for BWV 1030 are: the chromatic figure introduced in b. 13 of the opening Andante appears with a variety of slurrings (Example 69).

Example 69

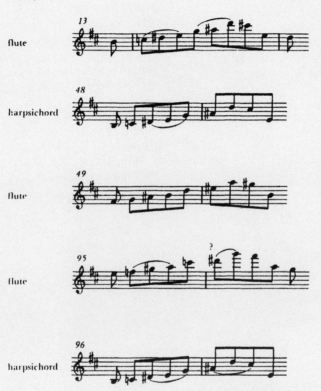

What is certain is that a *slurring* is to be applied, as is substantiated by the affective connotations of chromatic progressions (see p. 23 above). It may be significant that the first instance of this figure in b. 13 was originally as in Example 70 (see also Plate 8) and was subsequently

Example 70

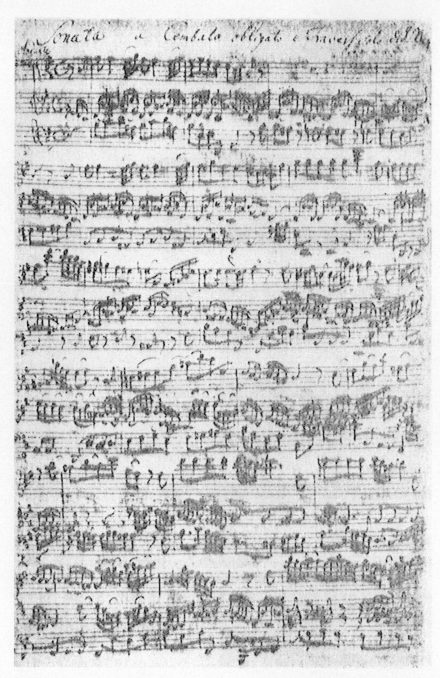

8 Sonata for flute and harpsichord in B Minor, BWV 1030, Andante, bb. 1-21; slur extension in b. 13. Mus. MS P 975

altered. This alteration may have been made (by Bach?) after the later marks had been written, reflecting a deeper consideration of the figural patterns involved.

Clearly the importance of articulation and its consistency varies according to the source and musical circumstances involved: Bach was not an *Urtext* editor, but neither was he oblivious to the musical significance of articulation.

INSTRUMENTAL CONSIDERATIONS

The seeming completeness of slurring in BWV 1027 relates to the bowing technique of the viola da gamba: articulation is influenced by the means of producing the sound.

The up-bow is the stronger stroke on the viola da gamba; apart from this reversal, the accentual implications of bowing are identical to those of the violin. The major repertory for the gamba – that of France – provides very complete performance directions, little adjustment being required for the bowing-scheme as dictated by the notated slurs (Robinson 1981 p. 279). If the Allegro ma non tanto is played 'as it comes', the string-crossing passage in b. 12 is comfortably played with an up-bow on the melody note (i.e. the first of each pair). Given, then, that Bach might have devised the bowing in bb. 5-11 to result in a stronger bowing for the sequence of b. 12, did he totally disregard the succession of accents in the earlier bars? The first beat of b. 8 receives an up-bow, but all subsequent beats until the g' in b. 11 receive the 'incorrect' down-bow. The 'strong' b' in b. 8, beat 1, and g' in b. 11 are in the same tessitura, the intervening notes being up to a seventh lower. It is in this very passage that the harpsichord takes over the line, maintaining the tessitura of the b', allowing it to drop sequentially to g' in b. 11. Then the gamba takes over the sequence with a strong up-bow (Example 71).

The sonata BWV 1030 (P 975) for flute and harpsichord employs some unusual slurs. The fugue subject of the Presto introduces a cross-beat slurring (Example 72). Appendix 2 does show a few examples of this pattern in string lines of the vocal works (1E, crossing the beat in instances involving notes of the half division of the beat). Indeed, the figuration in BWV 24/1, b. 8, is remarkably similar to that in the present instance. However, the most prominent example of 1E is in

Example 71

Example 72

BWV 232/1. In this movement the woodwind instruments are the most important, the strings never playing alone. Appendix 2 shows that in the vocal works cross-beat patterns are found almost as regularly with wind instruments as with strings (when, on the whole, less slurring is notated in wind parts).

Another striking example is the cross-beat and cross-bar slurring of b. 14f (Andante) (Example 73). This clearly represents a displacement

Example 73

of the standard paired slurring which returns with the metrical stress in b. 15, beat 3. Here then, the grouping of notes takes precedence over the metrical accent.

Bach was apparently experimenting with slurrings here: the return of the passage in b. 52 is slurred entirely according to the metre (i.e. a standard paired pattern, 1C). The slurs are especially faint (implying later addition at a time when the earlier cross-beat slurring had been forgotten?). Despite the preponderance of cross-beat figuration, the slurring for flute in BWV 1030 is otherwise predictable, in accordance with the character of the figures. Paired slurs are common in the Andante, for both the half division of the beat (b. 9) and the quarter division (b. 19). The opening slide: is equally common in string and, indeed, vocal music and could hardly be performed without a slur.

Four-note slurs are evident in the Largo e dolce (b. 10). These are omitted from earlier instances of demisemiquaver figuration (b. 5f) and might well be an afterthought. Their function is almost certainly accentual, complementing the single quaver chord per beat in the harpsichord part and preventing the player from subdividing each quaver pulse. Likewise slurs are added to figuration that has already been present in the Presto b. 102 (continuous conjunct semiquavers appeared first in b. 90). The markings in b. 102 reduce the number of flute accents, and, in effect, lessen the tone of the flute at the point where the harpsichord has the syncopated subject. Such a function of the slur, providing dynamic contrast to thematic material in another part, has been noted elsewhere (see p. 102 above).

Brandenburg Concerto 5, BWV 1050, which survives in the calligraphic autograph score Am.B.78 (1721) and the autograph parts of an earlier version (St 130, before 1721) provides a good opportunity to view flute and violin articulation within the same piece. The Affettuoso introduces many paired slurrings in all three instrumental parts.

The section from b. 24 is largely based on the *messanza* figure:

Both parts and score show a degree of inconsistency at this point. In the sequence bb. 24-5 the flute is slurred in pairs, the violin in fours (Example 74). The passage may be designed as a dialogue between the

Example 74

two slurrings of the same figure. However, Dadelsen (1978 pp. 99-102) doubts that this is the case and attributes the inconsistency to Bach's hurriedness, the four-note slurs being a shorthand for the paired slurs and the longer slurs in the harpsichord part (St 130) possibly derived from an earlier version. Both his wariness of a diplomatic interpretation and his observation that the paired slurs (b. 4) reflect the pulse of an extant earlier version (movement in quavers, without the semiquaver figuration) are convincing. His interpretation relates both to the wider textual problems and to the principles of figural composition, where the composer adds progressively more of the *Decoratio*. Furthermore, the 'shorthand' function of longer slurs is sometimes evident in the cantata sources (see pp. 130-1 above).

Fuchs (1985 pp. 154-6) interprets the markings more literally and considers the longer slurs to cover only the first three notes (1B). He consequently cannot accept the longer slurs as a shorthand for the pairs. However, his assertion that this figure (*messanza*) is seldom articulated with a four-note slur is not substantiated by the readings in Appendix 2 (slurs 1A and 1B). Whatever the solution to the problem of consistency, there seems to be no conclusive evidence in either autograph that the flute is to adopt an articulation style essentially different from that of the violin.

Throughout the concerto, articulation markings are used in the same way for flute as for violin. The only exception seems to be in the treatment of triplet patterns. In the first Allegro the sequence in triplets, b. 13f, is always marked with a three-note slur in the violin part, but not in the flute (Example 75). Clearly the slur is primarily a

Example 75

bowing direction here, the slurring causing a down-bow to fall on the tied minim. Such an indication would thus be irrelevant for flute.

Similarly in the final Allegro the violin slur, 2B: ⌢♩♩♩ (if this is the correct reading), suggests a strong down-bow on each beat. Bach presumably expected his flautist to devise his slurring to match that of the violin (depending on circumstances/acoustics?). Slurring is not so fundamental to the playing technique as in string playing. Only in instances such as b. 9, where the two instruments are playing simultaneously, is the precise articulation important. Here, then, both lines are marked (although only in the later source, Am.B.78) (Example 76).

Example 76

The 'Sonata sopra il soggetto Reale' from the Musical Offering, BWV 1079, likewise shows very little disagreement between markings for violin and flute. The differences that do exist may be the result of the engravers' carelessness (Example 77). However, Bach may have

Example 77 BWV 1079, Sonata, final allegro

considered that a separate tonguing on the top ab'' would be more accented than the violinist's weaker up-bow at this point. Whatever the reason for this difference, it is probable that both versions were designed to result in the same *sounding* articulation. One further difference is in the semiquaver phrase (bb. 11, 46 flute, 55 violin) (Example 78). In most other respects the markings for flute, violin

Example 78

and continuo parts are roughly compatible, suggesting that Bach considered the effect of slurs and strokes to be the same in all three media. Here, as in BWV 1050, the two parts share and discuss the same material.

In all the works concerned the articulation marking in the continuo matches that of the other voices. BWV 1027, 1030, 1050 furthermore employ an obbligato harpsichord; in every case the level and quality of slurring matches exactly that of the other melodic voices (Fuchs 1985 p. 24 observes that the keyboard player in ensembles is more bound ('gebunden') to specific articulation than in solo music). Indeed, in BWV 1027 the meticulous markings of the viola da gamba are paralleled directly in the harpsichord: even when the harpsichord receives a particular slurred figuration before the gamba it has the same 'bowing' (e.g. Allegro ma non tanto, bb. 1-4; Allegro Moderato, bb. 26-8).

Likewise in BWV 1030 all the major slurred figures noted for the flute appear also in the harpsichord (e.g. the cross-beat slurring of the fugue subject). The function of the slurs in the two media is similar: a notation of all the figuration which is to be slurred or grouped in a particular way, but not a complete system of markings or advice on performance technique (as is more the case in BWV 1027). In the Andante, the advisory nature of the slurs seems especially noticeable. A regular pairing of the disjunct figuration is specified in the first bar, but only sporadically later. The next markings occur in b. 4 and these four-note slurs coincide with more conjunct *groppo* figuration.

Paired slurs are reintroduced for specifically paired figuration in b. 10, as if as a reminder. The only other significant slurrings are those in bb. 40-2. These relate to the characteristic group of four descending notes so often noted in cases of 1A slurring in string and woodwind music (Example 79).

Example 79

There are significant and consistent discrepancies between gamba and harpsichord in BWV 1027, namely the initial figure slurred in pairs in the gamba, fours in the harpsichord (Example 80), and later instances of the same kind: Allegro ma non tanto, b. 4 harpsichord, b. 8 gamba (Example 81); Andante, harpsichord and gamba, b. 1 (Example 82). Significantly the paired/four-note discrepancy is the

Example 80

gamba

harpsichord

Example 81

harpsichord

gamba

Example 82

harpsichord

gamba

most common in the survey of the concerted vocal works (see p. 130 above). Such a consistent inconsistency between media here suggests a careful consideration of the implications of slurs in each. Four-note slurs for the harpsichord demand a sustaining of the notes within each group, creating a greater sonority; two-note slurs for gamba might imply that a great deal of bow should be used, likewise to enhance sonority. The gamba has far less projection than the violin, so Bach may well have written shorter slurs to achieve a full, fast bow-stroke. The resulting effect of the two markings is thus basically the same.

Nevertheless, the paired slurs at the opening of the Adagio do impart a special character to the opening motif (consisting of four descending conjunct semiquavers). When paired slurs are applied to quite foreign figuration (e.g. bb. 7-9 gamba) the character of the opening motif is effectively stamped on the more neutral figuration. The slurs thus act as a unifying motivic element in their own right.

Only in two passages does the gamba not have paired slurs for descending semiquavers: bb. 9-12 (Example 83) and bb. 21-3. Here

Example 83

there is continuous stretto between the gamba and both hands of
the harpsichord. The projection of one melodic line at the expense
of the other is therefore to be avoided, so the longer gamba slur creates
a softer, transparent tone. Furthermore, the character of the descending semiquavers is so well established by this stage that a change of
slurring does not obscure its identity. The alteration might further
underline the different function of the motif, now an imitative frag-
ment rather than a melodic component.

One further brief instance of a four-note gamba slur is at the return
of the opening in bb. 13–16 (Example 84). The return is disguised

Example 84

in the harpsichord part, the tonic being reached only half-way through
b. 13. The same ingenuity is shown in the gamba bb. 15–16: here the
paired slurring generally associated with the descending four notes is
heard with the 'anonymous' figuration at the end of b. 15, the actual
four-note figure receiving a single slur at the beginning of b. 16. Only
in the second half of the bar is the traditional paired slurring restored.

Thus the altered slurring in the gamba (b. 16) complements the altered musical structure in the harpsichord (b. 13); order is restored only in the second half of their respective bars.

An examination of the opening theme of the Allegro ma non tanto also shows certain superficial inconsistencies (Example 85). However, the first of the descending four-note figures in each example (bb. 3, 7, etc.) is a regular feature, as is the slurred trill and dot for the *corta* motif. Both these slurrings coincide with a form of appoggiatura. The differences in b. 98 and b. 108 (gamba) probably relate to the coordination with rhythmic devices in the harpsichord: *suspirans* in b. 98 and *corta* in b. 108. Coordination would have been much more difficult with a four-note slur (Example 86). The second four-note figure (b. 4, etc.) is not an accented appoggiatura and it is noticeable that this is far less consistently marked.

A comparison of woodwind, string and keyboard slurs often reveals which markings are included as performance aids (in the case of bow-

Example 85

Example 85 (*cont.*)

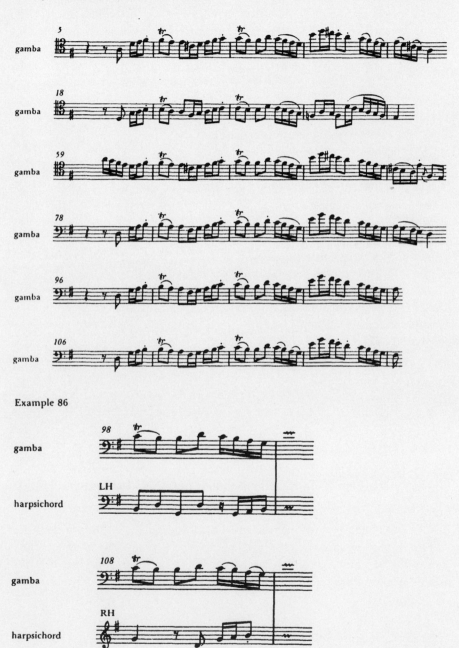

Example 86

ing slurs) and those which are more fundamental to the composition itself. There is no evidence that the *sounding* articulation of the instruments is different; indeed the consistent similarity of figuration and frequent swapping of musical lines suggests the contrary. The music is to be interpreted according to its intrinsic rhetorical content rather than to any specific instrumental style.

THE USE OF DOTS IN BWV 1027

One striking difference between articulation markings in BWV 1030 (P 975) and BWV 1027 (P 226/2) is the use of dots in the latter. This allows for the specification of three levels of articulation: slurred, unmarked and dotted. Three different functions of dots might be conjectured: (1) motivic associations (i.e. a figure which consistently appears with dots); (2) lightening the ends of groups or small-scale phrases; (3) complementing slurred patterns.

The first function, dots associated with certain figures, is most evident in the Adagio: the two quavers on the second beat of b. 1 receive a special identity throughout the piece, even in cases where they are displaced to the latter part of the beat (e.g. b. 12) (Example 87).

Example 87

The *corta* figure of the Allegro ma non tanto is also associated with a dot. This marking seems to emphasize the *anapaestic* nature of the figure: the accent falls on the two semiquavers, the quaver being played much more lightly:  This feature has already been observed in the vocal lines of the D major version of BWV 243 (see Example 10).

The same example introduces the second category of dots: the lightening of the ends of figures. Another instance is the end of b. 3 of the Adagio (Example 88). This prevents an undue accent on the

Example 88

bottom note and also allows the player time for the leap of a twelfth to the sustained a'.

The Allegro Moderato contains much figuration using dots in the third category: in regular conjunction with slurred patterns. In bb. 30-2 the marking reflects the note patterns: the three conjunct notes are slurred, the isolated note receives a dot. This style of articulation - one isolated note preceded or followed by three conjunct slurred notes - becomes as much an element of the piece as the rhythm or melodic motifs. In bb. 32, 110 and 135 it acquires autonomy and is no longer related to the original pattern of notes. It is unlikely that the use of dots in BWV 1027 implies a specific change of articulation practice since the time of the copying of BWV 1030 and 1050. It is probably symptomatic of Bach's habit of indicating his intentions ever more precisely, a trend that was at the centre of Scheibe's criticisms in 1737 (*Dok* vol. 2 pp. 286-7), exactly the period when this manuscript was prepared. The influence of French gamba writing must also have been strong. Bach may well have associated the precisely articulated motifs (particularly in the Adagio) with the finesse of French performance style.

SUMMARY

This study of selected chamber works substantiates points observed in the survey of the concerted vocal works. Bach's attention to articulation varies and is difficult to predict. Slurs are often added to specific figures in the *Decoratio* but comprehensiveness and accuracy of detail are not always evident. At the very least slurs act as a mnemonic reminding the player to give attention to the articulation of the figuration. When Bach takes string-playing technique into account the implications of articulation markings multiply. Here there are not only precise directions for the articulation of specific figural patterns but the accentuation of the music is influenced by the succession of bow-strokes. Slurs may also affect the dynamic and resonant qualities of the instruments involved. Despite the influence of playing technique on Bach's interpretation of his own music there is little evidence that the resulting effect of articulation in differing performance media varies in anything other than the smallest details.

11

Bach's keyboard articulation and the development of the keyboard idiom

NOTATED ARTICULATION IN MANUSCRIPT SOURCES OF DIDACTIC KEYBOARD WORKS

That articulation marks are closely related to the *Decoratio* – i.e. the ornamental rather than the structural level of the composition – is suggested by the unfinished prelude from the 'Orgelbüchlein': first Bach notated the cantus firmus in minims and only at a later stage added the intervening passing notes and slurs (see Example 31 and Plate 2 above).

Exactly the same function of slurs is shown in a finished work also based on a chorale: the second variation of Vom Himmel hoch, BWV 769, 'Alio modo in Canone alla Quinta' introduces paired slurs which suggest a continuation of the quaver pulse and outline through their accentual implications the paraphrased chorale (Example 89).

Example 89

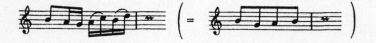

An examination of works in sources which Bach specifically designed for keyboard tuition, such as the music books of W. F. Bach (School of Music, Yale University) and A. M. Bach (P 224 and P 225) reveals the same trends. Slurs are found most often in the shorter, individual pieces which introduce a particular aspect of ornamentation or playing technique. Foremost are the short chorale settings with an ornamented solo line: 'Wer nur den lieben Gott läßt walten', BWV 691, in the Friedemann book, and 'Jesu, meine Zuversicht', BWV 728, in the

164

first Anna Magdalena book. Most slurs relate to specific ornamental patterns – generally of the *messanza*, *groppo*, or *tirata* type – which embellish a single note. Thus each note of the original chorale is defined by a slight break between slurred groups. The few slurs that occur in the draft of the first five French suites (the first Anna Magdalena book) likewise cover typical patterns of conjunct figuration, four-note descending appoggiaturas being particularly common. The prevalence of slurs in BWV 815 and 816 Sarabandes suggests their expressive connotations.

Clearly all these markings are not exhaustive and have a mnemonic function reminding the player of the significance and hierarchy of the diminution and also encouraging expression. Significantly Bach tends to add more slurs the more developed the work is – i.e. articulation markings are found more in revision scores than in composing scores. The manuscript of BWV 815 is possibly a revision rather than composing score, which would allow for more consideration of articulation markings; much of BWV 816 shows a rather later stage in Bach's handwriting (the middle of 1724), at least a year and a half later than the style of handwriting for the other suites (*NBA* 5/8 *KB* p. 16). By this later stage Bach was already engrossed in the first cycle of Leipzig cantatas. Thus he was now more attuned to other instrumental idioms and habitually indicating performance markings in instrumental parts. Significantly, this is the only suite to use dots, in Bourrée 2, b. 7.

The difference in markings between the two autographs of the Inventions and Sinfonias, BWV 772–801, is very noticeable (Wilhelm Friedemann book, Yale University, 1720, and P 610, 1723). All additions in the latter seem to contribute to the flow and momentum (in accordance with the exhortation to a 'cantabile' style on the autograph title-page?). Virtually every bar of BWV 774 receives a slur, implying one accent per bar (most slurs are of indeterminate length). This defines the piece as a one-beat 3/8 rather than three-beat. It may be that Bach feared that the player might accent the second quaver of the first bar since this is an appoggiatura (Example 90).

Example 90

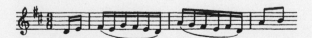

Longer groups of semiquavers are also implied in BWV 780, where continuous semiquavers of up to a bar's length are slurred together; this contrasts quite strongly with the shorter slurs (b. 4) in the Friedemann notebook, in which each beat is articulated (Example 91).

Example 91

There is no evidence that the earlier marking is a shorthand for the later, implying a 'general legato' (as Fuchs 1985 p. 112 affirms). Indeed, Bach seems more likely to have used longer slurs as a shorthand for shorter slurs (see pp. 130-1 above). The use of dots in the later volume of 'Das wohltemperierte Clavier', which often negate expected accents on 'good' notes (London autograph, GB Lbm Add. 35021, c. 1740-2) (Example 92), and the contrast between the two autographs of BWV

Example 92 BWV 879

772-801 both suggest that Bach was cultivating a lighter clavier style with longer phrases, in keeping with the call for a 'cantabile' style. Therefore the differences between the two versions suggest a new approach to articulation rather than a refinement of terminology. Shorter slurs - when they do occur - suggest the same style of articulation, related to the figuration of the music, that has been observed in other media.

The slurs in BWV 880 (GB Lbm Add. MS 35021) seem to constitute a rare 'model' example of how to play continuous passages of quavers. They occur in the first half of the prelude, which is copied by Anna Magdalena Bach (the second half is autograph). However, the markings in Anna's portion may derive from the composer himself since the ink colour and texture of the slurs does not quite match that of Anna's ties.

All figures which derive from the opening *suspirans* pattern are slurred in a similar fashion (Example 93). Those which are not

Example 93

preceded by a rest or tied note (often four-note descending appoggiaturas) are slurred in fours (Example 94). This might well suggest

Example 94

a holding of the first note of each figure, consistent with that indicated when two melodic parts are involved. Later the first two beats of continuous quaver passages are united by one slur, complementing the extension and development of motifs within the composition itself.

'STANDARD' NOTATED ARTICULATION IN
CLAVIERÜBUNG I

All the markings so far appear in manuscript sources which were originally designed for relatively private circulation. What does Bach do in the case of a more 'public' notation, such as in the six partitas of *Clavierübung* I?

The most common slurs in Bach's publication are those connected with suspensions and appoggiaturas: e.g. the opening of the Toccata from Partita 6 BWV 830. Bach clearly considered them necessary as an element of notation even though slurring is quite obvious to most players.

The remaining slurring patterns that appear and the types of notes to which they are applied are exactly the same as those observed in Bach's instrumental music. However, there are significantly fewer of them than in most of the ensemble works discussed. Common patterns are:

    1A: BWV 826, Sarabande, bb. 13-16
    1B: BWV 830, Toccata (b. 9 LH), and Air (b. 8 RH). Some ex-

amples of this pattern in the Toccata (bb. 21-2) and all of those in the Air (bb. 8-10) are manuscript additions made by Bach himself (in GB Lbm Hirsch III 37). In the first instance the slurring merely confirms a pattern already established. In the latter it could well be a further idea on Bach's part.

1C: is predictably very common (e.g. BWV 827, Burlesca, b. 10). The dotted form is evident in BWV 829, Sarabande. It seems that this slurring is distinguished from the traditional 'French Overture' dotting (as is evident in the unslurred openings of BWV 826 and 830) and might well influence the tempo since it is impossible to cut the second note short at fast tempi.

1D: is often related to *suspirans* figures and is very common in the keyboard music of Bach's contemporaries (see p. 57 above). It is surprisingly rare here, occuring only in BWV 826, Allemande, bb. 13-14, 29-30. Possibly Bach assumed that the players would recognize the *suspirans* rhythm inherent throughout the semiquaver figuration of this piece, but would be less likely to observe it in quavers. The slurring for semiquavers in b. 21 may denote an exception to a prevailing use of 1D (Example 95).

Example 95

The most interesting feature of *Clavierübung* I is the lack of slurs denoting triple patterns; none of the movements in compound time is slurred, nor the Rondeau of BWV 826 or the 9/8 section of the Ouverture to BWV 828. Evidently Bach did not consider players to require such markings in this keyboard collection.

The surveys of string and wind music revealed that slur patterns were more common with certain subdivisions of the pulse (see p. 113 above). Similar observations can be made here: slurs covering whole beats are connected only with suspensions or retardations, as in the cadences of BWV 827, Burlesca, or BWV 830, Sarabande. All such cases are in 3/4 time and generally involve only two notes. Triple metres are those in which slurs covering half beats are most common: BWV 827, Sarabande and Burlesca; BWV 829, Courante and Sarabande. These are generally confined to paired, two-note slurrings. In duple metres - BWV 827, Allemande, and BWV 830, Toccata - half-beat slurs are associated with suspensions and retardations. Most of the slurs denoting four-note motivic patterns cover notes of the

quarter pulse: triple-time in BWV 826, Sarabande, duple or quadruple
measures in BWV 826, Allemande, BWV 830, Toccata and Air. Some
notes of the eighth division of the pulse are slurred: BWV 826, Sinfonia
(Andante) and Allemande and BWV 830, Toccata. The last two examples are in ¢ time, so the aural effect is much the same as that
for slurred patterns covering the quarter pulse in C-time.

The rarity of dots in *Clavierübung* I is striking. In BWV 829,
Courante, b. 23 (RH), their function is probably cautionary (Example
96). Occurring after a more or less continuous stream of semiquavers

Example 96

they guard against holding the quavers too long; the second dot also
dictates a quick execution of the ornament. Dots may also define the
weak beats in the bar; the elegant phrasing of a minuet might be
evoked in BWV 828, Menuet, b. 1 (and 5, see also the example by
Couperin, Example 28) (Example 97). This dot was added as a later

Example 97

thought in the complete edition (1731), which suggests that Bach
considered the clarification important.

That the written length of notes in the keyboard works is notional
is implied by BWV 827, Burlesca (b. 22), where a dot appears over a
tied note (Example 98). This pattern is a particular feature of the

Example 98

movement (introduced in b. 5) and, coupled with the slurred paired
quavers (b. 10), seems to constitute a specific mood (in keeping with
the title 'Burlesca'?) which would not necessarily be assumed by the

player. Bach gave no such markings in his manuscript copy, P 225, and many of these markings do not appear in the 1727 impression of this partita. Do then the dots (present in only the complete edition) indicate a later style of performance, or do they merely reflect a style that was natural to Bach but deemed worthy of clarification in a 'public' edition? That the manuscript version is entitled 'Menuet' suggests it was Bach's conception of the piece itself that changed.

THE ROLE OF ARTICULATION IN THE ADOPTION OF OTHER INSTRUMENTAL FORMS AND STYLES

The most striking development in Bach's keyboard style is his adoption of ensemble forms and idioms, an innovation which had direct influence on his successors. First, probably through a court commission, Bach transcribed Italian concertos for organ and harpsichord during the middle-Weimar years (Schulze 1984 pp. 146-73). Brandenburg 5, BWV 1050, represents the next stage in the emancipation of the keyboard from its traditional role and repertory and this is followed by further keyboard concerti, cantata obbligati, sonatas for obbligato harpsichord and another instrument; organ sonatas in which all three lines are taken over by the keyboard; Italian concerto and French Overture in *Clavierübung* II.

It is precisely in these works that we find the most detailed articulation markings, already demonstrated in the study in chapter 10 of BWV 1027, 1030 and 1050. The organ obbligati in Leipzig cantatas and the harpsichord concertos – most being transcriptions from works for other instruments – provide further examples. Here the keyboard is not merely a partner with other instruments but dominates the ensemble.

Dreyfus (1985 pp. 237-47) conjectures that most of the organ obbligati, dating from 1726, were designed to be played by Bach himself. The organ lines in the autograph scores are transposed down a tone to sound at the pitch of the other instruments. The general absence of separate organ parts further suggests that the autograph score was used by the performer of the obbligato. Such a score – including all the instrumental lines – would surely have been used only by the director of the performance: Bach himself. This has striking implications for the indication of articulation marks. If the score was being used by the composer for his own performance, he would hardly have needed performance aids written into the notation. Such markings as there are, then, are probably part of the music itself, identified with its particular style and figuration. As many of these obbligati are string-like in style, articulation marks in the organ part seem to be a stylistic allusion to the musical implications of bowing rather than finite instructions to the player.

Some examples in the 1726 cantatas do suggest that articulation marks were not required for organ on the same level as they were for other instruments. In BWV 47/2 only very basic markings are given in the autograph P 163. In the parts, St 104, however, there is an autograph single-line part which is marked in far more detail, and to which an unknown hand has added 'organo'. This has every appearance of a violin part so it is doubtful whether these markings were ever intended for obbligato organ (*NBA* 1/23 *KB* pp. 182-4). The autograph score P 154 for BWV 170/5 is similarly sparsely marked: most slurs for organ relate to the most common figures found in Appendix 2: descending pattern of four notes with 1A and 1C and 'sigh' figures ending phrases. The parts, St 94, however contain a late autograph part for flute. This is slurred in considerable detail with many dots included.

In both cases, of course, the organ line in the autograph score is being compared with an autograph part for another instrument. Scores are generally less well marked than parts, so the difference in the level of markings between the two types of source is quite normal.

Nevertheless many of the 1726 obbligati show the organ surprisingly well marked. Such markings are hardly comprehensive – more allusive – but BWV 35/1 shows a subtlety of marking quite common in many of the instrumental works discussed. The first solo entry introduces several slurs which set the organ apart from the unslurred instrumental ritornello (Example 99). These slurs relate to typical figures: pairing,

Example 99

four-note appoggiatura and *messanza*. One slurring shared with the strings is that introduced by the oboe and violin in b. 27 (Example 100). This is adopted by the organ at the end of the episode bb. 68–76, a point of tension over the pedal F (Example 101). Here the slurring is developed along similar lines to the motifs: a slurring is first related to

Example 100

Example 101

a particular motivic pattern (here the group of six descending notes) and gradually adopted by other figures (b. 70f). Finally, by b. 72 the paired slurring is replaced by a longer pattern for exactly the same figures as b. 71 (which is an equally if not more justifiable slurring since it follows the grouping of the notes more closely). Then this longer slurring is applied to the new *messanza* figuration of b. 73, for which it is eminently appropriate. Thus these slurs have several functions: (1) linking the organ to the other instruments by the use of the same (slurred) figure; (2) the slurring itself becoming a subject for 'development' and bringing the organ into relief against the sustained chords in the instrumental parts (bb. 73-6, 93-7, 116-21); (3) acting as a dovetail (b. 72) between the two discrete forms of figuration in bb. 70 and 73.

BWV 169/1 and 49/1 are similar examples of concerto style where the organ is treated as if it were a solo violin. Indeed, Dreyfus notes that Bach's use of the organ in 1726 seems to be a special experiment, one that disappointed later commentators expecting the 'grand' organ style. The style seems more that of the overtly instrumental trio sonatas for organ, BWV 526-30, which may well date from the same period (*c*. 1727). As Dreyfus (1985 p. 242) comments about the obbligati, 'one of the most *galant* features of the organ solos is the clever manner in which the organ feigns identities other than its own'.

These observations also apply to the seven harpsichord concertos of the late 1730s (in autograph P 234). Here the harpsichord receives markings (including dots) which are characteristic of string music (Examples 102-6). These markings seem part of the 'transcription'

Example 102 BWV 1052, Allegro, b. 1

Example 103 Adagio, b. 1

Example 104 BWV 1053/1, bb. 12-13

Example 105

Example 106 BWV 1054/3, bb. 49-51

(both of the 'instrumental' concerto form *per se* and of actual violin concertos). This apparently new approach to keyboard style is made particularly clear in the organ obbligato to BWV 29/7 (27 August 1731).[1] This is a variation on the earlier aria with violin obbligato, BWV 29/3 (both set the words 'Halleluja, Stärk' und Macht sei des

Allerhöchsten Namen'). Here the organ part is a literal parody of the violin original, with an added, somewhat insolent, shake (Example 107).

Example 107

Thus slurs are used in obbligati and concerti as a stylistic feature. Since it is probable that Bach himself was the soloist in most of the works discussed, it follows that the slurs are part of the music rather than advice to the inexperienced player. The time from 1726 to the end of Bach's life seems to show developments both in the precision of nota-tion (cf. Appendix 2) and in the keyboard idiom. Nevertheless, the early Mühlhausen cantata, BWV 71/2 and 7 (1708), in a completely different and rather archaic style, shows frequent paired slurrings in the organ obbligato. These, particularly in BWV 71/2, seem a conscious parody of the paired vocal underlay. Apparently, then, the two elements normally associated with the later years - keyboard parody and detail of marking - are evident, in certain sources at least, in the earliest stages of Bach's development.

'INSTRUMENTAL' ARTICULATION FOR SOLO KEYBOARD

Turning now to keyboard solos with no accompanying instruments it is interesting to note that the style of articulation marking in the Italian Concerto of 1735, BWV 971, from *Clavierübung* II is closely compatible with that found in the keyboard obbligati and concerti. The work is a direct adaptation of the 'modern' instrumental concerto style to keyboard and with this comes the same dynamic form of arti-culation (Example 108). Nevertheless the level of slurring is far lower

Example 108 BWV 971 1, bb. 69-70

than that in the unaccompanied violin solos or BWV 1027: the level
is more that of the flute sonata BWV 1030; necessary figuration is
marked but the performer is left to apply the same markings to parallel
passages.

Slurs have a particular structural function in being associated with
the *piano* sections. Long slurs in the Presto are introduced for the
first *piano* section in b. 25 and for its return in b. 167. This also
emphasizes the contrast between the two manuals.

The distinction of musical style between this concerto and the accompanying Ouverture is quite marked. This could well lead us to
expect a very different style of articulation: the long melismatic solo line
of the central movement of the Italian Concerto is something quite
foreign to the French style. However, given the inevitable differences in
texture, much of the notated articulation is surprisingly similar. The
association of slurs with *piano* sections in the Italian Concerto is also
evident in the opening movement of the Ouverture and the Echo.
So great was Bach's concern that this slurring should be made clear that
he added the slur in b. 47 of the fugue in his personal copy.

Although the violinistic slurring of the Concerto with its combination of slurs and dots is less common in the Ouverture, extensive
examples do appear in Gavotte II and Passepied I (Examples 109 and
110). Similar detail is evident in certain instances in the third and

Example 109 Gavotte II

Example 110 Passepied I

fourth parts of the *Clavierübung* although comprehensive marking of
specific movements is rare.

Only one third of the movements in the fourth part of the *Clavierübung* ('Goldberg' variations), BWV 988, contain articulation marks
of any kind. Those without are generally in either a strict or a 'moto
perpetuo' style. Some markings, such as in Variation 13, b. 11, are very
detailed, consisting of both slurs and dots. These bear a strong likeness

to the 'instrumental' markings of the concerti and cantata obbligati. Bach's additional dots (Paris example) in Variation 14, Example 111

Example 111

(as exceptions, negating grammatical 'good' and 'bad' pulses?), might be a crucial clue to why so much earlier keyboard music – including *Clavierübung* I – was usually unmarked: players – unless otherwise informed – geared their articulation to the natural hierarchy of the pulse, and to their knowledge of the harmony and figuration.

Articulation marks also seem to indicate exceptions in *Clavierübung* III (1739) for organ. Other than slurs found in the slower, expressive, settings (paired slurs in BWV 678 and 682) as an affective device, most markings relate to extraordinary circumstances: Duets II and IV (BWV 803 and 805) contain slurs crossing the beat, denoting exceptions to the natural accents.

Dots also occur in some surprising places: the Fughetta, BWV 677, uses dots over its main quaver subject even though most notes are disjunct (a similar case is found in the episodes of the prelude BWV 544). Dots added in BWV 682 (b. 10) occur with the triplet semiquavers (all conjunct) denoting a somewhat unexpected articulation. Here the contrast with the unmarked quaver lines and the slurred 'Lombard' rhythm: 𝄞 results in complex, simultaneous articulation patterns. The markings here seem to underline the extraordinary eclectic nature of the piece: slurs contribute to the traditional 'pathetic' *Affekt* of penitence, as do the chromatic lines and severe canonic writing; however, the rhythms and detailed articulation also allude to up-to-date *galant* styles. The notation of this work surely reflects Bach's 'universal' view of composition, giving the supplicatory *Affekt* of the text 'Vater unser' both traditional and 'modern' qualities.

This example also shows Bach's tendency to define different components in the musical structure with different styles of articulation. Thus dots, in addition to indicating exceptions to expected articulation (as observed in Example 111 from BWV 988), help distinguish different *Affekt*s within the same piece.

The relation of articulation to structure is especially pronounced in the opening Prelude, BWV 552: Williams (1984 pp. 205-6) has recently observed that three styles of articulation – slurred, staccato and unmarked – characterize the three main elements of this prelude, and this contributes to the religious symbolism. Moreover, this precision of marking seems typical of the late 1730s (see pp. 115, 163 above).

Clavierübung III, with its diversity of style, shows more clearly than any other collection the relation of articulation marks to the 'modern' settings. None of the *stile antico* settings is marked (the only exception being the fairly strict fughetta BWV 677). Clearly some difference in performance style is implied, but the musical difference suggested by the notation is equally important: articulation marks as stylistic pointers are part of the documentary quality of Bach's later publications, reflecting an assimilation of all contemporary styles.

The six sonatas, BWV 525-30, have provided much material for previous studies of articulation marks. This is because they are, in places, marked in as much detail as is often found in calligraphic autographs of string and woodwind music. The study by le Huray and Butt (1985 pp. 185-206) suggests that scholars have often underestimated Bach's use of the autograph P 271 as a performance manuscript and that many of its articulation markings may have been added by Bach some time after the compilation of the manuscript in *c.* 1730. Furthermore, parts of the copy, P 272, by Wilhelm Friedemann and Anna Magdalena Bach, contain further articulation markings, probably dating from the period 1730-3. This manuscript contains considerably more autograph material than has hitherto been observed, in particular the titles and Italian directions in Anna's section of the manuscript.[2] A comparison with Bach's additions to instrumental parts of cantatas, often in a thinner nib, suggests that the articulation marks added to BWV 530/2 and 3 are autograph.

Bach's particular concern with the sixth sonata, BWV 530, around the time P 271 was compiled is clear from the structure of the manuscript, where the earlier gatherings have been engineered to meet up with the first, blank page of the sixth sonata. This might substantiate several hypotheses that this sonata was composed specially for organ, the others being compiled from previous material (Williams 1980 p. 51).

These sonatas, like the contemporary obbligati in cantatas and the harpsichord concertos, reflect an assimilation of instrumental styles by the organ and, with them, the agility of bowing and tonguing. Williams (1984 p. 204) has attempted to place slurrings into two categories: those in the 'old manner of "harmonic slurs or bowing-marks"' and those that 'might be associated in the new chamber music of the period with violinists' bowing or flautists' tonguing'. Although this description is slightly confusing – as 'bowing' is mentioned in both categories – Williams probably means that many slurs are of the traditional type (the paired slurs of BWV 526, Largo; the four-note descending patterns of BWV 527, Andante (b. 5) and BWV 530, Allegro (b. 77)) common to all instrumental media, and others are of the type found in well-marked string sources such as BWV 1027, derived as much from playing techniques as from the figuration. The latter type often 'interpret' the music, revealing qualities which are not immediately evident in the notes themselves. The two types of slurring are perhaps not as self-contained as Williams implies: the second type of 'modern' bowing is derived from the former and, as shown in the study of BWV 1027, a marking which is introduced in conjunction with a figure or harmonic feature often achieves independence as a rhythmic pattern later in the piece. Williams also notes the use of dots to clarify short slurred patterns (*ibid*. pp. 203–4) (Example 112). This likewise recalls the type of marking observed in BWV 1027.

Example 112 BWV 530. Lento (P 272)

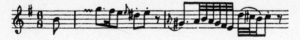

Another type of slurring is often found in the slow movements: the long slur of rather indeterminate written length, covering a melisma of faster note values (which is often structurally the 'ornamentation' of one or two beats). This reflects the trend towards longer sustained lines, already observed above in the discussion of clavier music (p. 166). Similar slurs are found in the solo lines of instrumental works (e.g. BWV 1046, Adagio, oboe solo). Perhaps the very vagueness of Bach's marking at such points suggests that a shaping or 'phrasing' is required rather than a detailed articulation (le Huray and Butt 1985 p. 191). However, a continuous legato, lasting for several bars, seems contrary to the implications of the majority of articulation marks in Bach's œuvre and obscures the basic structure of the music (see pp. 184–5 below).

The use of articulation marks to indicate 'exceptions' seems to be a particular feature of solo keyboard music. In the faster movements the player would presumably normally base his approach to articulation on the patterns of figuration and the grammar of the metre. In BWV 526, Vivace, bb. 44–5, the quavers are 'patterned' in an exceptional way (Example 113). Similarly, dots in BWV 527, Andante, may be used to negate an expected 'good' and 'bad' interpretation of quavers (Example 114).

Example 113

Example 114

The detail of the two manuscripts P 271 and P 272, although not comprehensive, suggests that Bach was educating his pupils in a more lively style of organ playing, one particularly suited to the music of BWV 525–30. Similar signs are clear in the organ obbligati of cantatas, where the organ is playing with other instruments and matches their manner of articulation. Likewise the upper line of the harpsichord part for the gamba sonata BWV 1027 achieves parity with the solo instrument; in BWV 525–30 both solo lines are given to the keyboard.

12

Bach and 'modern' articulation;
slurs as 'phrase marks'

In nineteenth-century music two levels of slurring are often used: smaller slurs indicate the details of articulation and larger slurs imply a general 'phrasing'. The term 'phrase' is increasingly evident in musical dictionaries of the late eighteenth century. Rousseau's definition in the *Encyclopédie* (1751-7 vol. 12 p. 530) seems to have been of tremendous influence, reappearing in the *Dictionnaire* (1768 p. 376). English translations are found in Grassineau (1767 p. 37) and Chambers (1783 vol. 3 'Phrase').[1]

There are no authentic instances of the simultaneous use of smaller and larger slurs in the music of Bach examined in this survey. A study of slurs unrelated to articulation or small-scale 'figural' and accentual grouping must be based on circumstantial evidence. Instrumental media in which no legato is possible will be examined first, then instances where Bach uses exceptionally long slurs. These might, on the one hand, indicate an unusually extensive legato style, on the other, a longer 'phrasing' which can be articulated in several ways.

Two works are of particular relevance to this study, since they relate to works and genres that will be discussed in chapter 13: the two suites for lute BWV 995 and 1006a. The autograph of the first (Brussels II 4085) dates from the period 1727-31 and comprises a very thorough arrangement of the cello suite, BWV 1011 (*NBA* 5/10 *KB* pp. 92, 102). The second (Musashino Music Academy, Tokyo; Littera rara vols. 2-14) is a later arrangement (1735-40) of the violin partita BWV 1006 (*ibid*. pp. 92, 161).

Only the very shortest of slurs could indicate a real legato on the lute (i.e. more than one note sounded during one plucking). Thus Bach may well have intended the slurs which match those in the original string versions to indicate a notional legato, the player ac-

centing within the slur as little as possible. The markings in BWV 995
follow roughly the same pattern as is found in Anna Magdalena's
copy of the cello suites (P 269). Most differences reflect a general
tendency toward longer slurs in the lute version (Example 115).

The most striking slur of all in BWV 995 is that found bb. 22-5 of
the Prelude (Example 116). This suggests a fairly free run to be played

Example 115

Example 116

'in one bow' with as little intermediate articulation as possible. Clearly
this long-term grouping of notes has something in common with later
concepts of 'phrasing'.

Slurs found in pizzicato passages in string music can be regarded
in the same light as lute slurs. Most of these, however, concern parts to
which the direction 'pizzicato' was a later addition (e.g. the continuo
parts to BWV 36b/7 St 15, BWV 213/5, St 65; BWV 248/15, St 112).
Nevertheless, in BWV 232/8 both the pizzicato direction and the few
slurs are also found in the autograph score P 180 (Example 117). These

Example 117

slurs coincide with the first appearance of the *superjectio* figure in the continuo line and clearly indicate the adoption of the same style of accent as is implied by the slurs in the other parts. Here some type of Lombard rhythm may be suggested, since some of the parts have been altered to reflect this (Herz 1974 pp. 90-7).

A similar instance is evident in the 'Et in terra pax', BWV 232/5 (Dresden parts): here the timpani receive a paired slurring mirroring that of the simultaneous trumpet parts (Example 118).

Example 118

Long slurs have already been discussed in the survey of vocal techniques. A long slur covering notes with staccato dots could be indicative of a phrasing direction if it were certain that the slur was not merely an indication of underlay (see pp. 24-5 above).

In instrumental parts it seems to be the oboe (and occasionally the transverse flute) which is given the longest slurs:

BWV 109. 5	17 10 23	b. 21	source St 56
249. 2	1 4 25	10	P 34, St 355; also later autograph version for flute
249. 9		14	
108 1	29. 4 25	4	P 82, St 28
72. 5	27/1. 26	38	St 2
207. 7	11/12 26	4	St 93 (flute)
112/2	8. 4. 31	3	St Thom
100/5	1732 5	3	St 97 (autograph)

All the markings which are not in autograph parts or score are in movements where Bach's editing is evident in the dynamic and ornament signs. None of these slurs extends for more than two bars, so all can easily be played in one breath. This suggests that they are genuine articulation markings indicating only a single tonguing; probably Bach considered the tonguing of the oboe to be rather too strong in certain circumstances and advocated a more legato style.

Long slurs in violin parts also imply experimentation in an unusually legato style. The slurs for violin and oboe in BWV 84/3 (*NBA* 1/7 *KB* pp. 37-8) have been added (hurriedly and possibly not in Bach's hand) to the parts (St 52) and suggest a new, flowing approach to the movement which was not at all evident in the score (P 108) (Example 119).

Example 119

Long slurs also cross ties in the parts (St Thom) for BWV 9/3 (1732–5). Only in BWV 248/54 (1735) are long slurs noticeable in an autograph score (P 32) (Example 120). The style here has much in common with

Example 120

that of the sonata from the late *Musicalisches Opfer*, BWV 1079, where entire bars of continuous quavers are slurred in the continuo line of the Largo. Slurs even cover tied notes in the Andante and final Allegro (Example 121). The longer slurs throughout BWV 1079 reflect a desire

Example 121 Final Allegro, violin, bb. 13-15

for evenness in the musical line, the smaller figures becoming subservient to the longer phrase. In the Andante the extensive legato lines also reflect the slower harmonic pulse of the more 'modern' style.

In the first movement of BWV 1041, bb. 112–16, long slurs are used as a means of sustaining a slow harmonic sequence where the same harmony is maintained for two bars (Example 122). Here, after much intricate articulation, all movement, harmonic and accentual, is apparently suspended. The slurred notes are purely an ornamental scale with no specific motivic content.

Example 122

All these markings can conceivably be played in one bow or tonguing. Thus they cannot be necessarily taken as phrase marks in the
full sense since they still affect articulation. Certainly they reflect a
trend for experimentation in a non-accented style (where conventional
points of articulation such as syncopations are ignored), which is part
of the general development of articulation throughout the eighteenth

century. This same trend is also reflected in the early classical style
where the musical phrase or sentence becomes more important than
a continuous harmonic rhythm.

The existence of long slurs in Bach's notation challenges the assertion that consecutive shorter slurs or inconsistent slurs imply a 'general
legato', particularly in keyboard works (Fuchs 1985, quoting Keller,
pp. 129, 146–52; Jenkins 1976 pp. 68–70). So often do articulation
markings in keyboard music accord with those of string and woodwind
parts that it is not likely that a continuous legato was ever intended.
On the other hand, a strict observation of the breaks before the first
note of the slur might sound absurd in such a piece as BWV 639 from
the 'Orgelbüchlein'. The accentual effect of such slurs in a cello part is
not the same as the articulation pause on the organ. These slurs for
organ probably indicate a varied or 'articulated' legato in the 'French'
manner (see p. 54 above) (Example 123). Inconsistent or careless

Example 123

slurring surely does not imply a general legato (which would often
obscure the basic tactus of the music) but demands that standard
slurring be applied (e.g. pairs or groups of four) in accordance with
metrical accents (see p. 132 above). This type of performance is important when the accentuation and articulation of every note of the
Decoratio is inappropriate (such as in *piano* sections or accompanying,
non-thematic voices).

Clearly, most slurs in Bach's music indicate that the notes are to
be grouped in some way. However, the exact function of the slur can
only be conjectured from its context: a few slurs are impossible to
play legato by virtue of their length or the technicalities of the instrument. Conversely, the harmonic circumstances may demand a legato
resolution or grouping of notes. Textbook definitions do not suffice
when the composer is working at speed and adding many markings
unconsciously.

13

Articulation marks in analysis and interpretation

This study has shown that the significance of Bach's notated articulation varies considerably between different sources and musical contexts. Nevertheless many norms have emerged showing that most markings are coherent with the structure of the *Decoratio*, conforming to certain metrical hierarchies, figurations and harmonic devices. In string playing slurs directly affect the mode by which sound is produced and consequently have further influences on the accentual flow of the music. This final chapter examines instances where Bach has marked articulation most precisely with the deepest consideration of all levels of implication. Here we can learn a great deal, not only about the performance of his music but also much about its structure and inner momentum. Such cases might also form a model for similar pieces which Bach left unmarked.

SLURS AND THE ACCENTUAL INFLUENCE OF PLAYING TECHNIQUE

Dadelsen cites the unaccompanied violin solos, BWV 1001–6 (P 967), as supreme examples of Bach's notated articulation:

Die autographe Reinschrift hat Bach sehr genau bezeichnet. Der Grund dazu liegt in der Musik selbst: Sie ist ganz vom Instrument und seiner Spieltechnik her komponiert. Intendierte, das heißt mit den Motiven fest verbundene Artikulation und die Erfordernisse einer geläufigen Bogenführung, die im Abstrich zugleich die Taktschwerpunkte markiert, stimmen miteinander überein. Das gilt besonders für die schnellen Sätze

(Bach has marked the autograph fair copy very exactly. The reason for this lies in the music itself: it is composed completely from the instrument and its

186

playing technique. Intended articulation, that is to say articulation which is closely connected with the motifs, corresponds with the requirements of a fluent bowing-scheme, in which the down-stroke marks the strong points of the bar. This is especially true of the fast movements)

(Dadelsen 1978 p. 105)

Dadelsen observes that generally only in the slower movements is the performer responsible for ensuring a satisfactory succession of bow-strokes, since there is more time to make adjustments to bow-direction, to accord with the metrical accent (*ibid.* p. 108). In the slow movements Bach marks only the figuration which needs to be identified by a slurred style, while in the faster movements his slurs result in a complete bowing-scheme dictating the succession of up- and down-bows. Bach obviously wrote BWV 1001–6 for the virtuoso, so the slurs are more didactic than advisory, limiting rather than merely assisting the player.

If, as Dadelsen claims, there is a circular relationship between playing technique, compositional style and articulation, the slurs should give us insight into the music itself. They might be regarded as Bach's interpretation of his own music, rather than simply as the technical and instructive means to play it.

Dadelsen briefly mentions instances where the relation of down-bows to strong beats is temporarily broken (*ibid.* p. 105). These offer insight into Bach's attitude towards phrasing and structure. The down-bow rule is also modified where there is one bow per bar or beat. Here every odd-numbered bar or beat will have a 'strong' down-bow.

The 'bar-rhythm' in the Presto of BWV 1001 is reflected by the shorter bar-line every other bar: two bars form one larger bar. This bowing suggests that Bach thought of b. 81 and not b. 80 (with its higher tessitura) as the peak of the phrase (Example 124).

Example 124

Quite often the slurring seems to *weaken* rather than emphasize the accents within a bar. Slurs crossing beats (e.g. BWV 1004, Giga, bb. 15, 16) reduce the number of accents per bar and thus enhance

the flow and momentum of the piece. In the Bourrée of BWV 1006 an
ingenious relation of bow-direction, slurring and dynamics is evident
when a repeated echo (with identical slurring) begins with the 'weaker'
up-bow (Example 125).

Example 125

Much of the momentum in Bach's melodic phrase structure is
derived from the ambiguity of the point at which one phrase ends and
another begins. Even if the phrasing superficially runs in four-bar
units, it is often difficult to establish the point at which the phrases
meet or overlap. The slurring often contributes to this technique:
BWV 1001, Presto, begins with two clear four-bar sequential phrases;
the first comprises disjunct notes, the second both conjunct and disjunct, the conjunct notes being delineated by slurs (bb. 1–8) (Example
126). The melodic line of the phrase, bb. 9–12, consists of four descending notes (Example 127). However, in b. 12 the line is displaced; the

Example 126

Example 127

f♯″ falls on the second and not the first quaver. The slur beginning on the *f♯″* (down-bow) provides the accent to clarify the voice-leading (many players would slur the appoggiatura, *g″-f♯″*, here). Moreover, all conjunct notes so far have been slurred, so the slurring here is coherent and predictable. Significantly, it identifies a new slurred figure which constitutes the sequential material for the next phrase (3H).

Thus one phrase ends at b. 12 (the accentual quality of the slur clarifies the line ending on *f♯″*); at the same time the sequential figuration (identified by the slur) begins the next phrase. This overlapping also prevents a strong caesura in the tonic which would be inappropriate at this stage in the movement. Bach's initial decision to slur conjunct notes not only prepares the ear for a new figure based on conjunct notes, it also belongs to the compositional decision to devise a dovetail between two sequences.

The conjunct-legato connotations of slurring in the next phrase throw the unslurred passages into more relief. Thus the harmonic sequence to E♭ major (by falling fourths) is given particular emphasis, with down-bows at the beginning of each bar (Example 128). Here the

Example 128

slurs provide a rhythmic figuration, based on conjunct notes within a sequence.

Many important junctions in the structure of a movement are accompanied by an increase in slurred patterns. The canons 'a2 Per motum contrarium' and 'a2 Quaerendo invenietis' from BWV 1079 introduce slurred patterns to mark the end of the canonic part (Examples 129 and 130). In realized performance these slurs often serve to

Example 129

Example 130

change the prevailing articulation just before cadences. Sometimes the slurs conflict with the bar-rhythm and harmony. Here the slurs are usually linked only to the grouping of conjunct notes (Examples 131 and 132). In Example 132 the melodic and harmonic sequence cor-

Example 131 BWV 1001, Presto, bb. 32 6 (modulation to D minor to end first half)

Example 132 bb. 117-21 (return to G minor at end)

responds to the bar accent, while the articulation pattern, linked with conjunct notes, constitutes its own sequence, ending exactly one semiquaver later. This is itself symmetrical, the number of unslurred notes (disjunct) and slurred (conjunct) following a consistent pattern: 3-3-1-5-3-3-1-5 (*slurred*=italics). All slurred groups receive the 'strong' down-bow.

The association of slurs with both conjunct motion and accentuation is demonstrated even more clearly in another chamber work, BWV 1017/4, Allegro - unfortunately not preserved in an autograph source.[1] Here the initial 1D slurring with its group of three conjunct notes becomes an element of syncopated development at the equivalent point in the second half of the movement (Example 133).

Example 133

The performance implications of slurs are thus of particular importance in the interpretation of the music. They may relate to features which are already inherent in the notes, such as a sequence of conjunct notes which seems to run against the metrical pulse. Slurs confirm that this melodic grouping is also rhythmically important. Clearly Bach is acting here as the supreme interpreter of his music. His activity as a performer is literally a further stage in the compositional process, deriving deeper implications from the 'superficial' *Decoratio*.

THE AFFECTIVE IMPLICATIONS OF SLURS

Slurs might often be used to evoke a particular *Affekt*. Here the slurs confirm something which is already evident in the notes, or impose a particular *Affekt* on notes which could have been interpreted in a number of ways.

Sometimes the character of a particular dance might influence the rhythmic structure of a movement. The Giga of BWV 1004 is consistently articulated with a 2B slur regardless of the layout of notes (also observed by Fuchs 1985 p. 74). Similarly the Gavotte of BWV 1006 is characterized by the double upbeat. Paired slurs often confirm this rhythmic *Affekt* by turning four even quavers at the end of the bar into two crotchet pulses (Example 134). That this rhythm is funda-

Example 134

mental to the music is suggested by Bach's autograph transcription of this piece for lute (see p. 180 above). Here the two crotchet pulses are confirmed by chords.

Nowhere is affective contrast more evident than in the paired movements of BWV 1002. Each of the four Doubles is essentially a more continuous, running version of the previous dance. In this way the regular slurred pairs of Double 1 (paired with the Allemande) contrast with the sharp dotted rhythms and uneven succession of notes in the Allemande itself. These paired slurs bear no relation to pre-existent paired figuration; they impose a slurred *Affekt* which accents the first note and shortens the second in each group (generating crotchet accents). The Corrente is characterized by a subtle use of three-note slurs. Its Double contains virtually no slurring, and, with its continuous, fiery semiquavers, complements the grace of the former. The continuous 9/8 (unslurred) movement of the third Double seems intentionally bland after the emotive style of the Sarabande. A relationship between the Borea and Double is also evident: the former derives its momentum from contrasts of rhythm and tessitura, the latter partly from its slurring, imposing a pattern on a succession of even notes. This slurring often covers short motifs taken directly from the Borea (e.g. b. 4).

Slurs impose a change of *Affekt* in BWV 1004, Ciaccona, bb. 72-3. Here the running figuration is virtually the same for the two bars. However, the disappearance of slurs at the exact point where the next four-bar variation begins suggests that a definite contrast is implied and that the slurring should not automatically be continued by the player; articulation has become an element of the variation technique.

In these last examples, then, Bach's slurrings reflect the composer in the role of musical interpreter, imposing a specific *Affekt* on 'neutral' notes.

SLURS AND SPECIFIC FIGURES

Throughout this survey it has been suggested that singers and players would have recognized certain figures within the music, through their knowledge of improvised ornamentation. Moreover some figures may well have received a particular delineation or articulation. However, such is the complexity of Bach's music that specific figures are often integrated into the structure of the work and developed in such a way that their original identity is obscured.

An interesting relationship between slurs and developing figuration is evident in the canon 'a4' from BWV 1079. Here (bb. 3-4) the *suspirans* is defined by the tied note (without slurs) (Example 135). In b. 5, however, this figure is contracted without a tied minim (Example 136). Here the slurs underline the rhythmic diminution of the motif; the *suspirans* is engulfed by the four-note figure (initially identified with closer, conjunct movement). The reverse is evident in

Example 135

Example 136

Contrapunctus 8 from BWV 1080. Here the first version is slurred (bb. 5-6), the subsequent contracted version unslurred (bb. 7-8) (Example 137). Thus slurs act as a marker for Bach's development and rhythmic contraction of thematic material.

Example 137

Analysis of slurs and specific figuration is made more complex by the fact that slurs may perform a specific rhythmic or affective function – often associated with the playing technique – which is not necessarily related to the figuration constituting the musical line. The slurring in BWV 1005, Allegro Assai, for instance, is related to the rhythm and not directly to the figures used. In b. 5, the first beat could be termed a *messanza*, the second a *groppo* or turn, the third a *messanza* similar to the first (Example 138). However, some figures

Example 138

may derive from the playing techniques involved, particularly note groupings which require a long down-bow followed by a short up-bow, 1B (i.e. three conjunct notes followed by a leap): BWV 1005, Largo (b. 1).

Figures of the *messanza* type (i.e. comprising both conjunct and disjunct motion) are often found in triple metres, where three conjunct slurred notes are followed by a leap, 3C: BWV 1001, Presto, b. 25. Here this pattern is regularly maintained, the slur crossing the subdivisions of the beat, creating excellent forward-drive.

However, it should not be assumed that traditional figures necessarily require a slurred style. The *suspirans* of Printz and Walther (never identified with a slur in such writings) is displayed unslurred in its early occurrences in BWV 1005 Largo (Example 139). Later it is slurred (Example 140, Plate 9). It could be argued that this was slurred

Example 139

Example 140

in its second instance as an afterthought to the first (i.e. the slurring is not part of the composition, but an incidental marking).[2] This view would assume that the notes and slurs were written in the direct sequence of the manuscript. Certainly in BWV 1004, Ciaccona, b. 244, the slurring has clearly been extended by one note from 2C to 5C. In the ensuing bars the slurring appears in its later form without alteration, so it is likely that these slurs were added in the sequence of the manuscript.

On the other hand, several stages in the inclusion of slurs are evident in BWV 1005, Allegro assai (Plate 9). Here the first slur in b. 5 has been extended to the left to cover the first note. At the equivalent point in the second half (b. 47) there is even more visible evidence that the same slur has been extended. However, all other instances of the pattern follow the later version without alteration, implying that the first slurs to be inserted were those in bb. 5 and 47, the others being filled in later. This case suggests that it is unwise to assume automatically

9 Sonata 3 for solo violin in C Major, BWV 1005, Largo; Allegro assai (p. 196),
bb. 1–56 (1); slur extensions in bb. 5, 47. Mus. MS P 967

9 (cont.)

that additions to slurring in the course of a movement in a fair copy reflect afterthoughts.

Although it is difficult to account for the inconsistency of articulation for the *suspirans* in BWV 1005, Largo, a succinct example from a similar fair copy, St 145, for the concerto BWV 1041 shows how the changing musical role of the *suspirans* might be reflected in the articulation (Example 141).

For the first four bars the *suspirans* is characteristically slurred; however, in b. 28 the expected slur is absent. It is at this very point that the next musical sequence begins (these three semiquavers are thus a 'Janus' figure, belonging to both phrases). Now that the *suspirans* (b. 29) is incorporated into a longer sequence it is 'disguised' by the absence of the slur. The three-note slur itself as a musical element in its own right is transferred to the first beat of the bar where it now features as a downbeat accent (rather than as the previous upbeat accent of the *suspirans*). It imparts the three-note flavour of the original figure to an 'anonymous' scale. At b. 32 this slur becomes associated with a new three-note figure, which, as the inversion and equivalent of that in b. 28 beat 2, functions as the end of one sequence and the beginning of the next. Even here the slur is not constantly tethered to the one figure: the three-note figure features at the beginning of every bar, but each cell of the sequence is two bars long. The slur (as an accent) occurs on every 'strong' bar (32, 34, 36, etc.). This

Example 141

Example 141 (*cont.*)

accent occurs on two bars in succession, bb. 40-1, underlining the
bar-rhythm of the head-motif of the ritornello, which returns in
the accompaniment. The slurring is also here a fundamental tool in
articulating the phrase structure: the first phrase, bb. 25-8, is a regular
four-bar sequence, the second appears to be four bars – bb. 29-32 – but
with hindsight b. 32 is in fact the beginning of the new sequence,
bb. 32-9 (4 + 4). However, the slurring in b. 32 satisfies the ear's expectations of a fourth bar of the same sequence even though musically
this represents the start of a new phrase. This subtlety of phrasing
is typical of Bach's style, arousing expectations and fulfilling them,
but in an unexpected way. Just as Bach seldom uses the same figure
incessantly in a continuous movement, but integrates it into what is
superficially a seamless line, the slurring is not blindly regular; it reflects some of the underlying subtleties of the music itself.

The 'figural' slurring mentioned so far has been discussed mainly
for its accentual and delineating properties. An 'expressive' (legato?)
slurring is more usually associated with figures which comprise some
form of harmonic accent, such as the appoggiatura. As with the study
of vocal articulation, the close *accentus* figures are those most commonly associated with slurs (particularly in slower movements).

The association of the dotted *anticipatione della nota* with slurs is
particularly strong; it dominates the character of BWV 1005, Adagio.
The legato effect might be lost later on in the movement, where large
chords are spread. Perhaps what is important is the shaping implied
by the weight of the bow and the inevitable shortening of the second
notes. More definitely legato are the slurred pairs of stepwise even
notes (b. 5).

Longer slurred figures are often associated with appoggiaturas.
That at the beginning of BWV 1001, Siciliano, is a typical example
(Example 142). This slurring is consistently maintained in cases where

Example 142

the figure begins with an appoggiatura, on the beat. However, Bach is
prepared to allow paired slurring for ease of performing a lower part
when the appoggiatura is essentially a passing note (i.e. it has a weaker
accent) (Example 143).

Example 143

SLURS AND THE STRUCTURE OF MOVEMENTS

Slurs perform several functions in well-marked sources: they create a rhythmic system of accents which often reveals the true structure of a passage, its voice-leading and phrasing. They identify a specific *Affekt* in a movement (i.e. one of colourful rhythmic bowings or one of slurred expressive phrasing). They identify or delineate particular motifs within the musical structure. This concluding study of the Corrente from BWV 1002 examines the significance of slurs within the context of an entire movement to determine whether the slurs can assist us in our interpretation of the music.

BWV 1002, Corrente (Plate 10)

Slurred motifs (Example 144)

Example 144

10 Partita 1 for solo violin in B Minor, BWV 1002, Corrente. Mus. MS P 967

10 (cont.)

A three-note slur covering arpeggiated 10th (disjunct motion!) b. 2, etc. Always distinguished from subsequent notes which change direction and/or comprise conjunct notes.

A¹ three-note slur covering triad (bb. 28 and 31), clearly derived rhythmically from A but seldom so distinctive (i.e. subsequent note often proceeds in the same direction).

B slurs covering conjunct figures of the *circolo mezzo* type. More changeable than A, e.g. compare bb. 9 and 18.

X bb. 48, 77-8, etc. Three-note slur with rhythmic character of A but the conjunct motion of B.

Y bb. 72-3. Long slur of a bar + 3 notes. Rhythmic character of A, with three-note rhythm, but conjunct notes of *circolo mezzo* figure of B.

Slurs are not the only interpretative feature of the notation. Bach has marked every other bar with a half-length bar-line. This implies a strong-weak pairing of bars (as in the Presto of BWV 1001). The slurs and related figuration show an initial affinity with this two-bar grouping. In bb. 1-6 the 'strong' bars (1, 3, 5) consist of a rising arpeggio (unslurred) which presumably receives the grammatical bar accents (three beats). The 'weak' bars (2, 4, 6), however, contain the slur (over a descending 10th) which bisects the bar; this creates a syncopated upbeat to the next bar.

Bars 7-8 introduce a sequence. Bar 9, although outside the sequence, sounds as the consequent of bb. 7-8. The B slur and chord in b. 9 provide an 'extraordinary' accent on the second beat, punctuating the I-V progression. The three bars (7-9) are also motivically unrelated to those surrounding them, so they stand out as a three-bar unit, preparing for the return to 'normal' figuration in b. 10, a 'weak' bar with slur A. The accentual quality of the B slur and the association of A slurs with 'weak' bars underline this caesura. The whole of the section bb. 1-10 acts as an 'imperfect cadence' which is rhythmically prepared by the strong-weak relationship between the first two bars of the piece, chords I-V. This phrase is thus structured as indicated in Example 145. Bar 10, although the end of one phrase, provides material (i.e. the A slur) which is fundamental to the next phrase.

The use of an extra A pattern in b. 13 is interesting, since it implies, by association, a group of three 'weak' bars. This balances the three-bar 'strong' group bb. 7-9 (Example 146).

Bars 11-18 complement bb. 1-10 with the cadence in D on the 'weak' bar (18). The position of the B slur is interesting: in b. 9 it was part of the 'strong' bar of the cadence; in b. 18 it is part of the second 'weak'

Example 145

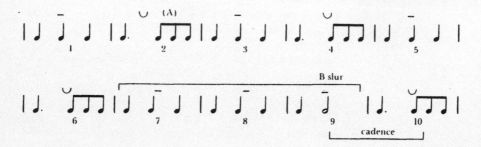

Example 146

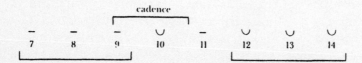

bar. The syncopated nature of the B slur acts as a long upbeat to the next phrase, the notes reaffirming the tonic by the reintroduction of the leading-note. This opens with the A slur on the *strong* bar (b. 19). Although bb. 20-5 contain none of the 10th figures and associated A slurs, this A slur in b. 19 lends the entire phrase a rhythmic instability, with the 'strong' and 'weak' bars apparently reversed. Bar 26 reintroduces the expected A slur on the weak bar, but it is immediately followed by three more bars of A and A¹. This leaves the accentual nature of A reversed, right up to the end of the first half of the movement. That Bach intended this reversal to characterize the central tonality (f♯ minor – presumably to create instability at the central point of the movement) is substantiated by the use of the slur A¹, in b. 31. Here the slur confirms the reversal of accents suggested by the presence of the A slur in bb. 27 and 29. The use of four slur patterns in a row, bb. 26-9, creates the same sense of expectancy as the group of three bars 7-9 ('strong') and the slurs in bb. 12-14 ('weak'), where they did not lead to an eventual reversal of the accents.

The A¹ slurs also perform a melodic role. The *a″* in b. 26 is prominent as it occurs at the beginning of the first slur for six bars. The A¹ slurs in bb. 28 and 31 – made conspicuous by their association with ascending motion – complete the melodic progression downwards to f♯, the central dominant chord (Example 147).

Example 147

The second half of the movement continues the rhythmic instability of the first, with A on the 'strong' bar in b. 35. It is restored to the 'weak' bar in bb. 36 and 38, but here it is transferred to the second beat. This element of syncopation is evident in the harmony of b. 34 and, of course, in the first major caesura in b. 9 (the 'B' slur accenting the second beat of the bar). Bars 39-72 constitute the important modulating section, leading back to b minor. Here most aspects of rhythm and slurring are entirely regular, so that the rapid harmonic changes (through flatter keys) are not obscured. Even the equivalents of the three unexpected 'strong' bars of bb. 7-9 are regularized - bb. 41, 43 - with a 'weak' A bar after each (42, 44).

Only two features of the slurring are unusual here. First, b. 48 introduces the slurring X. The usual A slur is rhythmically expected at this point, but the figuration it covers is conjunct, like that of B. The A^1 slur (bb. 28 and 31, a triad) provided an intermediate three-note slur, so that this conjunct use does not sound totally unexpected. This X slur, created through the temporary dissolution of the relationship between melody and rhythm, becomes especially significant in the closing bars of the piece. Secondly, b. 49 introduces the A slur on the 'strong' bar. This time the slur is necessary for melodic and harmonic, rather than rhythmic reasons. The leading-note of e minor was heard as the first note of the slur in b. 46 (weak bar), and b. 49 provides the equivalent slur and leading-note for A major (strong bar - these two

A slurs are, incidentally, the only ones to exceed the standard interval of a 10th). It is the harmonic rhythm here that is irregular, and this causes the slur - delineating leading-notes - to fall in the 'wrong' place. This is particularly characteristic of a swiftly modulating section.

The coda, bb. 72-80, performs no harmonic function necessary to the piece as a whole. Rather it expands the single-voice concept of the piece by transversing the octaves of the tonic on either side of b' and resolves the rhythmic tensions of the structure. The slurs show - by crossing bars and introducing syncopation - how the inevitable 'strong-weak' cadence of bb. 71-2 generates the momentum which is so characteristic of the piece (as is evident at earlier cadences, e.g. bb. 9-10 and 17-18).

The inevitable 'weak' slur in b. 72 is extended by a whole bar (Y). It has the rhythmic function and character of A but the conjunct figuration of B. This conjunct use of three-note slurs (here with the addition of a bar) complements X in b. 48. The Y slurs are thus a 'caricature' of A, first in their rhythmic position at the beginning of 'weak' bars (bb. 72, 74), and in their three-note character. By b. 77 the ear is accustomed to the three-note A slur, transformed to the conjunct X slur. Now the metrical associations are also removed (anticipated by the A slurs on the second beat, bb. 36, 38?) and the groups of three create a rhythmic hiatus across the bar-line. This element of syncopation acts as the 'rhythmic cadence' of the piece, the transference of the accent to the 'strong' bar, b. 79. This is the first 'strong' cadence in the tonic.

Slurs then perform an extremely important function in the structure of this piece. They are consistently connected with specific figures and, in turn, reveal how the position of such figures varies according to their place in the rhythmic, harmonic and melodic structure. Although the slurs are often developed in their own right like other features in the structure, what might appear to be initially spontaneous, improvised slurrings, such as A^1 and X, are shown to have a structural significance later in the piece.

These performance markings are then the clearest evidence we have of Bach's own interpretation and analysis of his music. They provide a crucial clue to the relationship between harmony, melody and rhythm. All three elements might be initially related, but developed out of phase with each other. It is the resolution of these conflicts and the dovetailing of the musical sentences that give this music its particular quality and momentum. Its 'rhetoric' is considerably more developed than that of most music of the age.

Conclusion

Descriptions of *Musica Practica* and testimonials for young players suggest that the more talented musicians in Bach's environment were educated in both composition and performance. They would have been able to develop and rewrite much of the music they performed; indeed the concept of musical 'interpretation' might have implied some element of composition. The rhetorical analogies frequently made in music are useful in this context: an orator writes his speech (*Inventio*) and delivers it (*Elocutio*) in the manner most appropriate to its content. In delivering a speech by someone else, he must follow the basic plan (*Dispositio* or *Elaboratio*) but may alter or elaborate the details (*Decoratio*).

Writers constantly emphasize the importance of interpreting correctly the *Affekt* of a piece, and here the performer's choice of appropriate articulation is vital. Conventional 'figures of speech' in the music may well have been associated with a particular articulation or delineation. Some such 'figures' may further have received different stresses or pronunciation according to their place in the musical structure. In all, the performance required the same clarity of pronunciation as would have been necessary in a verbal delivery.

The notated articulation is perhaps the closest evidence we have of how Bach himself interpreted his own music. Just as he notated all details of superficial figuration, taking away the performer's prerogative and rendering such figuration more structurally coherent, he also limited the performer's choice of articulation by adding slurs and dots. It is perhaps in this desire to record as much of his achievement on paper as possible rather than in ephemeral performance that Bach's enduring quality resides: for the very act of notation leads to a

more definitive version of the music, one which generates a further
sophistication and refinement of style.

Bach's attention to articulation markings is discerned by tracing
their role within the compositional process. To begin with, Bach
recorded many basic slurrings in the earliest stage at which he commit-
ted the notes to paper. These are most often related to standard figures
in the music itself, such as dissonances and paired figuration. Many of
these 'early' slurrings serve to delineate the rhythmic flow of the music
and underline the harmonic rhythm. Furthermore, Bach developed
slurring in the course of composition. A new figure might be derived
from one that is introduced at the beginning of the movement. The
two figures may have been slurred in the same fashion initially but, as
the movement progresses, the newer figure acquires its own slurring.
The slurs in such circumstances are part of Bach's technique of
thematic development: an initial idea breeds others, the characters of
which are 'discovered' by Bach the interpreter after they have actually
been developed.

That these early slurrings are not random choices is suggested by
the fact that Bach seldom altered them during subsequent editing of
both scores and parts. When he augmented slurrings he worked
primarily as a performer and elaborator, interpreting if not analysing
his own creations. The later compositional stages may also reveal
elements in the structure which were not necessarily evident in the first
notated draft.

In the editing stage, Bach often added details of ornamentation
and interpretation: ornament symbols, dynamics and articulation
marks. In the 1730s he spent more time on editing and indeed copying
out parts; articulation marks from this period are particularly detailed
and informative. Furthermore, Bach habitually revised his own music
in his later years. Each piece has its unique qualities, structure and
relationships which Bach himself was ever trying to realize and
interpret.

Slurring is most often associated with the levels of diminution
relating to the *Decoratio* of the music. Just as much of Bach's unique
musical quality lies in the close relationship between the figures in the
Decoratio and the underlying contrapuntal structure, the accentual
and delineating qualities of slurs bring us to a deeper understanding
of the music. In string music the function of a slur might vary widely
according to context, implying accentuation, dynamic shading or a
negation of expected pulses. Bach progressively applied more string-

like slurring to vocal, wind and keyboard music, as these, in turn, became influenced by string figuration. It is the 'modern' works for keyboard, such as the Leipzig cantata obbligati, the harpsichord concertos and the six sonatas BWV 525-30 which contain the detailed articulation marks, not the standard keyboard forms such as the fantasia and fugue. The latter in particular owes more to the character of the *stile antico*, where articulation may be governed primarily by metrical hierarchy and harmonic accents. Here the 'ornamental' figures often lead directly from one structural note to the next and do not require detailed interpretation.

Since the technical implications of the violin family influence Bach's figural style to such a great extent, it seems to be no mere chance that one of Bach's most detailed and calligraphic manuscripts should be of works for unaccompanied violin. The detailed slurrings in the autograph of BWV 1001-6 are of immense value in adding to our understanding of the particular quality of Bach's music: that inevitability which is somehow unexpected. Some slurs can be regarded as motifs in their own right, developing as the music progresses; some imply a rhythm which is different from that of the harmony or barline; some underline a melodic line which would otherwise be obscured in the figuration; others suggest tempo and dynamics. The music often comprises the interplay of several elements: metrical and harmonic rhythm, figural and melodic consistency and proportion. It is often the ambiguity as to which element has priority at any one point that gives the music its particular quality. Slurs often give us an insight into how this is achieved, reflecting the momentum and symmetry of the music; sometimes they perform several interpretative tasks simultaneously. Clearly many slurrings in string works are technical instructions, but to ignore these on the assumption that they do not affect the interpretation of the music is to miss the essential connection between composer and performer; the technical means are geared to realize musical implications.

Dots are less important to the structure and quality of the music; far fewer movements are marked with extensive passages of dots. Although most dots are found in the higher tessituras (like slurs), the note values most likely to have dots are generally larger than for slurs: principally the half and whole pulse. This may reflect the respective function of slurs and dots: slurs relate to accentuation, voice-leading and general colouring of the line; dots suggest more the lightening of the pulse and shortening of notes, and are far less likely to be associated with the 'ornamentation' in the music. Dots clarify rather than interpret textures in the music.

Although the detail and complexity of marking is greater than most that is to be found in the music of Bach's contemporaries, there are still the severe problems of consistency and completeness. The study of sources clearly implies that ambiguities relate to the circumstances and time spent in preparation, as Dürr and Dadelsen have convincingly shown. Clearly some contexts demand a change in the expected articulation, a special effect related to the development or role of a motif; different instrumental media might also demand some minor alteration to the notated slurring. Above all it is the varying importance of articulation according to the musical style and the forces involved which is a clue to the problem of consistency. When clarity of counterpoint and voice-leading is less important than the metrical and harmonic momentum, articulation marks do not 'interpret' the music. Generally slurs in such circumstances (often the common paired patterns such as 1C) remind the player to observe standard metrical accents, but reduce the degree of detail implicit in unslurred performance. In such cases exact consistency might indeed render such parts too prominent.

It is hoped that this study will give enough guidance on the implications of markings and reflect the statistical norms for certain regular patterns in different media to render it a useful tool in the interpretation of ambiguous or poor sources. The music will not be destroyed by unidiomatic articulation, but so many more levels of detail and meaning can be discerned if we 'edit' and 'interpret' the music with at least some of the care and insight that Bach himself has shown.

Appendix 1

Manuscript and printed sources

Abbreviations

P/St: Partitur/Stimmen (Score/parts);
See P. Kast, *Die Bach-
Handschriften der Berliner
Staatsbibliothek, TBSt* vol. 2/3
(Trossingen, 1958).
manuscripts that are currently housed
in the Deutsche Staatsbibliothek,
Berlin/DDR - Musikabteilung, are
designated here as ds
manuscripts in the Staatsbibliothek
Preußischer Kulturbesitz, Berlin/
West - Musikabteilung, are
designated here as spk
manuscripts in the Biblioteka
Jagiellońska, Kraków, are
designated here as bjk

St Thom: parts left by Anna Magdalena
Bach to the Thomasschule, Leipzig,
now housed in the Archiv der Stadt
Leipzig.

Other locations

bl: British Library, London
Coburg: Kunstsammlung, Veste Coburg
Copenhagen: Det Kongelige Bibliotek,
Copenhagen
Darmstadt: Hessische Landes- und
Hochschulbibliothek, Darmstadt
Dresden: Sächsische Landesbibliothek,
Dresden/DDR
Morgan: Pierpont Morgan Library,
New York
New York: New York Public Library
Paris: Bibliothèque Nationale, Paris
Private: private possession
Riemenschneider: Riemenschneider
Bach Institute, Berea, Ohio
Sacher: Paul Sacher Stiftung, Basel
(Private)
Scheide: Collection of William Scheide
(Private), housed in Princeton
University Library
Washington: Library of Congress,
Washington DC
Wien: Österreichische
Nationalbibliothek, Vienna

Sources for concerted vocal works (see Appendix 2)

* source examined from original
| | source used exclusively for later performance
The chronology is based on those found in Dürr 1976; Dadelsen 1958.

Work (BWV)	Date of earliest performance (with some of surviving sources)	Score	Parts
71	2/4/08	ds P 45/1*	ds St 377*
182	25/3/14	spk P 103	ds St 47*; St 47a*
12	22/4/14	spk P 44/7	spk St 109*
199	12/8/14	Copenhagen [ds P 1162]	spk St 459
185	14/7 15 (score partly autograph)	spk P 59*	ds St 4
134(a)	1/1/19	Paris MS 2 [spk P 44/3]	ds St 18
23	7/2/23 (earlier origin?)	spk P 69	ds St 16
59	16/5/23?	spk P 161	[spk St 102*]
76	6/6/23	ds P 67*	spk St 13b*
24	20/6/23	spk P 44/4	spk St 19*
147	2/7/23 (first chorus 20/12/16)	spk P 102	spk St 46*
48	3/10/23	ds P 109	ds St 53
109	17/10/23	ds P 112	ds St 56
194	2/11/23 (earlier origins)	ds P 43/3	spk St 48*; St 346* (earlier)
40	26/12/23	ds P 63	spk St 11*
81	30/1/24	ds P 120	ds St 59*
245	7/4/24 (later score partly autograph)	[spk P 28]	spk St 111
67	16/4/24	ds P 95*	spk St 40*
44	21/5/24	ds P 148	spk St 86*
20	11/6/24	Sacher	St Thom
2	18/6/24	Private	St Thom
10	2/7/24	Washington	St Thom
94	6/8/24	ds P 47/2	St Thom
33	3/9/24	Private	St Thom
114	1/10/24	Private	St Thom
96	8/10/24	ds P 179	St Thom
5	15/10/24	bl loan 65/1*	St Thom
26	19/11/24	ds P 47/1	St Thom
116	26/11/24	Paris MS 1	St Thom
62	3/12/24	spk P 877	St Thom
91	25/12/24	spk P 869	St Thom; spk St 392*
232/III (Sanctus)		ds P 13/1	spk St 117*
121	26/12/24	bjk P 867	St Thom; spk St 390
133	27/12/24	ds P 1215	St Thom; spk St 387
122	31/12/24	spk P 868	St Thom; spk St 391*
41	1/1/25	spk P 874	St Thom
123	6/1/25	bjk P 875	St Thom; spk St 395*
124	7/1/25	spk P 876	St Thom; spk St 396*
3	14/1/25	Private	St Thom; spk St 157*

Sources for concerted vocal works (see Appendix 2) (cont.)

Work (BWV)	Date of earliest performance (with some of surviving sources)	Score	Parts
92	28/1/25	spk P 873	St Thom
127	11/2/25	spk P 872	St Thom; spk St 393*
249	1/4/25	[spk P 34]	spk St 355
6	2/4/25	spk P 44/2	ds St 7*
42	8/4/25	ds P 55	ds St 3
85	15/4/25	ds P 106	ds St 51
103	22/4/25	ds P 122	spk St 63*
108	29/4/25	ds P 82*	spk St 28*
87	6/5/25	ds P 61	ds St 6*
128	10/5/25	Private	spk St 158*; P 892
183	13/5/25	ds P 149	spk St 87*
175	22/5/25	ds P 75	spk St 22*
176	27/5/25	ds P 81	Scheide
36(a-c)	4-5/1725	ds P 43/2	[ds St 15*; spk St 82*]
168	29/7/25	ds P 152	spk St 457*; Scheide
164	26/8/25	spk P 121	ds St 60
79	31/10/25	ds P 89	spk St 35
110	25/12/25	ds P 153*	ds St 92*
57	26/12/25	ds P 144*	spk St 83*
151	27/12/25	Coburg	Coburg; St 89*
28	30/12/25	ds P 92	spk St 37
16	1/1/26	ds P 45/7*	ds St 44
32	13/1/26	ds P 126	ds St 67
13	20/1/26	ds P 45/4*	ds St 69*
72	27/1/26	ds P 54	ds St 2
43	30/5/26	spk P 44/6	ds St 36
39	23/6/26	ds P 62	spk St 8*
88	21/7/26	spk P 145	spk St 85*
170	28/7/26	spk P 154	spk St 94
187	4/8/26	ds P 84	spk St 29*; Scheide
45	11/8/26	ds P 80	spk St 26*
35	8/9/26	spk P 86	ds St 32
17	22/9/26	ds P 45/5*	spk St 101*
19	29/9/26	ds P 45/8*	spk St 25a*
27	6/10/26	spk P 164	spk St 105*
47	13/10/26	ds P 163	ds St 104*
169	20/10/26	spk P 93	spk St 38*
56	27/10/26	spk P 118	spk St 58*
49	3/11/26	ds P 111	ds St 55
98	10/11/26	spk P 160	spk St 98*
55	17/11/26	spk P 105	spk St 50*
52	24/11/26	spk P 85	spk St 30*
207	11/12/26	spk P 174	spk St 93* [St 347*]
58	5/1/27	spk P 866	St Thom; spk St 389*
82	2/2/27	spk P 114	ds St 54
84	9/2/27	ds P 108*	spk St 52*

Sources for concerted vocal works (see Appendix 2) (cont.)

Work (BWV)	Date of earliest performance (with some of surviving sources)	Score	Parts
174	6/6/29	spk P 115	spk St 57 St 456*; Rie-menschneider
201	c. 1729	spk P 175	spk St 33a*
51	17/9/30	ds P 104	spk St 49*
112	8/4/31	Morgan	St Thom
29	27/8/31	ds P 166	spk St 106
177	6/7/32	ds P 116	St Thom
232 I	21/4/33?	spk P 180	Dresden Mus. 2405; D21 Aut. 2
213	5/9/33	ds P 125	ds St 65*
97	c. 1734	New York	ds St 64
211	c. 1734	ds P 141	Wien SA.67.B.32
215	5/10/34	ds P 139	ds St 77
248 I	25/12/34	spk P 32	spk St 112/1*
248 II	26/12/34	spk P 32	spk St 112/2*
248 III	27/12/34	spk P 32	spk St 112/3*
248 IV	1/1/35	spk P 32	spk St 112/4*
248 V	2/1/35	spk P 32	spk St 112/5*
248 VI	6/1/35	spk P 32	spk St 112/6*
14	30/1/35	ds P 879	St Thom; ds St 398
11	19/5/35	spk P 44/5	bjk St 356
9	1732-5	Morgan	St Thom
100		ds P 159	spk St 97
244	30/3/36	ds P 25	spk St 110
30(a)	28/9/37	ds P 43/1; [spk P 44/1]	[ds St 31]
195	1735-50 (later score, only partly autograph)	ds P 65	spk St 12*
234		Darmstadt	spk St 400*

Other sources examined in the original

Location	Work	Catalogue number
ds	BWV 61	P 45/6
	BWV 71	Mus. 11495 (printed parts)
	BWV 525-30	P 271/1
	BWV 769	P 271/3
	BWV 831	P 226/9
	BWV 1027	P 226/2
	BWV 1079 (Ricercare)	P 226/1
spk	BWV 136	St 20
	BWV 179	St 348
	BWV 525-30	P 272

Other sources examined in the original (cont.)

Location	Work	Catalogue number
bl	'Das wohltemperierte Clavier' II	Add. MS 35021
	BWV 71	Hirsch III 620 (printed parts)
	Clavierübung I	k.10.a.1
		k.10.a.30
		Hirsch III 37
	Clavierübung II	k.8.g.7
		k.8.g.21
		Hirsch III 38
	Clavierübung III	k.10.a.2
		k.10.a.42
		Hirsch III 39
	Olavierübung IV	k.10.a.41
		Hirsch III 40
	BWV 769	Hirsch III 74
	BWV 645-50	k.10.a.23
Cambridge University Library	Clavierübung I	MR 340.b.70.1

Other sources examined from facsimile or microfilm

BWV 115	Fitzwilliam Museum, Cambridge, Mus. MS 631
BWV 214	ds P 41/2; St 91
BWV 243	ds P 38; P 39
BWV 599-644	ds P 283
BWV 645-50	Scheide
BWV 691	Anna Magdalena Notebook, ds P 224; Friedemann Notebook, Library of the School of Music, Yale University
BWV 728	Anna Magdalena Notebook, ds P 224
BWV 772-801	Friedemann Notebook, Yale, ds P 610
BWV 812-16	Anna Magdalena Notebook, ds P 224
BWV 988	Paris, MS 17669
BWV 995	Royal Library, Brussels, II 4085
BWV 1001-6	spk P 967
BWV 1006a	Musashino Music Academy, Tokyo, Littera rara vols. 2-14
BWV 1011	spk P 269
BWV 1030	ds P 975
BWV 1041	spk St 145
BWV 1046-51	ds Am.B.78; St 130
BWV 1052-8	ds P 234
BWV 1079	Original Engraving, 1747
BWV 1080	Original Engraving, 1751; ds P 200

Appendix 2

Regular slur patterns in concerted vocal works

B: figuration under slur is always disjunct, or at least contains a substantial leap

C: mixed figuration, some of which may include a leap, some of which might cover an indeterminate (i.e. non-motivic) group of notes

r: regular use

s: sporadic use (only one or two instances throughout the entire movement)

If figuration can be identified it is designated thus:

<: notes under slur ascend in conjunct motion

>: notes under slur descend in conjunct motion

AP: appoggiatura function of figure

TNF: three-note figure:

FNF: four-note figure (i.e. conjunct self-contained group, e.g. *groppo, circolo*):

FvNF: five-note figure

SNF: six-note figure

SvNF: seven-note figure

LP: one of the above figures with a single leap within its span

Mes: *messanza*, conjunct three-note figure followed/preceded by leap:

corta: *corta* rhythm:

step: stepwise motion (i.e. every second note repeated):

sigh: sighing, appoggiatura figure, usually followed by rest:

superjectio:

arpeg: arpeggio motion

Pastorale: 'Pastorale' rhythm:

tied: one note, generally that outside the slur, tied

2nds, 3rds, etc: notes under slur move in intervals thus designated

OSC: oscillating intervals

ONC: one note constant within slur:

DFU: dot for unslurred note(s):

RFU: rest for unslurred note(s)

X: some discrepancy in sources: inconsistency or later version

EXAMPLE

1A

182/4   25/3/14   C   3   Q   vl   Cr FNF/LP 3rds X: some parts lC

Column 1: Cantata 182, movement 4

    2: first performed with some of existing material: 25/3/1714

    3: C time

    4: slur (1A) first occurs at b. 3 in autograph score

    5: no reference for parts: slur therefore also occurs at b. 3 in parts (' – ' would indicate omission)

    6: quarter pulse: i.e. slur covers semiquavers

    7: instrument: violin 1

    8: Cr: mixed figuration, regular slurring throughout movement; FNF: four-note figure features among this figuration; LP 3rds: some leaps involved, particularly thirds

    X: inconsistency in the use of this pattern: some instances of this figuration marked with paired slurs (1C)

NB. Each pattern is, for convenience, specified in quaver values. However, the exact note values used vary and are discerned by relating 'Metre' and 'Division of pulse'.

Regular slur patterns in concerted vocal works

(see Appendix 1 for complete list of cantatas and sources consulted)

Work (BWV)	Date	Metre	First instance 1: Score	2: Parts	Division of pulse	Instruments	Type
			1A				
71/6	4/2/08	C	14		Q	rs, obs (vl)	Cr FNF/LP Mes X: all 1D?
71 7		C	3		Q	vl, obl	As < X: some 1B
182. 4	25/3/14	C	3		Q	vl	Cr FNF/LP 3rds X: some parts lC
182/5		C	5		Q	fl	Cs arpeg FNF/LP
182. 6		3/4	..	69	Q	bc	Cr FNF > LP X: some lC
12/1	22/4/14	C	--	12	Q	ob	Ar FNF some corta
134a./4 (134)	1/1/19	¢	3		E	vl	Br arpeg X: lB in parts/later score
23/4	7/2/23	C	—	4	Q	ob2 (l)	Cr paired 3rds Mes some corta FNF/LP

Regular slur patterns in concerted vocal works (cont.)

Work (BWV)	Date	Metre	First instance 1: Score	First instance 2: Parts	Division of pulse	Instruments	Type
59/4	16/5/23	C	1		Q	vl	Ar >AP
76/2	6/6/23	C	4		Q	vl, 2	Cr some FNF/AP X: many 1C
76/8		C; 3/4	2		Q	obdm	As >AP
24/1	20/6/23	3/4	8	6	Q	vl, 2, vla	Cr < > FNF some LP
24/5		C	28	3	Q	obsdm	Cr < > FNF Mes 3rds
24/6		C	...	2	Q	obsdm	Cs step. arpeg X: many 1C, esp ob2
109/1	17/10/23	C	1		Q	vl, cor, obs	Cr FNF >AP
109/5		3/4	10		Q	obl (2)	Ar >AP
194/5	2/11/23	¢	3	2	Q	vl	Cr FNF. LP > some corta
40/1	26/12/23	C	–	10	Q	vl, 2	Ar FNF
81/1	30/1/24	C	...	3	H	bc (vl, 2, rs)	Ar >
81/3		3/8	2		Q	vl	Cr > FNF LP
245/1	7/4/24	C	1		Q	vl, 2 (stgs, fls, obs)	Ar FNF some LP (Mes)
245/21b		6/4	[2]		Q	fls, obs	Cr > FNF Mes
245/25b		6/4	[1]		Q	fls, obs	Cr > FNF Mes
245/35		3/8	[37]	2	Q	fls (obs, bc)	Ar Mes
44/6	21/5/24	C	2		Q	vl (2) obs	Ar FNF
20/1	11/6/24	C; 3/4	53		Q	vl, 2, obs	As >AP
20/3		3/4	...	55	Q	bc	As >
20/5		C	1		Q	obl (2, 3, bc)	Ar >some AP
20/8		C	3		E	vl, obl	Ar FNF DFU quaver
2/5	18/6/24	C	2		H	stgs, obs	Ar < > X: most 1B?
94/1	6/8/24	C	4		Q	vl, fl, ob	Ar >AP X: some 1C
94/2		C	7	1	Q	bc	Cr < > FNF
94/4		C	6		E	fl	Ar FNF/LP
94/7		C	5		Q	obdm	Ar >AP
114/2	1/10/24	3/4	11	6	Q	fl	Bs arpeg
114/5		C	14	2	Q	stgs, ob	Cr < FNF
26/4	19/11/24	C	4		Q	obl	Ar >
			15		H	obl	Ar >AP
133/2	27/12/24	¢	–	61	E	bc	Cs FNF >
133/4		¢	10		E	vl	Ar > AP
			5		Q	vl, 2	Cs < > X: some 1B
123/3	6/1/25	C	...	1	Q	obdml (2, bc)	Cr </LP FNF/LP *superjectio* X: some 1B
123/5		C	–	2	Q	fl	Cs FNF >
124/3	7/1/25	3/4	26	1	Q	obdm	Cs FNF/LP >AP X: some longer

Regular slur patterns in concerted vocal works (cont.)

Work (BWV)	Date	Metre	First instance 1: Score	2: Parts	Division of pulse	Instruments	Type
3/1	14/1/25	C	21	3	Q	obsdm, stgs	Cr FNF < >
92/2	28/1/25	C	19	17	Q	bc	Ar FNF
249/9	1/4/25	C	3	8	Q	obdm (stgs)	Cr >some AP arpeg
6/3	2/4/25	C	1		Q	vclpicc	Ar FNF
42/3	8/4/25	C	5	2	Q	obs	Cr FNF/LP OSC 2nds X: some OSC 1C
103/3	22/4/25	6/8	2		Tw	fl (or v)	Cr > FNF/LP X: most 1D
87/3	6/5/25	C	2		H	obsdc	Bs X: some 1C
			9	8	Q	obdc2 (1)	Cs >
			1		Q	bc	Br arpeg X: slur extended (one part)
183/4	13/5/25	3/8	1		Q	obsdc, vl	Ar FNF/LP
175/1	22/5/25	C	1		Q	rsl-3	Ar FNF some LP
176/4	27/5/25	3/4	—	10	Q	bc	Ar FNF
36c/1 (36)	4-5/1725	3/4	3	1	Q	obsdm, vl	Ar >AP X: some 1C
164/3	26/8/25	C	1		Q	fl1 (2)	Cr > FNF/LP X: some 1C
110/4	25/12/25	3/4	2		Q	obdm	Ar >AP
151/1	27/12/25	12/8	2		Tw	fl	Cr Mes FNF/some LP X: most Mes=1B/D
16/5	1/1/26	3/4	—	4	Q	obdc (or violetta)	Cs FNF/LP/AP
32/1	13/1/26	C	8	5	E	ob	Ar Mes
			—	2	Q	ob	As >AP
72/5	27/1/26	3/4	—	1	Q	ob	Cr FNF Mes
43/1	30/5/26	C	5		Q	vl, ob1	As FNF
43/9		3/4	49	1	Q	obs	Cr FNF Mes FNF/LP > X: most Mes 1B
170/5	28/7/26	C	10	2	Q	fl or org, (obdm, stgs)	Ar >AP X: some 1C
187/5	4/8/26	C	—	18	E	ob	As >
17/3	22/9/26	C	33	—	Q	v2	As > X: 1C in parts
17/5		C	8		Q	v1	Cs FNF/LP
19/3	29/9/26	C	—	3	Q	obdm1 (2, bc)	Cr Mes FNF > X: most Mes=1B
27/3	6/10/26	C	9		Q	obdc	As FNF/LP
47/1	13/10/26	¢	122	108	Q	bc, v2 (obs)	Cs > FNF
47/2		3/8	27		Q	v (or org)	Cr ONC > X: changed to 1D in parts + DFU
47/4		C	1		Q	v (bc, ob)	Ar >

Regular slur patterns in concerted vocal works (cont.)

Work (BWV)	Date	Metre	First instance 1: Score	2: Parts	Division of pulse	Instruments	Type
169/2	20/10/26	3/8; C	—	37	Q	bc	Ar < >
56/2	27/10/26	C	1		Q	vcl	Br arpeg
98/1	10/11/26	3/4	—	4	Q	vl	Br arpeg
58/5	5/1/27	2/4	18	5	Q	obl, vl	Cr Mes > X: Mes = 1D?
82/3	2/2/27	C	62	8	H	fl or ob (vl)	Bs arpeg X: some 1C
201/7	c. 1729	¢	126		Q	vl, 2 (bc)	Ar >AP
201/11		¢	13	5	Q	vl, 2 (bc)	Cr >AP FNF
201/13		3/4	39	6	Q	bc (fls)	Cr < > FNF X: some 1B
201/15		2/4	—	20	Q	ob2 (1, fls, stgs)	Cr > FNF
174/4	6/6/29	¢	—	6	E	stgs	Cr FNF < X: some longer esp. score
			11		Q	stgs	Ar >
51/4	17/9/30	3/4	1		Q	vl (v2, bc)	Ar >AP
112/3	8/4/31	C	20		Q	vl, 2	Cs > FNF/LP
112/4		2	5		Q	vl (bc)	Br arpeg
232/1	21/4/33	C	—	48	Q	obl	As Mes
232/9		3/4	7		Q	fll (2)	Cr FNF some LP >
232/12		3/4	21		Q	fls, obs (stgs)	Cr FNF > X: many 1C esp. stgs
213/3	5/9/33	2/4	—	1	Q	vl, 2 (bc)	Cr >AP Mes FNF/LP
213/13		2	1		Q	vl (bc, corl, obl)	Cr arpeg >AP FNF
97/4	c. 1734	C	7		E	v	Br Mes
211/10	c. 1734	¢	3		Q	bc (vl, fl)	Cr >AP arpeg X: some 1C
			6		E	fl	Ar < most cover next crotchet
215/7	5/10/34	2/4	5	4	Q	fls	Cs > FNF
			3		H	fls	As FNF X: most 1B
248/7	25/12/34	3/4	—	1	Q	bc, obs	Ar >AP
248/8		2/4	4		Q	tr, vl, fl	As >AP
248/19	26/12/34	2/4	1		Q	vl, 2 (bc) obsdm and dc	Cr >some AP FNF/LP Mes
248/31	27/12/34	2/4	—	6	Q	bc	Ar >
248/42	1/1/35	3/4	—	4	Q	corl	As >
248/43	2/1/35	3/4	107		Q	vl (obsdm)	As >
248/47		2/4	7	4	Q	obdm	Cr < >AP FNF/LP X: some > = 4B
248/57	6/1/35	3/4	1		Q	vl (stgs, obdm)	Cr >AP < FNF

Regular slur patterns in concerted vocal works (cont.)

Work (BWV)	Date	Metre	First instance 1: Score	2: Parts	Division of pulse	Instruments	Type
248/62	6/1/35	2/4	15	4	Q	bc (obsdm)	Cr FNF/LP > OSC 2nds X: most 1C
			19		H	obdml (2)	Cr >AP FNF/LP X: many 1C; >AP 1D?
248/64		C	9		Q	trl	As >AP
14/2	30/1/35	3/4	—	2	Q	cor (stgs)	Cr < FNF
11/3	19/5/35	C	—	9	Q	bc	As >AP
11/7		C	8		Q	bc	As >
11/11		6/4	--	2	Q	trl, obl (2, fls)	Ar >
9/5	1732-5	2/4	49	1	Q	fl, obdm	Cr FNF/LP >
244/27a	30/3/36	C	--	8	H	fl2 (1, obs)	Cs FNF
244/33		C	—	7	Q	bc	As >
244/49		3/4	14		Q	fl	As < >
30a/1 (30)	28/9/37	2/4	27	13	Q	ob2 (1, fls, stgs)	Ar > some AP X: some 1C
195/1	1735-50	C	[-]	7	Q	obs	As >
234/3	1735-50	C	1		Q	vl (bc)	Cr > arpeg FNF X: some extend to next quaver (see 4B)

1B

71/6	4/2/08	C	1		Q	vcl (stgs, rs)	Br arpeg
182/5	25/3/14	C	2		Q	r	Cr > arpeg
76/8	6/6/23	C; 3/4	15	3	Q	vladg (obdm)	Cr FNF Mes
245/13	7/4/24	3/4	[-]	10	Q	vl (2)	Ar FNF DFU (parts)
245/30		3/4	[-]	36	Q	vladg	As Mes
2/5	18/6/24	C	2	—	H	stgs (obs)	Ar < > X: some 1A
10/1	2/7/24	C	3		Q	v2 (1), obl (2)	As FNF
10/2		C	--	3	Q	v2 (1, obs)	Ar FNF X: some 1A
94/2	6/8/24	C	—	1	Q	bc	Cr FNF Mes X: some 1A esp. score
114/2	1/10/24	3/4	54	12	Q	fl	Ar Mes LP AP DFU (parts)
96/3	8/10/24	C	1		H	fl (bc)	Ar < +LP DFU (parts)
			7	5	Q	fl	Cr < FNF DFU (parts)
5/3	15/10/24	3/4	—	3	Q	vla	Ar > X: score 1A
133/4	27/12/24	¢	4		Q	vl, 2, vla	Ar < >

Regular slur patterns in concerted vocal works (cont.)

Work (BWV)	Date	Metre	First instance 1: Score	2: Parts	Division of pulse	Instruments	Type
123/3	6/1/25	C	—	2	Q	obdml (2, bc)	Cr arpeg < > FNF/LP X: most 1A?
124/1	7/1/25	3/4	9		Q	obdm	Ar Més
92/4	28/1/25	C	1		Q	obdml (2, bc)	Ar Mes
127/3	11/2/25	C	6		Q	ob	Bs Mes LP AP
249/5	1/4/25	3/4	1		Q	fl	Cr arpeg, Mes
42/1	8/4/25	C	1		Q	vl, 2 (vla, obs, fag)	Ar Mes some DFU (parts)
42/6		¢	12		E	vl, 2	Ar FNF/LP
108/2	29/4/25	3/4	5		Q	v	Cr arpeg Mes AP X: some 1D
183/2	13/5/25	C	1		Q	vclpicc	Ar < (FNF/LP)
175/4	22/5/25	¢	1		Q	vclpicc	Ar FNF
151/3	27/12/25	¢	5	3	Q	obdm, stgs	Ar < > X: score orig. 1C
43/9	30/5/26	3/4	49	1	Q	obs	Cr Mes FNF X: some 1A/4G
45/1	11/8/26	¢	13		Q	fl1, 2, ob2	As FNF/LP
17/5	22/9/26	C	32	1	H	vl	Ar FNF
19/3	29/9/26	C	6	3	Q	obsdm (bc)	Ar Mes
47/2	13/10/26	3/8	—	5	Q	v (org)	Ar < > some ONC DFU (part)
169/1	20/10/26	C	1		Q	vl	Ar Mes
98/1	10/11/26	3/4	9		Q	vl	Br corta + leap DFU (parts)
58/3	5/1/27	C	--	9	Q	v	Br arpeg DFU (parts)
			---	16	H	v	As >
201/11	c. 1729	¢	113	111	H	vl, 2	Ar < DFU (parts)
201/13		3/4	13	8	Q	fls	Cr < FNF DFU unslurred often at pitch of 1st
201/15		2/4	--	4	Q	vl (2), fls, obs	Ar FNF/LP DFU (parts)
174/1	6/6/29	C	2		Q	vl-3 (stgs)	Ar Mes FNF
29/3	27/8/31	¢	10		Q	v	Br arpeg
177/2	6/7/32	C	—	39	Q	bc	As FNF/LP
177/4		C	1		Q	v (fag. bc)	Cr arpeg < FNF Mes
			71		H	bc	Bs arpeg
232/1	21/4/33	C	—	56	H	vl, fls, obs	As Mes < >
232/2		C	5		Q	vl, 2	Ar < DFU
213/3	5/9/33	2/4	—	7	Q	vl	Cr FNF/LP Mes DFU (parts)

Regular slur patterns in concerted vocal works (cont.)

Work (BWV)	Date	Metre	First instance 1: Score	First instance 2: Parts	Division of pulse	Instruments	Type
213/13	5/9/33	2	1		Q	vl (bc)	Br arpeg X: some 1A?
211/2	c. 1734	C	1		Q	vl, 2	Ar DFU OSC 2nds
215/7	5/10/34	2/4	2		H	fls	As FNF
248/7	25/12/34	3/4	—	6	Q	ob, obdm	Cr Mes FNF X: some 1A
248/31	27/12/34	2/4	17		Q	v	Br arpeg
248/41	1/1/35	C	—	7	H	v2 (1)	Bs DFU (parts)
248/47	2/1/35	2/4	1		H	bc (obdm)	Cs Mes FNF DFU
248/47		2/4	23		Q	obdm	Cs < FNF/LP some DFU
248/51		2/4	5		Q	v	Br arpeg
14/4	30/1/35	C	—	1	H	obs, bc	Ar < > FNF/LP Mes DFU (parts)
11/4	19/5/35	C	3		H	vl, 2	As >
11/11		6/4	—	4	Q	fl2 (1, obl)	Ar Mes DFU (parts)
36b/5 (36)	1732-5	C	—	11	Q	vl	Ar FNF/LP
100/1	1732-5	¢	108	27	Q	fl	Ar FNF DFU (parts) unslurred at pitch of 1st
100/6		C	—	24	Q	obdm	As Mes
244/5	30/3/36	C	1		Q	fls	Ar > DFU (parts)
244/42		C	12		Q	v	Bs arpeg
244/49		3/4	13		Q	fl	Bs DFU
234/3	1735-50	C	5		Q	v	Ar Mes DFU

1C

Work (BWV)	Date	Metre	First instance 1: Score	First instance 2: Parts	Division of pulse	Instruments	Type
71/4	4/2/08	3/4	1		H	rs, obs (fag, vcl)	Cr < > FNF/LP
71/6		C	2		H	rs, obl (2, stgs)	Ar dotted
			1		Q	fag (obs, rs)	Br
71/7		C	1		Q	vcl, fag (rs, ob2, vl)	Cs FNF/LP
182/2	25/3/14	C	5		Q	v (vlas, r)	Cr FNF >
182/4		C	1		Q	vl (stgs)	Cr FNF Mes step paired 3rds X: many 1A
182/5		C	1		Q	r	Cr AP arpeg
182/6		3/4	—	1	Q	bc	Cr FNF >
			17		H	bc	Cr superjectio
182/7		¢	39	38	H	vlas (vcl)	As >
			40		Q	vla2 (1, vcl)	Cr FNF

Regular slur patterns in concerted vocal works (cont.)

Work (BWV)	Date	Metre	First instance 1: Score	2: Parts	Division of pulse	Instruments	Type
12/1	22/4/14	C	1		Q	vl, 2	Ar FNF
12/4		C	6		Q	ob	As *superjectio*
199/2	12/8/14	C	1		Q	ob	Cr sigh/step
199/4		3/4	3		H	vl, 2 (stgs)	Cr FNF < >
199/6		C	1		Q	vla	Cs >
185/1	14/7/15	6/4	[–]	4	Sx	bc	Ar SNF/LP X: some 3A
185/3	14/7/15	C	[2]		Q	vl (2, ob)	As >
			[12]		H	vl (ob)	As sigh
147/1	20/12/16	6/4	10		H	v2 (stgs, obs)	Cs FNF/LP >
134a/2 (134)	1/1/19	3/8	--	61	H	vl	As FNF
23/3	7/2/23	3/4	4		H	bc (stgs, obs)	Cr > SNF X: some 3G/3I
23/4		C	–	1	Q	vl	Ar sigh
59/1	16/5/23	C	31		Q	vl, 2	Ar *superjectio*
59/4		C	33		Q	vl	As *superjectio*
76/2	6/6/23	C	9	5	Q	vl, 2	Cr some ONC FNF > X: some 1A/D
76/3		C	2		Q	v	Cr sigh arpeg
76/5		C	15		Q	vl (2)	Cs AP Mes
76/7		C	–	13	H	v2, vla	Cs FNF/LP
76/8		3/4	5		Q	vladg	Ar >AP
24/1	20/6/23	3/4	55	5	H	vl, 2, vla	Cr > *superjectio*
24/1		3/4	–	6	Q	vl, 2, vla	Cr > FNF X: many 1A
24/3		3/4	–	72	H	v2, ob2 (1, stgs)	As OSC 2nds
24/5		C	–	2	Q	obdml (2)	Cr < > FNF *superjectio* paired 3rds X: many 1A
24/6		C	2		Q	vl, 2, vla, obs	Cr step arpeg
147/2	2/7/23	C	18		H	vl, vla	Cs step
147/3		3/4	4		H	obdm (bc)	Cr arpeg > FNF/LP
147/8		C	–	1	Q	obdm	Ar *superjectio* X: score and obdc have 3G
48/4	3/10/23	3/8	46	14	H	ob	Bs 4ths
109/1	17/10/23	C	11		Q	vl	Cs < >
109/3		C	1		H	v2, vla, bc	Ar > dotted
109/5		3/4	–	8	H	obs	Ar < > OSC 2nds
194/1	2/11/23	3/4	33		H	vl, obl (2, stgs)	Cr 3rds < > SNF step X: some 3A
194/5		¢	1		Q	vl (2, vla)	Cr >AP arpeg X: many 1A
194/10		3/4	4		H	bc	Br > paired 3rds

Regular slur patterns in concerted vocal works (cont.)

Work (BWV)	Date	Metre	First instance 1: Score	2: Parts	Division of pulse	Instruments	Type
40/1	26/12/23	C	5	2	Q	cor2 (vl, 2, obs)	Cr ONC 3rds, FNF X: most unmarked
40/5		C	1		Q	vl, 2, vla	Br arpeg
81/1	30/1/24	C	7	2	H	stgs	Ar >
245/1	7/4/24	C	1		H	vla	Br OSC leaps > arpeg
245/13		3/4	[3]		H	vl, 2 (stgs)	Cr dotted
245/16d		C	[--]	13	H	v2	Cs FNF/LP
245/20		12/8	[1]		Sx	vlasdm	Cr > SNF/AP dotted OSC 2nds
245/21b		6/4	[--]	1	Sx	vl (stgs)	Ar >AP
245/23f		C	[--]	4	Q	v2 (obdm2)	As FNF
245/24		3/4	[··]	·13	H	vl	Br > paired 3rds
245/25b		6/4	[-]	1	H	vl (stgs)	Ar >AP
245/27b		3/4	[--]	22	H	vl (2), vla, fls, obs	Ar step
245/30		C	[2]		Q	vladg	Cr dotted < > FNF
245/35		3/8	[7]	5	H	fls, obsdc	Cr Mes step, arpeg X: some arpeg have dots
245·39		3/4	[1]		H	stgs, fls, obs	Cr > arpeg, X: some longer
67/1	16/4/24	¢	49		H	bc (v2, vla, fl, obdm2)	As dotted >
			··	3	Q	vla	As >
67/2		C	2		H	vl, 2, obdm	Ar sigh
67/6		3/4	10		H	stgs (fl, obsdm)	Cr dotted OSC FNF < > some LP
44/2	21/5/24	C	31	11	Q	vl, ob	Cs > step
44/3		3/4	7		H	bc	Bs dotted
44/6		C	3		Q	vl (stgs, obs)	Ar step < >
20/1	11/6/24	3/4	46		H	vl, 2, obs	Br falling 3rds
20/3		3/4	4	1	H	stgs	Cr SNF/LP *superjectio*
20/5		C	20	4	H	obs	Cs sigh
			··	9	Q	obl (2, 3, bc)	Cs 3rds
20/6		3/4	62	26	H	stgs	Cr < > Mes
10/6	2/7/24	C	10		Q	vl, 2, vla	Br OSC 3rds 4ths
94/1	6/8/24	C	3		Q	vl, obl	Ar >AP X: some 1A
94/3		3/8	1		H	obl (2, bc)	Br 3rds
94/6		C	--	1	H	stgs	Cr dotted < FNF arpeg
33/1	3/9/24	3/4	--	12	Q	obs (vl)	Ar sigh

Regular slur patterns in concerted vocal works (cont.)

Work (BWV)	Date	Metre	First instance 1: Score	2: Parts	Division of pulse	Instruments	Type
33/5		3/4	–	3	H	obs (bc)	Cs ḞNF/LP step >
114/2	1/10/24	3/4	10		Q	fl	Ar *superjectio* X: changed to Lombard rhythm in parts
114/5		C	2		Q	ob (stgs)	Cs step FNF
			18		H	ob	Cr step arpeg
96/3	8/10/24	C	6	1	H	fl (bc)	Ar sigh < >
			–	10	Q	fl	Ar FNF
96/5		3/4	1		H	stgs, obs	Cr dotted > arpeg
5/1	15/10/24	C	11	2	Q	vl, 2, obs	Cr OSC 2nds > arpeg
5/3		3/4	1		H	bc (vla)	Cr step < > arpeg
			··	6	Q	vla	Br ONC
5/5		C	6		Q	vl, 2, obs	Ar step
116/2	26/11/24	3/4	2		H	obdm (bc)	Cs arpeg, step >
62/1	3/12/24	6/4	···	7	Sx	obs (bc, v2, vla)	Ar step sigh < >
62/2		3/8	2		H	vl, obl (2)	Ar >AP X: some 3G
91/3	25/12/24	3/4	6	1	H	obs, bc	Cr dotted < > FNF arpeg
91/4		C	3		Q	vl, 2, vla	As ONC
			10		H	vl, 2, vla	Cr
232 III	25/12/24	C	1		H	vl, 2	Br dotted arpeg
121/4	26/12/24	C	18		Q	vl	Cr > ONC FNF
			–	71	H	vl	As AP
133/2	27/12/24	¢	·	4	H	bc	Ar FNF
122/1	31/12/24	3/8	117	5	H	v2 (1), vla, obs	Cr SNF Mes 3rds
41/1	1/1/25	3/4	105		H	vl (stgs)	Cs OSC 2nds
124/1	7/1/25	3/4	27		H	bc (vla)	As dotted FNF X: most omitted
124/3		3/4	6		H	bc (stgs)	Cr dotted step OSC 2nds > FNF/Mes
3/1	14/1/25	C	11	2	Q	vl, obsdm	Cr >
			5	4	H	vl	Ar sigh
3/5		C	24		H	vl, 2, obsdm	Ar sigh
127/1	11/2/25	C	30		Q	obs (fls)	As dotted OSC 2nds X: most missing?
127/3		C	2		Q	ob (rs)	Cr step AP >
127/4		C	13		Q	vl, 2	As Mes
249/1	1/4/25	3/8	12		H	vl, obs	As OSC 2nds
249/3		3/8	49		H	obl (vl)	Cs FNF/LP
249/5		3/4	3		Q	fl	As OSC 2nds
			5		H		As AP

Regular slur patterns in concerted vocal works (cont.)

Work (BWV)	Date	Metre	First instance 1: Score	2: Parts	Division of pulse	Instruments	Type
249/7	1/4/25	C	1		Q	vl, rl (2, bc)	Cr OSC 2nds Mes arpeg X: some written as 1A
			1		H	v2 (r2, bc)	Cr OSC 2nds FNF X: some written as 1A
249/8		C	—	3	Q	bc	Ar OSC 2nds
249/9		C	69		H	obdm	As AP/sigh
		C	—	2	Q	obdm (vl)	Cr OSC 2nds Mes
249/11		C	43	41	H	obs	As FNF/SNF X: vl = 3C
6/1	2/4/25	3/4	—	4	H	bc (stgs, obs)	Cr Mes < >
6/2		3/8	—	8	H	obdc or vla	Cr Mes 3rds X: Mes = 3G in vla version
6/5		C	1		H	vl (2, bc)	Cr arpeg
42/1	8/4/25	C	24		Q	ob2 (1), fag	Cr step paired 3rds
			—	27	H	ob2, fag (stgs)	Cs FNF X: many omitted?
42/3		C	11	10	H	vl, 2, vla	Br 3rds, 4ths
			22	1	Q	ob2 (1)	Ar OSC 2nds
42/4		3/4	—	4	H	bc, fag	Ar semitones
85/1	15/4/25	C	35		Q	vl	As *superjectio*
85/3		3/4	1		H	ob1 (2, bc)	Cr dotted, < step X: many omitted?
103/1	22/4/25	3/4	—	23	H	bc (stgs, fls, obs)	Cr > arpeg step 3rds Mes X: some longer
103/5		C	41		H	vl, 2, obsdm	Ar sigh
108/1	29/4/25	C	1		Q	obdm (stgs)	Cr dotted 3rds
108/4		¢	—	3	E	bc (stgs)	Cr OSC 2nds
			—	16	Q	bc, vla (stgs)	As >
87/1	6/5/25	C	—	31	Q	v2	Bs falling 3rds
87/3		C	5	1	H	obsdc	Cr sigh < > 3rds
87/4		C	—	6	H	bc (vl)	Cs >
128/3	10/5/25	3/4	26	16	Q	vl, 2	Cs > AP paired 3rds
			—	70	H	stgs	Cs
128/4		6/8	—	5	Sx	obdm	Cs Mes
183/4	13/5/25	3/8	12		H	vl (obsdc)	Bs dotted
			11		H	vl (2) obsdc	As step
175/4	22/5/25	¢	79		H	bc	Cs step arpeg
175/5		C	9		Q	vl, 2	Cr OSC 2nds *superjectio*
176/1	27/5/25	C	41	2	H	bc (stgs, obs)	Cr step chromatic

Regular slur patterns in concerted vocal works (cont.)

Work (BWV)	Date	Metre	First instance 1: Score	2: Parts	Division of pulse	Instruments	Type
176/3		¢	1		Q	stgs	Br 3rds some dotted
			2		H	vl, 2, vla	Ar sigh
176/5		3/8	–	14	H	obs	Ar step
36c/1 (36)	4–5/1725	3/4	25	3	Q	vl, 2, obsdm	Cr FNF > X: many 1A, esp. early score (P 43)
36c/3		3/8	–	87	H	bc	Cs 3rds FNF/LP
36c/5		C	–	9	Q	bc	Cr FNF >
36c/7		12/8	3		Sx	v	Br ONC
168/2	29/7/25	C	–	15	Q	obsdm	Bs paired 3rds some AP
164/3	26/8/25	C	1		Q	fll (2, bc)	Cr step arpeg
110/4	25/12/25	3/4	4		H	obdm (bc)	Cr dotted step
57/3	26/12/25	3/4	1		H	vl (bc)	Cr step semitone pairs
151/3	27/12/25	¢	1		Q	obdm	Cs FNF/LP X: 1D in parts
28/1	30/12/25	3/4	–	2	Q	vl (2)	Cr >AP FNF X: many omitted, some 1A
16/5	1/1/26	3/4	9		H	obdc or vltta	As sigh
		3/4	1		Q	vltta (or obdc)	Cr arpeg paired 3rds
32/1	13/1/26	C	2		Q	ob	Cr step some LP
13/3	20/1/26	C	1		Q	vl, 2	Cr paired 3rds FNF/LP
13/5		C	1		H	v, rs	Cr step chromatic
72/1	27/1/26	3/4	7		H	obl (2, stgs)	Cr FNF/LP step arpeg
72/3		C	–	5	H	bc (vl, 2)	Ar sigh
			–	78	H	bc	Cr FNF/LP
72/5		3/4	–	12	Q	v2	Cs >
43/1	30/5/26	C	2		Q	vl, obl	Cr >AP Mes step
43/5		C	–	15	Q	stgs, obs	As OSC 2nds X: most missing
43/7		C	–	22	H	bc	Cs FNF Mes
39/1	23/6/26	C	100		H	obs	Ar sigh < >
			105		Q	vl, 2	Cs >AP FNF/LP
39/3		3/8	18	8	H	v (ob)	Cr SNF/LP step
88/1	21/7/26	¢	127	118	H	corl (2, obdml, vl)	Cr dotted arpeg OSC 3rds
88/3		3/8	–	89	H	obdm (vl)	Cr > *superjectio* 3rds arpeg

Regular slur patterns in concerted vocal works (cont.)

Work (BWV)	Date	Metre	First instance 1: Score	2: Parts	Division of pulse	Instruments	Type
170/5	28/7/26	C	2		H	obdm (fl, vl)	As sigh
			1		Q	vl, obdm, fl	Cr >AP 3rds X: some 1A
187/1	4/8/26	C	—	107	H	vl	As *superjectio*
			—	90	Q	vl	As >
187/5		C	12		Q	ob	Bs step dotted
187/6		C	15	14	H	vl, 2	As step
35/1	8/9/26	C	34		Q	v2, vla (vl) obs	Cr Mes < > FNF
35/7		3/8	30	2	H	vl (stgs, obs)	Ar >AP (four notes)
17/5	22/9/26	C	1		Q	bc	Ar OSC semitones
			2		H	vl, 2, vla	Cr dotted sigh
19/3	29/9/26	C	—	47	H	obsdm	As Mes
27/1	6/10/26	3/4	6	5	Q	obs (vs)	Ar step
			1		H	stgs (obs)	Cr arpeg dotted OSC 2nds < > step
27/3		C	32		H	obdc	As sigh
47/1	13/10/26	¢	2		H	vl, 2 (stgs) obs	Ar sigh
47/2		3/8	—	33	H	v (or org?)	As <semitones
47/4		C	1		H	v (ob)	Ar FNF Mes X: some 1D
47/4		C	—	52	Q	ob	As *superjectio*
169/1	20/10/26	C	108		H	vl (2) obl (2)	As step sigh
			85		Q	obs	Cs step
169/2		3/8	5		H	bc	Ar SNF/LP
56/1	27/10/26	3/4	2		H	vl, vla (stgs) obs	Ar step X: few in parts
56/4		3/4	12	8	H	vl, 2, vla (bc)	Cr step
49/4	3/11/26	C	1		Q	vclpicc (bc, obdm)	Cr >AP
			10		H	vclpicc (obdm)	Ar sigh < >
98/1	10/11/26	3/4	4		H	v2, vla	Br disjunct AP
			—	13	H	bc	Cs > arpeg
			—	16	Q	vl	Bs
98/3		3/8	15	4	H	ob	Cr step >
55/3	17/11/26	C	3		Q	fl	Ar step chromatic < >
52/3	24/11/26	C	29		Q	bc	Cs FNF
207/1	11/12/26	6/8	78		Sx	vl	As FNF step
207/7		3/4	3		H	fl2	Cs FNF/LP X: most longer
207/9		2	64		Q	fls	Cr FNF/some LP
58/1	5/1/27	3/4	1		H	stgs (obs)	Cr dotted FNF SNF *superjectio* < >

Regular slur patterns in concerted vocal works (cont.)

Work (BWV)	Date	Metre	1: Score	2: Parts	Division of pulse	Instruments	Type
58/3		C	1		H	v	Cr 2nds LP
82/3	2/2/27	C	3		H	vl (stgs) or obdc or fl	Cr > Mes arpeg sigh
82/5		3/8	1		H	ob, vl, bc	Cr < > SNF/LP X: some longer
84/1	9/2/27	3/4	1		H	ob (vl, bc, stgs)	Cr dotted < >
84/3		3/8	—	1	H	v	Br ONC 3rds
201/5	c. 1729	3/8	141	7	H	vl (2) fl, obdm	Cs > FNF/AP X: some longer
201/7		3/8	9	3	H	vl, 2 (bc)	Cr 3rds step
201/11		¢	11		Q	vl, 2	Cr FNF >AP
201/13		3/4	1		H	bc (fls)	Cr Mes OSC 3rds, 4ths step
			18	2	Q	fls	Cr OSC 2nds < superjectio 3rds
201/15		2/4	8	1	H	fls, obl (2, stgs)	Cr FNF/LP Mes
			—	32	Q	fls	Cs 3rds > OSC 2nds X: many 1A
174/4	6/6/29	¢	1		H	stgs	Cr > LP
112/2	8/4/31	6/8	—	7	Sx	obdm (bc)	Bs 3rds
112/4		2	—	21	Q	vla (v2)	Cs > FNF
177/1	6/7/32	3/8	—	31	H	vl	As >AP
177/2		C	1		H	bc	Ar sigh < >
			3		Q	bc	Br step OSC 3rds chromatic
177/4		C	—	48	Q	bc	As OSC 2nds
			—	72	H	bc	Cs >
232/1	21/4/33	C	1		H	fl2 (1) obdm2 (1), stgs	Cr sigh < > step
		C	—	4	Q	vl	Cs >
232/2		C	2		Q	vl, 2	Cr superjectio FNF/LP > arpeg
232/3		¢	30		H	vl, 2, fls, obsdm (vla)	Cs < >
232/5		C	2		H	vl, 2 (tutti)	Cr step FNF
			47		Q	fll, obl	Cs > arpeg
232/6		C	2		Q	v, vl (stgs)	Cr step >AP
232/8		C	1		Q	fl (stgs)	Ar superjectio
			8		H	vl, 2, vla	Cr sigh < >
232/9		3/4	1		H	vla (vl, 2)	Cr OSC 3rds arpeg < >
			22		Q	fll (2)	Cr step, 3rds arpeg
232/10		6/8	8		Sx	obdm (vl)	Cr 3rds >AP superjectio

Regular slur patterns in concerted vocal works (cont.)

Work (BWV)	Date	Metre	First instance 1: Score	2: Parts	Division of pulse	Instruments	Type
232/11	21/4/33	3/4	1		H	fags .	Cr step > X: some > =1A
232/12		3/4	21	11	Q	vl, 2 (vla, fls, obs)	Cr FNF >AP *superjectio* X: many 1A
213/3	5/9/33	2/4	2		H	vl (stgs)	Cr step LP
			—	3	Q	vl (2)	Cs >AP FNF/LP X: most 1A
213/9		3/8	13	3	H	v	Cr >AP OSC semitones rising 3rds
213/11		3/8	5		H	vlas (bc)	Ar step
213/13		2	—	13	H	ob2	As < step
		2	9		Q	vl (bc)	Cr >AP ONC
97/1	c. 1734	C	45		H	vl, 2, vla	Cs sigh arpeg
			—	72	Q	vl	As >
97/4		C	3		Q	v (bc)	Cr step arpeg
97/8		2/4	5		Q	obs (bc)	Ar step 3rds
211/2	c. 1734	C	6		Q	vl (2, bc)	Cs paired 3rds
			3		H	stgs	Ar sigh X: some staccato
211/4		3/8	5		H	fl	Cr step >some AP (four notes)
211/10		¢	13	1	Q	vla (vl, fl)	Cr FNF paired 3rds ONC
215/3	5/10/34	C	19		Q	vl, obsdm	As >
215/5		3/8	123		H	v2, vla	As step
215/7		2/4	6		H	fls	As < >
248/1	25/12/34	3/8	14	13	H	bc	Cr *superjectio* Mes 3rds
248/3		C	4		H	obsdm	Cr step arpeg
248/4		3/8	13		H	v (bc) obdm	Cr OSC semitones Mes rising 3rds arpeg
248/7		3/4	12		H	ob, obdm (bc)	Cr 3rds arpeg step >
248/15	26/12/34	3/8	82		H	bc	Br ONC
248/19		2/4	1		H	bc (stgs, obsdm, dc, fl)	Cr step AP arpeg
248/24	27/12/34	3/8	39		H	tr (fls)	Cs > 3rds X: most 3G
248/29		3/8	5		H	obsdm (bc)	Ar step
248/31		2/4	6		H	vl	Ar sigh <
			—	6	Q	bc	As >AP
248/36	1/1/35	3/8	—	12	H	corl (2, obs, stgs)	Cr OSC 2nds >AP Mes X: most obs 3G
248/38		C	—	10	H	vl, 2, vla (bc)	Cr FNF/LP arpeg
248/40		C	3	2	H	bc (stgs)	Cr FNF/LP arpeg

Regular slur patterns in concerted vocal works (cont.)

Work (BWV)	Date	Metre	First instance 1: Score	First instance 2: Parts	Division of pulse	Instruments	Type
248/42		3/4	1		H	cors (obs, vl, 2)	Cr 3rds < step
248/43	2/1/35	3/4	106	74	Q	vl (obdml)	Cs *superjectio* 3rds >
248/47		2/4	6		H	obdm (bc)	As < >
			7		Q	obdm	Bs 3rds
248/57	6/1/35	3/4	1		Q	obdm, vl (stgs)	Cr < > some AP 3rds X: some 1A
248/61		C	4		Q	obsdm (bc)	Br 3rds
			18		H	obsdm	Cs *superjectio* .sigh/LP
248/62		2/4	1		H	obsdm (bc)	Cr sigh, 3rds
			4		Q	obsdm (bc)	Ar OSC 2nds X: some 1A
14/1	30/1/35	3/8	—	6	H	vla (stgs)	Cr FNF/LP < >
14/2		3/4	--	41	Q	bc	Ar *superjectio*
11/3	19/5/35	C	—	9	Q	bc	Cs > arpeg
11/4		C	31		H	v	Ar > sigh
11/7		C	—	17	Q	bc	Cs <
100/1	1732-5	¢:	1		Q	vl, 2 (stgs) cors (fl, obdm)	Cr < > step sigh
			114		E	vl (obdm)	Cs >
100/4		2/4	13		Q	v2	As OSC 2nds
100/6		C'	—	20	H	corl	As sigh <
244/4e	30/3/36	C	—	43	H	vl, 2, vla	Bs paired 3rds
244/8		C.	1		H	vl, 2 (stgs) fls	Ar sigh >
			34		Q	fl	Bs 3rds
244/11		6/4	29		Sx	vl (stgs)	Cr SNF Mes < >
244/13		6/8	5		Sx	obsdm (bc)	Br 3rds
244/14		C	11		Q	vl, 2	As <
244/19		C	1		H	rs, obsdc (bc)	Cr FNF < sigh X: some 1D
244/20		C	3		H	ob, bc (stgs)	Cr FNF Mes OSC 2nds
244/27a		C	7		H	fll (2) obl	Cr step arpeg
244/29		C	2		H	vl, 2, vla (obsdm, fls)	Cr step 3rds
			1		Q	fls (bc, stgs, obsdm)	Cr step arpeg
244/30		3/8	39	31	H	v2 (stgs)	Cr > some AP SNF
244/33		C	7		Q	bc	As >
244/35		C	1		H	vladg	Br
244/36a		C	10		Q	vl, 2	Cr FNF/LP
244/42		C	28	4	H	vl, 2	Ar sigh < >
244/49		3/4	4		H	obsdc	Cr dotted SNF
			32		Q	fl	Cs step

Regular slur patterns in concerted vocal works (cont.)

Work (BWV)	Date	Metre	First instance 1: Score	2: Parts	Division of pulse	Instruments	Type
244/52	30/3/36	3/4	1		H	vl, 2, bc	Br dotted arpeg
244/57		C	8		Q	bc	As dotted < >
244/60		C	1		H	obsdc	Ar dotted OSC 2nds
			5		Q	obsdc (bc)	Cr step < > some arpeg
244/64		C	1		H	v2, vla	Cr arpeg
244/65		12/8	4		Sx	vl, obdcl (2)	Cr step X: some 3C
244/66b		C	17		H	vl, 2, vla, fls, obs	As sigh
244/67		C	2		Q	fl (vl, vla, obl)	Cs > arpeg
			2		H	v2, vla (vl, obl)	As sigh
244/68		3/4	3		H	vl, 2 (vla) fls, obs	Cr step >
30a/1 (30)	28/9/37	2/4	15	7	Q	fll, vl (2, obl)	Ar >AP X: some 1A
30a/3		3/8	3		H	vl	Ar >AP X: some 3I
30a/8		2/4	5		H	v, vl (2), obdm	Ar step sigh
195/2	1735-50	C	12		Q	bc	Br step arpeg
195/3		2/4	[2]		Q	vl, obdml (2, vla)	Cr OSC 2nds >AP Lombard rhythm
			[6]		H	vl, 2 (obsdm)	Br Lombard rhythm
			[19]		H	vla (v2, bc)	Cs
195/5		3/4	[118]		H	vl (stgs) obs, fls	Cr step
234/1	1735-50	3/4	1		H	vl, 2 (stgs) fls	Cr dotted FNF/LP arpeg > X: some 3G
			5		Q	vl (fls)	Cr step FNF arpeg *superjectio*
		3/8	129		H	vla	As > X: some 3G
234/2		3/4	10		H	fls (stgs)	Cr dotted arpeg FNF/LP Mes X: some longer
234/4		3/4	10		H	fls	Cr OSC 2nds *superjectio*
234/5		6/8	1		Sx	vl, 2, vla	Cr FNF/LP (DFU) step OSC 2nds

1D

Work (BWV)	Date	Metre	First instance 1: Score	2: Parts	Division of pulse	Instruments	Type
71/6	4/2/08	C	2		Q	rl (2), obl (2, vl)	Ar FNF/LP > some tied
71/7		C	2		Q	vcl, violone, fag	Ar < RFU

Regular slur patterns in concerted vocal works (cont.)

Work (BWV)	Date	Metre	First instance 1: Score	2: Parts	Division of pulse	Instruments	Type
199/2	12/8/14	C	3		Q	ob	Cr Mes < > some RFU/tied
76/2	6/6/23	C	5		Q	vl (2)	Ar < > Mes
147/8	2/7/23	G	--	1	Q	obdm	Ar TNF RFU X: obdc and score 3G
194/5	2/11/23	¢	5		Q	vl (bc)	Ar > X: some 1A?
81/1	30/1/24	C	1		H	vl, 2, vla (bc) rs	Cr some RFU Mes >
245/16d	7/4/24	C	[−]	11	Q	vl, fl	Ar Mes
10/2	2/7/24	C	18		H	stgs	Cr RFU < >
			--	1	Q	vl (stgs)	Ar FNF/LP DFU (parts) X: 1A in score
94/7	6/8/24	C	14	5	H	bc	Cr RFU < > TNF/LP
			7		Q	obdm	Ar >
33/3	3/9/24	C	34	1	Q	vl	Ar tied Mes
114/2	1/10/24	3/4	4	2	Q	fl	Cr Mes arpeg some tied some DFU (parts)
114/5		C	−	2	Q	ob (v)	Ar Mes
96/3	8/10/24	C	2	1	H	bc	Cr some RFU DFU (parts) FNF
			−	10	Q	fl	Ar > DFU (parts)
5/3	15/10/24	3/4	−	3	Q	vla	Ar > some DFU (parts)
5/5		C	8	7	Q	vl, obs	Ar Mes
91/5	25/12/24	C	19		H	bc	As RFU TNF
121/2	26/12/24	3/4	−	48	Q	obdm	Bs Mes LP
133/1	27/12/24	¢	64		E	vl (2. vla) obsdm	Ar Mes slurred notes constant X: some 1A in score
3/1	14/1/25	C	1		Q	obdm2 (1)	Cr arpeg < some RFU/tied
3/5		C	−	48	Q	vl. 2 (obsdm)	Ar < > some tied
249/2	1/4/25	3/4	14		Q	ob	Cs > Mes some tied
249/5		3/4	4		Q	fl (or v)	Ar < >
249/9		C	--	7	Q	obdm	Cr arpeg < > some tied X: some extended to 4G
42/1	8/4/25	C	9		Q	obs (fag)	Cr RFU/tied TNF/LP < >
103/3	22/4/25	6/8	2		Tw	v or fl	Ar > DFU

Regular slur patterns in concerted vocal works (cont.)

Work (BWV)	Date	Metre	First instance 1: Score	First instance 2: Parts	Division of pulse	Instruments	Type
108/2	29/4/25	3/4	9	1	Q	v	Cr tied > X: some 1A (score)
87/3	6/5/25	C	8		Q	obdc2 (1)	Ar > unslurred constant
			2	13	H	obsdc	Cs some RFU arpeg X: most 1A
87/4		C	–	6	Q	v	As TNF
			–	7	H	vl (stgs)	Cs > RFU
183/3	13/5/25	C	–	1	Q	obsdm, obsdc	Br RFU TNF/LP
151/3	27/12/25	¢	11	1	Q	vl, 2, vla, obdm	Ar < > DFU some RFU (parts) X: score 1C
16/5	1/1/26	3/4	10	3	Q	vltta or obdc	Cr < tied DFU (parts) Mes RFU
32/5	13/1/26	C	1		Q	vl (ob)	Cr Mes FNF/LP >
43/1	30/5/26	C	–	1	Q	bc, vl, obl	Ar < RFU or tied
43/5		C	–	3	Q	vl (obl)	Ar < tied
88/5	21/7/26	C	3	1	H	vl, 2, bc, obsdm	Cr RFU or tied TNF Mes < >
170/5	28/7/26	C	–	7	E	fl	Ar Mes DFU (part)
		C	–	10	Q	fl	Cs < Mes tied
47/2	13/10/26	3/8	–	27	Q	v	As DFU (parts) ONC > X: 1A in score
47/4		C	9	1	H	v, ob, bc	Ar FNF/Mes DFU (parts) slurred constant X: score 1C
169/1	20/10/26	C	66		H	obl	As > RFU
98/1	10/11/26	3/4	–	13	Q	vl	Ar > DFU
207/3	11/12/26	¢	9		Q	vl (obdm)	Ar < > RFU
			–	50	E	vl	As Mes RFU or tied
58/3	5/1/27	C	3		Q	v	Ar tied > X: score often 1A
58/5		2/4	5		Q	vl, obl	Ar Mes DFU (parts)
82/3	2/2/27	C	–	1	H	bc (stgs, obdc)	Cr > DFU (parts) FNF some tied
201/15	c. 1729	2/4	–	32	Q	fls	As <
51/4	17/9/30	3/4	7	–	Q	v2 (1)	Cs Mes
112/3	8/4/31	C	18		Q	vl (2)	Cr tied
112/4		2	64		Q	v2	As > tied
29/3	27/8/31	¢	13		Q	v	Ar DFU ONC (unslurred) >
232/1	21/4/33	C	6		Q	vla (stgs) obdml, fll (2)	Cr tied Mes >
			7		H	vl, 2 (stgs) fls, obsdm	Ar some tied < >

Regular slur patterns in concerted vocal works (cont.)

Work (BWV)	Date	Metre	First instance 1: Score	2: Parts	Division of pulse	Instruments	Type
232/2		C	5		Q	vl, 2	Ar > DFU ONC (unslurred)
232/6		C	3		Q	v (vl, 2)	Ar DFU rhythm:
97/6	c. 1734	C	7		Q	vl (bc)	Ar > DFU (parts)
211/2	c. 1734	C	21		Q	vl	Ar < DFU/RFU
211/10		¢	20		Q	fl	As < >
215/3	5/10/34	C	9		H	bc (stgs, obsdm)	Cr > DFU some RFU
215/7		2/4	6		Q	bc	As DFU
248/19	26/12/34	2/4	17		H	vl, obsdm	As Mes DFU (parts)
			114		Q	stgs (obdm)	Ar < RFU
248/21		C	—	25	H	vl, 2, vla, fls	Br RFU arpeg
248/31	27/12/34	2/4	17		H	v	Ar DFU >
248/40	1/1/35	C	—	16	H	vl	Bs RFU arpeg
248/47	2/1/35	2/4	3		H	bc	As >
			6		Q	bc (obdm)	Cr < > arpeg RFU/tied
248/51		2/4	5		Q	v	Cr Mes < > DFU some step
248/61	6/1/35	C	8		H	obsdm	Cs > arpeg
248/62		2/4	18		H	obdml (2)	Cr < > RFU
248/64		C	5		Q	trl (stgs)	Ar < > DFU ONC
14/4	30/1/35	C	—	6	H	obl (2, bc)	As < > DFU (parts) some RFU
			—	47	Q	bc	As < >
9/1	1732-5	3/4	7	3	Q	obdm (fl)	As <
100/4	1732-5	2/4	39		H	vl	As > RFU
244/8	30/3/36	C	5		H	bc (stgs, fls)	Ar > DFU some step
244/19		C	1		H	fls, obs	Br some RFU X: some 1C
244/20		C	5		H	bc (stgs, fll, ob)	Cr < > some un-slurred tied
			45		Q	ob	As <
244/27a		C	14		H	fls (obs)	Cr arpeg > some tied DFU (parts)
244/29		C	9		H	vl (2, vla)	Cs tied < >
244/42		C	12		Q	v	As >
244/48		C	1		Q	obsdc	Ar Mes unslurred tied
244/49		3/4	4		Q	fl	As < >
244/52		3/4	39		Q	v	As <
244/59		C	1		Q	obsdc	Br unslurred tied

Regular slur patterns in concerted vocal works (cont.)

Work (BWV)	Date	Metre	First instance 1: Score	2: Parts	Division of pulse	Instruments	Type
30a/8 (30)	28/9/37	2/4	—	99	H	obdm (bc)	As < >
			14		Q	vl, 2 (obdm)	Ar DFU ONC > some unslurred tied
234/3	1735-50	C	12	1	Q	bc	Ar > unslurred tied

1E

♩♩♩♩

Work (BWV)	Date	Metre	1: Score	2: Parts	Division of pulse	Instruments	Type
182/7	25/3/14	¢	50		Q	vlal	As RFU (lst)
24/1	20/6/23	3/4	85	8	H	vl, 2, vla	Ar <
81/1	30/1/24	C	1		H	vl, 2, vla	Ar X: most 1D?
10/1	2/7/24	C	—	9	H	vl (2, obs)	Ar >
94/7	6/8/24	C	13	2	H	bc	Ar > corta under slur
249/2	1/4/25	3/4	—	41	Q	ob	As > with 4L X: some longer in score
151/3	27/12/25	¢	8	4	Q	vl, 2, vla (obdm)	Ar < > *superjectio* some corta
207/3	11/12/26	¢	—	53	Q	vl	Cr < > LP, RFU (lst) DFU (2nd)
58/3	5/1/27	C	8	7	Q	v	Ar > with 4L
232/1	21/4/33	C	5		H	fll (2) (stgs) obdml (2) (fag)	Ar < > slurred notes constant in sequence
211/6	c. 1734	C	1		H	bc	Ar < DFU (parts) some RFU (lst)
248/62	6/1/35	2/4	65		H	obsdm	As < > RFU (both)
11/4	19/5/35	C	3		H	v	Ar < > with 4L
244/20	30/3/36	C	6		H	ob	Ar < > DFU (both)
244/58d		C	56		H	vl, obl	As < X: some 1B
234/3	1735-50	C	5		Q	v	Ar Mes, 1st un-slurred tied, 2nd DFU

2A

♩♩♩

Work (BWV)	Date	Metre	1: Score	2: Parts	Division of pulse	Instruments	Type
199/8	12/8/14	12/8	2		T	ob (stgs)	Cr < TNF arpeg X: many 2B
23/1	7/2/23	C	1		Sx	obs (bc)	Cr TNF < > TNF/LP
76/12	6/6/23	9/8	2		T	obdm (vladg) bc	Cs < > TNF/LP X: some 2B?
24/5	20/6/23	C	14		Sx	obsdm	As <
147/5	2/7/23	C	4	2	Sx	v	Br X: score gen 2B

Regular slur patterns in concerted vocal works (cont.)

Work (BWV)	Date	Metre	First instance 1: Score	2: Parts	Division of pulse	Instruments	Type
147/6		3/4	1		T	vl, obs	Cr TNF/LP step < > arpeg
109/3	17/10/23	C	38		Sx	vl	As >
194/3	2/11/23	12/8	1		T	vl, 2 (stgs) ob	Cr TNF < > X: often 2B in score
194/8		C.	—	52	T	bc	As < >
44/3	21/5/24	3/4	—	3	T	ob (bc)	Cr < > TNF/LP step
44/6		C	1		Sx	vl, obl (2, bc)	Ar < dot for quaver
20/8	11/6/24	C	4		Sx	tr	Ar TNF
2/3	18/6/24	3/4	2		Sx	v	Cr TNF >arpeg
94/1	6/8/24	C	3		Sx	fl, obl, vl	Ar >
94/4		C	5		Sx	fl	As < >
94/6		C.	2		T	vl (stgs)	Cr > TNF X: some 2B esp. score
96/1	8/10/24	9/8	1		T	stgs, obs	Cr TNF < > arpeg pastorale X: some 2B or 5B
5/5	15/10/24	C.	10		Sx	tr (obs, vs)	Cr TNF <
26/2	19/11/24	6/8	8	2	T	bc (v)	Cr with repeated notes > TNF/LP
232/III	25/12/24	C	1		T	trl, 2 (stgs)	Ar <
41/2	1/1/25	6/8	1		T	obsl-3 (bc)	Cr pastorale < > TNF/LP arpeg X: some 2B
123/1	6/1/25	9/8	18	1	T	stgs (obs, fls)	Cr < > TNF arpeg step pastorale
249/3	1/4/25	3/8	1		W	v2, vla, ob2 (1)	Cr < > X: many 2B?
249/5		3/4	58	14	Sx	fl or v	Ar >
249/11		C	2	1	T	stgs (obs, trs)	Cr TNF/LP < > X: TNF/LP 2B?
6/5	2/4/25	C	3		Sx	vl (2, bc)	Ar < >
42/3	8/4/25	C	7		Sx	obs	Ar <
85/5	15/4/25	9/8	1		T	stgs	Cr arpeg < > step
108/5	29/4/25	6/8	1		T	stgs	Cr TNF < > X: some 2B
87/6	6/5/25	12/8	1		T	vl (stgs)	Cr dotted TNF arpeg < > X: some 2B
128/4	10/5/25	6/8	1		T	obdm (bc)	Ar < > X: some 2B
175/2	22/5/25	12/8	1		T	rs	Cr < > TNF/LP X: many 2B
176/3	27/5/25	¢	8		Sx	vl	Cr TNF/LP >arpeg X: some 2B?

Regular slur patterns in concerted vocal works (cont.)

Work (BWV)	Date	Metre	First instance 1: Score	2: Parts	Division of pulse	Instruments	Type
176/5	27/5/25	3/8	—	3	W	bc	Cr TNF >
36c/1 (36)	4–5/1725	3/4	2	1	Sx	vl (obsdm)	Ar < >
36c/5		C	17	5	Sx	vl, fl	Ar TNF DFU quaver
36c/7		12/8	1		T	vl or fl (bc)	As > X: most 2B?
168/1	29/7/25	C	4		Sx	vl (stgs)	Cr TNF AP < > arpeg
164/1	26/8/25	9/8	1		T	vla, bc (stgs)	Cr < > pastorale
110/1	25/12/25	9/8	28		T	stgs (obs, fag)	Cr TNF/LP step < X: most step 2B, some extended
110/4		3/4	8	6	T	obdm	Cr > TNF
151/1	27/12/25	12/8	—	20	T	v2 (1, obdm)	Cr < arpeg X: often 2B in score
		¢	—	32	Tw	fl (obdm, vl)	Cr TNF < arpeg
32/3	13/1/26	3/8	5		T	v	Cr < TNF arpeg
13/1	20/1/26	12/8	3	1	T	fls, obdc (bc)	Cr TNF < >
88/1	21/7/26	6/8	1		T	stgs, obsdm	Cr < > pastorale arpeg X: some 2B
170/1	28/7/26	12/8	1		T	stgs, obdm	Cr repeated < > pastorale
19/5	29/9/26	6/8	32		T	tr	As < pastorale
55/1	17/11/26	6/8	1		T	fl, obdm (vl, 2, bc)	Cr < TNF step X: most 2B, esp. score
52/1	24/11/26	C	2		T	cor2 (1)	Cs repeated arpeg
174/2	6/6/29	6/8	1		T	bc	Cr TNF >
201/1	c. 1729	3/8	1		T	stgs (fls, obs)	Cr < > TNF arpeg
201/5		3/8	12		T	vl (bc, fl, obdm)	Cr < > step TNF/LP
201/9		12/8	6	1	T	bc (obdm)	Cr < > TNF some AP LP X: many 2B
51/3	17/9/30	12/8	1		T	bc	Ar <
112/2	8/4/31	6/8	—	13	T	obdm	As >
112/4		2	13		Sx	vl (2, vla)	Ar < > step
213/1	5/9/33	3/8	223	3	W	stgs, obs (cors)	Cr < > TNF arpeg X: some arpeg 2B?
213/5		6/8	2		T	obdm	Cr TNF/LP < > arpeg X: many 2B
211/4	c. 1734	3/8	1		T	fl (bc)	As < >
211/8		6/8	—	24	T	bc	Cr TNF > arpeg X: some 2B
248/10	26/12/34	12/8	1		T	vl, 2, fls (stgs, obsdm, bc)	Cr dotted arpeg pastorale step TNF
248/18		C	5		Sx	bc	Br arpeg
248/23		12/8	2	1	T	v2 (1) vla, bc (fls, obs)	Cr pastorale step dotted TNF arpeg

Regular slur patterns in concerted vocal works (cont.)

Work (BWV)	Date	Metre	First instance 1: Score	2: Parts	Division of pulse	Instruments	Type
248/24	27/12/34	3/8	25		W	vl, 2	Bs X: most 2B (esp. score)
248/36	1/1/35	3/8	3		W	corl (2) obs, stgs	Cr < > arpeg TNF X: mòst 2B?
248/39		6/8	7		T	ob (bc)	Cr < > TNF/LP X: some 2B?
14/1	30/1/35	3/8	37	10	W	bc (stgs, cors, obs)	Cr < > pastorale X: some 2B
11/10	19/5/35	3/8	3		W	fl (ob, stgs)	Cr < TNF X: most TNF 2B
9/3	1732-5	12/16	4		T	v (bc)	Cr < > TNF X: most TNF 2B
100/5	1732-5	12/16	1		T	bc, obdm	Cr TNF some LP < > pastorale
244/1	30/3/36	12/8	3		T	v2 (stgs, fls, obs)	Cr < > TNF arpeg X: some 2B
244/6		3/8	17		W	bc (fls)	Cr < > TNF
244/12		C	1		Sx	obsdm	Ar < > step ONC
244/23		3/8	2		W	vl, 2, bc	Cr < > TNF X: some 2B?
244/39		12/8	5		T	stgs	Cr < > step TNF some dotted
244/65		12/8	1		T	vl, 2, vla (bc) obsdc	Cr pastorale < step, arpeg X: some 2B?
30a/3 (30)	28/9/37	3/8·	4		T	vl (stgs)	Ar >
30a/10		9/8	2	1	T	vl, 2, bc	Cr < > arpeg TNF some 2B
195/2	1735-50	C	—	2	Sx	bc	Ar TNF

2B

Work (BWV)	Date	Metre	First instance 1: Score	2: Parts	Division of pulse	Instruments	Type
199/8	12/8/14	12/8	1		T	ob (stgs)	Cr TNF < > X: some 2A
76/12	6/6/23	9/8	2	1	T	obdm, vladg	Cr < > LP
147/5	2/7/23	C	2		Sx	v	Br arpeg X: parts mainly 2A
48/1	3/10/23	3/4	2		W	vl (stgs)	Cr < > AP
48/6		3/4	3		W	ob (stgs)	Cr > arpeg some corta
194/1	2/11/23	3/4	80		W	vla (stgs, obs)	Cs AP arpeg
194/3		12/8	1		T	vl, 2 (vla) ob	Cr TNF OSC < > X: many 2A
40/4	26/12/23	3/8	56	6	W	vla (stgs) obs	Cr < > some RFU
40/7		12/8	2		T	obs	As TNF
245/32	7/4/24	12/8	[—]	1	T	bc	Br

Regular slur patterns in concerted vocal works (cont.)

Work (BWV)	Date	Metre	First instance 1: Score	First instance 2: Parts	Division of pulse	Instruments	Type
10/5	2/7/24	6/8	2		T	bc	As
94·3	6/8/24	3/8	-	2	W	bc	Ar >
94/6		C	2		T	vl (2, vla)	Cr > arpeg TNF X: some 2A
96/1	8/10/24	9/8	4	3	T	stgs, obs	Cr TNF < > arpeg X: many 2A or extended to 5B
96/5		3/4	9		W	vl, 2, vla (obs)	Ar >AP RFU sigh
26/2	19/11/24	6/8	...	13	T	v, fl	Bs
133/4	27/12/24	12/8	61		T	vl	Bs
122/1	31/12/24	3/8	1		W	vl, 2, vla, obs	Cr < > TNF
41/2	1/1/25	6/8	1		T	obs	Cr TNF/LP < > X: most 2A
249/3	1/4/25	3/8	1		W	v2, vla (bc)	Cr < > X: many 2A
249/11		C	2		T	trs (tutti)	Cr < > TNF/LP X: many < > 2A some extended to 5B (oboes)
108/5	29/4/25	6/8	1		T	stgs	Cr TNF arpeg AP some RFU X: some 2A
87/6	6/5/25	12/8	1		T	vl (stgs)	Cr dotted X: most 2A?
128/4	10/5/25	6/8	1		T	obdm (bc)	Cr < > X: some 2A
183/4	13/5/25	3/8	61		W	vl	Cs TNF RFU/tied
175/2	22/5/25	12/8	1		T	rs	Cr < > X: some 2A
176/3	27/5/25	¢	8		Sx	vl	Cr TNF/LP > X: most 2A?
176/5		3/8	58	2	W	obs	Ar > sigh/AP some RFU
36c/7 (36)	4-5/1725	12/8	1		T	v (bc)	Cr >LP X: some 2A
110/1	25/12/25	9/8	24		T	v2, ob2 (1, stgs)	Cr < step X: some extended
110/4		3/4	6		T	obdm	Cr < corta
57/1	26/12/25	3/4	20		W	vl, obl (2, stgs)	Ar >AP RFU
57/3		3/4	80	3	W	vla (bc, v2)	Br < arpeg
151/1	27/12/25	12/8	2		T	vl, 2, vla (bc) obdm	Cr arpeg <
32/3	13/1/26	3/8	1		W	v	Ar >
			11		T	v	Br
13/1	20/1/26	12/8	—	7	T	rs	Cs TNF X: most 2A?
88/1	21/7/26	6/8	1		T	vl, 2 (stgs) obsdm	Cr < > arpeg X: many 2A
187/3	4/8/26	3/8	15		W	vl, 2, vla, ob	Ar <
19/5	29/9/26	6/8	--	22	T	vl, ob	Cs dotted < >
27/5	6/10/26	3/4	3		W	vl (2, vla)	Cs < > corta

Regular slur patterns in concerted vocal works (cont.)

Work (BWV)	Date	Metre	First instance 1: Score	2: Parts	Division of pulse	Instruments	Type
49/3	3/11/26	3/8	8		W	v2, vla	Bs
55/1	17/11/26	6/8	1		T	fl, ob (stgs)	Cr < TNF X: most 2A?
84/3	9/2/27	3/8	–	3	W	ob (v)	Br leap 6th
201/5	c. 1729	3/8	9	1	W	stgs, obdm, fl	Cr < > arpeg X: some 2A
201/9		12/8	19	1	T	obdm, bc	Cr < > X: most 2A? TNF LP some DFU (parts)
29/5	27/8/31	6/8	1		T	vl, ob	Bs dotted
177/3	6/7/32	6/8	3		T	obdc (bc)	As < >
232/10	21/4/33	6/8	3		T	stgs, obdm	Cr < > TNF arpeg unslurred tied
213/1	5/9/33	3/8	3		W	bc (stgs, obs, cors)	Ar < > TNF X: most 2A
213/5		6/8	2		T	obdm (bc)	Cr TNF LP < > arpeg some RFU X: most 2A
213/9		3/8	108	104	W	bc	Bs
213/11		3/8	1		W	vlal (2)	Ar < dotted
97/2	c. 1734	6/8	1		T	bc	Br step
211/8	c. 1734	6/8	–	25	T	bc	Br arpeg X: many 2A
248/4	25/12/34	3/8	–	1	W	v (obdm)	Br
248/15	26/12/34	3/8	3		W	bc	Cr > TNF/LP arpeg
248/24	27/12/34	3/8	4		W	trl, fls, obs, stgs	Cr dotted arpeg
248/29		3/8	1		W	obdml (2)	Ar dotted
248/36	1/1/35	3/8	3		W	stgs, cors, obs	Cr < > arpeg some DFU (parts) X: some 2A?
248/39		6/8	2		T	ob (bc)	Cr TNF LP arpeg < > some RFU X: some 2A
248/42		3/4	30		W	vl (obs)	Bs
248/54	6/1/35	3/8	32	17	W	obl (2, stgs)	Cr < arpeg TNF/LP some RFU
11/10	19/5/35	3/8	1		W	fls, v, vla (ob)	Cr TNF octave leap
9/3	1732-5	12/16	3		T	v (bc)	Br arpeg step
244/1	30/3/36	12/8	3	1	T	stgs, obs, fls	Cr < > TNF/LP DFU X: some 2A
244/6		3/8	2		W	fls (bc)	Cr LP ONC TNF some tied < > X: 2A for TNF/ < >?

Regular slur patterns in concerted vocal works (cont.)

Work (BWV)	Date	Metre	First instance 1: Score	2: Parts	Division of pulse	Instruments	Type
244/11	30/3/36	6/4	19		W	vl, vla, bc	Ar < >
244/13		6/8	3	2	T	obsdm (bc)	Ar < > AP RFU/ unslurred tied
244. 23		3/8	2		W	vl, 2, bc	Ar < > some RFU or tied X: many 2A
244/39		12/8	16		T	v (vl, 2, vla)	Cs AP < > X: most < > 2A
244/65		12/8	1		T	vl, 2 (stgs, obsdc)	Cr TNF/LP < > arpeg X: some 2A
30a/5 (30)	28/9/37	C	---	12	T	vl, fl	Cs > arpeg
30/10		9/8	11	1	T	vl, 2	Br arpeg X: many 2A

2C

109/5	17/10/23	3/4	2		W	obs	Ar dotted
40/4	26/12/23	3/8	58		W	obl	As < RFU
123/1	6/1/25	9/8	---	9	T	vl, 2, vla (obdms, fls)	As < RFU or tied
57/1	26/12/25	3/4	---	7	W	vl. obl	As >AP unslurred tied
32/3	13/1/26	3/8	29		T	v	Ar slurred notes constant
13/1	20/1/26	12/8	22	1	T	bc	Ar < some RFU
187/3	4/8/26	3/8	11		W	v2. vla	Cr < > RFU
35/7	8/9/26	3/8	---	17	W	vl, 2, vla, obs	Cr corta > arpeg RFU X: most missing
98/3	10/11/26	3/8	.	1	W	ob	Ar dotted
55/1	17/11/26	6/8	2		T	vl, 2 (bc, obdm, fl)	Ar > some RFU
201/5	c. 1729	3/8		17	W	vla	Bs < > arpeg
29/5	27/8/31	6/8	3		T	vl, ob	As dotted:

232/10	21/4/33	6/8	7	3	T	obdm (stgs)	Cr < > unslurred tied, some arpeg
248/54	6/1/35	3/8	201	185	W	obl (2)	Cr < arpeg RFU
14/1	30/1/35	3/8	.	1	W	vla (stgs)	Ar < > RFU
9/3	1732-5	12/16	4		T	v (bc)	Cr < > arpeg RFU or tied
100/3	1732-5	6/8	1		T	fl	Ar < dotted
			5		T	bc	Br arpeg
244/1	30/3/36	12/8	14	13	T	vl (obs, fls)	As < >

Regular slur patterns in concerted vocal works (cont.)

Work (BWV)	Date	Metre	First instance 1: Score	2: Parts	Division of pulse	Instruments	Type
244/30		3/8	1		W	vl (stgs) fl, obdm	Ar dotted <
244/65		12/8	2		T	vl, 2 (bc) obsdc	Ar < > unslurred tied

3A

Work (BWV)	Date	Metre	First instance 1: Score	2: Parts	Division of pulse	Instruments	Type
185/1	14/7/15	6/4	[4]		H	bc	Cr SNF/LP arpeg X: some parts 1C
23/3	7/2/23	3/4	17	1	H	vl (2, vla) obs	Cr < X: often 1C
147/3	2/7/23	3/4	32		H	obdm	Br arpeg
194/1	2/11/23	3/4	34		H	vl (stgs) obl (2)	Cr SNF/LP OSC 2nds X: many 1C
245/9	7/4/24	3/8	[3]		H	fls	Cr > TNF Mes arpeg
245/24		3/8	[--]	19	H	vl, 2, vla (bc)	Cr < > SNF/LP
245/39		3/4	[4]		H	vl (bc) fls, obs	Cr > arpeg
20/3	11/6/24	3/4	3		H	bc (vl)	Cs SNF > X: many SNF 1C
94/6	6/8/24	C	22		Sx	vl	Cs SNF/LP arpeg
26/2	19/11/24	6/8	1		Sx	fl (v, bc)	Cr > SNF/LP
62/2	3/12/24	3/8	4		H	vl (2) obl (2)	Cr < > SNF
122/1	31/12/24	3/8	2		H	bc (vl, vla, obs)	Cr < SNF 3rds X: most 3rds 1C
41/1	1/1/25	3/4	—	106	H	vl (2, obc)	Ar SNF
124/5	7/1/25	3/8	...	53	H	bc	As <
249/3	1/4/25	3/8	11		H	vl (stgs) obl	Ar <
249/11		3/8	—	73	H	obl	As SNF X: some appear as 1C
36c/3 (36)	4-5/1725	3/8	93	5	H	obdm (bc)	Cr < arpeg SNF/LP
128/4	10/5/25	6/8	30	3	Sx	obdm	Cr < > SNF
176/5	27/5/25	3/8	48	29	H	obs (bc)	Cr > SNF/LP+ <
57/1	26/12/25	3/4	—	7	H	v2, ob2, bc (stgs, obl)	Ar SNF/LP
13/1	20/1/26	12/8	...	3	Sx	obdc	Cr < > SNF/LP Mes
43/3	30/5/26	3/8	17		H	vl, 2	Ar < >
39/5	23/6/26	6/8	2		Sx	rs	Cr SNF/LP arpeg
88/1	21/7/26	6/8	5		Sx	vl, obl (2, bc)	Cr SNF some LP
170/1	28/7/26	12/8	4		Sx	v2, vla (vl, ob)	Cr > SNF/LP+ <
45/3	11/8/26	3/8	—	102	H	vl	As SNF last = quaver
169/2	20/10/26	3/8	3		H	bc	As >
49/1	3/11/26	3/8	72		H	vs (bc) obdm	As >
49/2		3/8	17		H	bc	As SNF/LP

Regular slur patterns in concerted vocal works (cont.)

Work (BWV)	Date	Metre	First instance 1: Score	First instance 2: Parts	Division of pulse	Instruments	Type
98/3	10/11.26	3/8	.	5	H	ob	Cr < arpeg
207 1	11.12.26	6/8	8	1	Sx	trs (obs, stgs)	Ar OSC 2nds + FNF
207 7		3/4	8		H	fll (2)	As < > X: most ext over next bar (parts)
82.1	2 2.27	3/8		142	H	vl, 2	As SNF/LP
82.5		3/8	10		H	ob (vl)	Cr SNF/LP < X: some 1C
84 3	9/2 27	3/8	25	17	H	v (ob)	Cr < SNF/LP
177/3	6/7/32	6/8	2		Sx	obdc (bc)	Cr SNF/LP >
232/10	21.4/33	6/8	8		Sx	obdm	Cr < > SNF/LP
213/5	5.9/33	6/8		96	Sx	obdm	As SNF
213 9		3/8	42		H	v, bc	Cs > SNF
248/1	25.12/34	3/8	174		H	bc	Cs SNF X: most 1C
248.4		3/8	42		H	v, obdm, bc	Cr > SNF arpeg
248/15	26.12/34	3/8	8		H	bc	As SNF
14.1	30/1/35	3/8		45	H	bc	Cr < > SNF some LP
11./10	19/5/35	3/8	81		H	vl, 2, vla	As SNF
244/13	30/3/36	6/8	2		Sx	bc (obsdm)	As < >
244./30		3/8	5		H	v2	Ar >
244/68		3/4	1		H	vl, 2 (stgs), fls, obs	Cr > SNF corta X: many variants esp. 1C
234/1	1735 50	3/8	122		H	bc (fl)	Cs SNF < >

3B

245.9	7/4/24	3/8	[1]		H	fls	Ar < X: some 3A
128.4	10/5/25	6/8	61		Sx	obdm	Bs arpeg

3C

FO = first only

SO = second only

199/4	12/8/14	3/4	21		H	vl	As TNF (SO)
134a/2 (134)	1/1/19	3/8	149	147 later score (P 44)	H	vl	Cs arpeg TNF (FO)
23/3	7/2/23	3/4	43		H	obl (vla)	Cs TNF > X: most 3A
147/3	2/7/23	3/4	15		H	obdm	Cs arpeg TNF/LP
48/1	3/10/23	3/4	1		H	vl (2)	Ar < > (FO)

Regular slur patterns in concerted vocal works (cont.)

Work (BWV)	Date	Metre	First instance 1: Score	2: Parts	Division of pulse	Instruments	Type
40/4	26/12/23	3/8	1		H	vl (bc)	Ar TNF (FO)
245/9	7/4/24	3/8	[5]		H	fls	Cr TNF/LP (FO) X: most 3A
94/3	6/8/24	3/8	41		H	obl	Bs (FO) arpeg
62/2	3/12/24	3/8	9		H	vl (ob)	Ar < (FO) DFU (parts)
122/1	31/12/24	3/8	5		H	vl	As (FO) < X: most 1C
249/1	1/4/25	3/8	41		H	vl	Cr < > TNF (FO) some DFU (parts)
249/3		3/8	1		H	vl, obs	Ar > (FO) DFU
249/11		3/8	—	70	H	vl	As </TNF (FO) X: ob 1C
6/2	2/4/25	3/8	--	5	H	vla or obdc	Cr < arpeg (FO) dot for note 4
36c/7 (36)	4-5/1725	12/8	2	1	Sx	v	Cr < TNF (FO)
128/4	10/5/25	6/8	11	7	Sx	obdm	Cr < > arpeg (FO)
176/5	27/5/25	3/8	43	3	H-W	obs	Cr < arpeg (FO) some FO = quaver + semiquaver
57/3	26/12/25	3/4	15	9	H	vl (2)	Ar < X: often 1C in score
57/7		3/8	--	35	H	v	Bs (FO) arpeg
88/3	21/7/26	3/8	—	29	H	obdm	As (SO or FO) < >
98/3	10/11/26	3/8	—	3	H	ob	Bs arpeg + > X: some 3I?
			—	10	H-Q	ob	Ar (FO) corta + DFU + tie:

Work (BWV)	Date	Metre	First instance 1: Score	2: Parts	Division of pulse	Instruments	Type
82/1	2/2/27	3/8	6	4	H	vl (2, ob)	Cs < > TNF some FO/SO
82/5		3/8	11		H	ob (or fl) vl, 2	Ar TNF/LP + >
84/3	9/2/27	3/8	—	3	H	v	Cr arpeg > (FO)
201/5	c. 1729	3/8	5		H	fl, ob	Ar (SO) >
201/7		3/8	--	41	H	vl, 2	Bs arpeg (FO)
232/10	21/4/33	6/8	1		Sx	obdm	Cr (SO) TNF arpeg; rest/tie for 1st group
248/15	26/12/34	3/8	13		H	fl (bc)	Cr (FO) < arpeg some DFU
248/29	27/12/34	3/8	12		H	bc	Ar TNF+ > X: some parts 1C/3G
248/36	1/1/35	3/8	45		H	obl (vl)	As (FO) TNF X: some 1C (parts)

Regular slur patterns in concerted vocal works (cont.)

Work (BWV)	Date	Metre	First instance 1: Score	2: Parts	Division of pulse	Instruments	Type
100/3	1732–5	6/8	4		Sx	bc	Cr TNF (SO) X: some 3I
244/11	30/3/36	C	25		Sx	vl (bc)	Ar TNF (FO)
244/13		6/8	1		Sx	obsdm (bc)	Ar (FO) TNF
244/65		12/8	4		Sx	vl, obdcl	Ar (FO) < +DFU+ >:
244/68		3/4	1		H	fls, obs, stgs	Cr (both, FO, SO) < > TNF/LP some RFU X: many 3A
30a/10 (30)	28/9/37	9/8	2		Sx	vl (2)	Ar > (SO) first = tied, dotted quaver

3D

134a/2 (134)	1/1/19	3/8	59 later score (P 44)		H	vl	As >
147/3	2/7/23	3/4	6		H	obdm	Ar >
194/10	2/11/23	3/4	7		H	ob2 (1, bc)	Ar < > RFU or tie
245/7	7/4/24	3/4	3		H	ob2 (1, bc)	Cr arpeg > +corta
245/39		3/4	[3]		H	vl (stgs) fls, obs	Cr < > arpeg some RFU
33/5	3/9/24	3/4	..	13	H	ob2	Cs FvNF/LP
133/4	27/12/24	¢	63	62	Sx	vl	Cr > FNF + leap arpeg
41/1	1/1/25	3/4	.	109	H	ob2 (3)	As FvNF/LP
92/1	28/1/25	6/8	10	9	Sx	obsdm (vs)	Ar FvNF RFU
92/8		3/8	32		H	obdm	Cr arpeg +TNF > X: many 3A
6/1	2/4/25	3/4	16		H	ob2 (1)	Ar > X: most 1C
103/1	22/4/25	3/4	..	27	H	picc (obsdm)	Cr < > chromatic some RFU/tied
87/5	6/5/25	3/8	19	3	H	bc	Ar >
128/4	10/5/25	6/8	30	20	Sx	obdm	Cr > RFU/tied FvNF/LP
176/5	27/5/25	3/8	-	25	H	obs (bc)	Ar < some RFU or tied
168/3	29/7/25	3/8	--	93	H	obdm	As FNF/LP
57/1	26/12/25	3/4	--	1	H	vl, ob1 (2, stgs)	Ar FvNF some LP RFU or tied
57/3		3/4	--	39	H	vl	As FvNF tie for note 1 X: most 1C

Regular slur patterns in concerted vocal works (cont.)

Work (BWV)	Date	Metre	First instance 1: Score	2: Parts	Division of pulse	Instruments	Type
57/5		3/4	—	87	H	vl (bc)	As > 1st tied X: 1C in score
57/7		3/8	—	152	H	bc	Ar > RFU
88/3	21/7/26	3/8	—	41	H	obdm (bc)	Cr < ·> FvNF un-slurred often tied
170/1	28/7/26	12/8	6		Sx	vl, obdm	Cr < RFU or tied
187/3	4/8/26	3/8	69		H	vl, ob	As < RFU
35/5	8/9/26	3/8	84		H	vl, 2, obs	As >
19/5	29/9/26	6/8	84		Sx	vl, ob	Ar FvNF/LP
27/5	6/10/26	3/4	—	5	H	vl	Cs·< FvNF 1st often tied
98/3	10/11/26	3/8	26	13	H	ob	Cr FvNF RFU <
207/9	11/12/26	3/4	18		H	fls (bc)	Cr > FvNF many extended to next bar; most unslurred tied
82/1	2/2/27	3/8	—	15	H	ob (vl)	Cr < > FvNF most unslurred tied
201/7	c. 1729	3/8	—	101	H	vl, 2	As < > unslurred tied, one DFU
112/2	8/4/31	6/8	—	9	Sx	obdm	Cr FvNF > RFU unslurred often tied; many extend to further beat
177/1	6/7/32	3/8	7		H	v2 (vla)	As <
177/3		6/8	2		Sx	obdc (bc)	Cr < > FvNF 1st often tied X: some 3A
232/9	21/4/33	3/4	5		H	vl (2, vla)	Cs FvNF < tied X: many 1C
213/1	5/9/33	3/8	—	138	H	vl	As FvNF RFU
213/9		3/8	41		H	v (bc)	As >
211/8	c. 1734	6/8	96	54	Sx	vl	Cr < > arpeg, some tied
248/4	25/12/34	3/8	41		H	v, obdm	As >
100/3	1732-5	6/8	9		Sx	bc (fl)	Cr < >
244/68	30/3/36	3/4	2		H	bc (stgs, fls, obs)	Br arpeg
234/4	1735-50	3/4	1		H	fls (v, vla)	Ar FvNF some tied/ LP RFU

3E

248/15	26/12/34	3/8	9		H	fl	Ar FNF DFU

Regular slur patterns in concerted vocal works (cont.)

Work (BWV)	Date	Metre	First instance 1: Score	2: Parts	Division of pulse	Instruments	Type
244/30	30/3/36	3/8	43		H	vl	As FNF lst unslurred tied
244/68		3/4	30		H	vl (obs, fls)	As FNF tied

3F

rrrrrr

Work (BWV)	Date	Metre	First instance 1: Score	2: Parts	Division of pulse	Instruments	Type
245/24	7/4/24	3/8	[–]	9	H	vl	Ar TNF slurred notes constant in sequence
6/2	2/4/25	3/8	–	2	H	obdc or vla	Ar Mes DFU (lst, parts)
42/3	8/4/25	C	–	58	Sx	bc	Ar TNF DFU (lst, in parts)
79/2	31/10/25	6/8	22	–	Sx	ob or fl	As < RFU (lst)
72/5	27/1/26	3/4	–	35	H	vl, ob	As Mes
39/3	23/6/26	3/8	1		H	ob (v)	Br <AP slurred notes constant in sequence X: many 3C in parts
47/2	13/10/26	3/8	3	1	H	v (or org, bc)	Cr > Mes DFU (lst, parts)
82/1	2/2/27	3/8	9		H	vl, 2 (ob)	Cr < > TNF
248/15	26/12/34	3/8	5		H	fl (bc)	Cr > TNF DFU (lst) arpeg
244/68	30/3/36	3/4	6		H	vl (2) fls, obs	Cr TNF/LP tied unslurred
234/5	1735-50	6/8	3		Sx	vl, 2, vla	Ar > DFU

3G

rrrrrr

Work (BWV)	Date	Metre	First instance 1: Score	2: Parts	Division of pulse	Instruments	Type
182/8	25/3/14	3/8	53		H	r (v)	As >AP unslurred = tied quaver
134a/2 (134)	1/1/19	3/8	157	23	H	vl, obs	Cs FNF >AP
134a/6		3/8	229		H	vl, vla (obs)	As >AP unslurred = tied quaver
23/3	7/2/23	3/4	80	17	H	vs (obs)	Ar < > X: most lC
194/3	2/11/23	12/8	2		Sx	vl, ob	Ar >AP unslurred = quaver FNF X: some 3A
194/10		3/4	1		H	obs (bc)	As FNF/LP unslurred = crotchet

Regular slur patterns in concerted vocal works (cont.)

Work (BWV)	Date	Metre	First instance 1: Score	2: Parts	Division of pulse	Instruments	Type
33/5	3/9/24	3/4	68	15	H	ob	Ar FNF some LP X: some 1C
96/1	8/10/24	9/8	92		Sx	vl	As >AP unslurred = quaver
26/2	19/11/24	6/8	11		Sx	fl (v)	Cs Mes < >
62/2	3/12/24	3/8	30	2	H	vl (2) obs	Cr >AP FNF unslurred = quaver X: some 1C
122/1	31/12/24	3/8	10		H	vl (2) obs	Cr >some AP FNF unslurred = quaver
92/1	28/1/25	6/8	—	26	Sx	v2 (stgs, obsdm)	Cr > FNF 1st = quaver
92/8		3/8	23		H	obdm	Cs < X: most 3A?
249/1	1/4/25	3/8	—	15	H	obs	As > unslurred = quaver
249/3		3/8	7		H	v2, ob2 (trl)	As FNF/some LP unslurred = quaver
249/11		3/8	—	64	H	obl (vl)	Cs FNF >AP unslurred = quaver
36c/3 (36)	4-5/1725	3/8	38	1	H	obdm (bc)	Cr >some AP FNF unslurred = quaver
176/5	27/5/25	3/8	—	12	H	bc	Ar < > unslurred = quaver
110/4	25/12/25	3/4	11		Sx	obdm	Cr < > FNF unslurred = quaver
57/5	26/12/25	3/4	—	87	H	vl (2, vla)	Cs < > FNF X: most 1C
13/1	20/1/26	12/8	—	2	Sx	obdc (rs)	Cr Mes > RFU/ quaver
72/2	27/1/26	3/8	—	8	H	bc	Cr >AP/FNF
88/3	21/7/26	3/8	—	26	H	obdm	As > unslurred = quaver
170/1	28/7/26	12/8	1		Sx	vl, obdm	Cr FNF < RFU
45/3	11/8/26	3/8	2		H	vl (2)	Ar >AP unslurred = quaver
49/1	3/11/26	3/8	30		H	vl, 2, obdm	Cr < > some AP FNF/LP RFU/quaver
207/1	11/12/26	6/8	68		Sx	v2 (1, obsdm, fls)	As FNF unslurred = quaver
207/7		3/4	3		H	bc (fls)	Cr > FNF/LP unslurred = crotchet some ext over next beat (parts)

Regular slur patterns in concerted vocal works (cont.)

Work (BWV)	Date	Metre	First instance 1: Score	2: Parts	Division of pulse	Instruments	Type
84/3	9/2/27	3/8	60	7	H	v (ob)	Ar < >AP unslurred = quaver
201/7	c. 1729	3/8	–	73	H	vl, 2	As >AP X: most 1C
201/9		12/8	17		Sx	obdm	Cr >AP FNF unslurred = quaver
232/10	21/4/33	6/8	12		Sx	obdm (vl)	Ar > X: some orig. 1C
232/11		3/4	34	2	H	fags	Cr > FNF X: many 1C
213/1	5/9/33	3/8	–	95	H	obl (vl)	As >some RFU/ quaver
213/5		6/8	18		Sx	obdm (bc)	As > unslurred = quaver
213/9		3/8	5		H	vl (bc)	Ar >AP unslurred = quaver
213/11		3/8	110		H	bc	As >
97/2	c. 1734	6/8	–	7	Sx	bc	Cr < FNF/LP unslurred = quaver
248/1	25/12/34	3/8	154		H	v2 (1, vla, obs, fls)	Ar >AP unslurred = quaver
248/4		3/8	5		H	v (bc) obdm	Ar >AP unslurred = quaver
248/15	26/12/34	3/8	1		H	fl (bc)	Ar > unslurred = quaver
248/24	27/12/34	3/8	7		H	vl, 2 (obs, trs, fls)	Cr < >some AP FNF
248/36	1/1/35	3/8	22		H	cor (obl, vl)	Ar >AP some RFU/ quaver
248/39		6/8	18		Sx	ob, bc	As >AP unslurred = quaver
248/54	6/1/35	3/8	1		H	vl, 2, vla (tutti)	Cr FNF/some LP >AP
11/10	19/5/35	3/8	3		H	ob (fl)	Ar >AP unslurred = quaver
244/6	30/3/36	3/8	4		H	bc (fls)	Cr < > FNF AP unslurred = quaver
244/68		3/4	11		H	vl (2) fls, obs	Ar > X: some 1C
234/1	1735–50	3/8	120	–	H	vl	As > X: some 1C
234/5		6/8	18		Sx	bc (stgs)	As FNF

3H

| 6/2 | 2/4/25 | 3/8 | – | 6 | H | vla (or obdc) | Cs > Mes DFU (last, in part) |

Regular slur patterns in concerted vocal works (cont.)

Work (BWV)	Date	Metre	First instance 1: Score	2: Parts	Division of pulse	Instruments	Type
103/3	22/4/25	6/8	1		Sx	v or fl (bc)	Ar > Mes X: most slurs longer
43/3	30/5/26	3/8	9		H	vl, 2 (bc)	Ar Mes
234/5	1735-50	6/8	2		Sx	vl, 2, vla	Cr arpeg < DFU TNF

31
♩♩♩♩♩♩

Work (BWV)	Date	Metre	First instance 1: Score	2: Parts	Division of pulse	Instruments	Type
134a/2 (134)	1/1/19	3/8	—	5	H	obl	Br arpeg
147/3	2/7/23	3/4	14		H	obdm	Cs arpeg X: some 1C
94/3	6/8/24	3/8	41		H	obl	Bs arpeg X: score 3C?
62/2	3/12/24	3/8	5	3	H	vl, obl	Cr < >AP DFU unslurred = quaver
122/1	31/12/24	3/8	—	58	H	taille	As FNF X: most 1C
249/3	1/4/25	3/8	--	131	H	ob2 (vl)	Cs >
36c/7 (36)	4-5/1725	12/8	2	1	Sx	vl (bc)	Ar SNF/LP X: most 3C
187/3	4/8/26	3/8	--	7	H	vl, ob	Ar < unslurred = tied quaver (last)
98/3	10/11/26	3/8	--	3	H	ob	Bs arpeg visually 3C?
207/7	11/12/26	3/4	24	2	H	fls, bc	Cr SNF < X: some 3A
82/5	2/2/27	3/8	2		H	ob (vl, bc)	Cs < >AP some unslurred = quaver DFU (parts) X: some 1C
112/2	8/4/31	6/8	--	51	Sx	obdm	Bs Mes unslurred = quaver
213/9	5/9/33	3/8	19		H	v	As >AP X: some 1C unslurred = quaver
248/1	25/12/34	3/8	178		H	bc	As > X: most 1C
248/4		3/8	3		H	v, obdm	Ar >AP unslurred = quaver
248/54	6/1/35	3/8	4		H	trl (2, obs, stgs)	Cr < >AP FNF some groups constant in sequence unslurred = quaver
100/3	1732-5	6/8	--	4	Sx	bc	Ar dotted quaver for first note X: many 3C
244/6	30/3/36	3/8	5	1	H	fls	Ar > some AP unslurred = tied quaver

Regular slur patterns in concerted vocal works (cont.)

Work (BWV)	Date	Metre	First instance 1: Score	2: Parts	Division of pulse	Instruments	Type

					3J		
42/4	8/4/25	3/4	--	1	H	vcl, fag	Ar < semitones 2nd slur only; some DFU (parts)
128/4	10/5/25	6/8	28		Sx	obdm	As *superjectio*
176/5	27/5/25	3/8	71	70	H	obs	As > first only
72/5	27/1/26	3/4	−	3	H	vl, ob	Ar > semitones X: some 1C
187/3	4/8/26	3/8	11		H	vl, ob	Ar < 2nds DFU (parts)
97/7	c. 1734	3/4	−	4	H	bc	Ar > semitones 2nd slur only; some DFU
234/5	1735-50	6/8	9		Sx	vl, 2, vla	Ar > semitones some cross-bar DFU

					4A		
5/3	15/10/24	3/4	1		Q	vla	Ar FvNF
85/2	15/4/25	C	1		Q	vclpicc	Cr < > FvNF
108/2	29/4/25	3/4	9-10		Q	v	Bs arpeg over bar-line
19/3	29/9/26	C	−	46	Q	obs	As <
98/1	10/11/26	3/4	36	13	Q	vl	Ar FvNF dot for last slurred note (with 1D)
177/4	6/7/32	C	−	78	Q	bc	As Mes

					4B		
147/3	2/7/23	3/4	16		Q	obdm	Ar < +four more notes; last note = quaver
122/2	31/12/24	¢	--	2	E-Q	bc	Ar < last note = quaver
6/3	2/4/25	C	6		Q-H	vclpicc	Ar > last note = quaver
108/4	29/4/25	¢	−	18	E	vla (stgs)	Cr < FNF SNF OSC
28/1	30/12/25	3/4	87	3	Q-H	v2 (1)	Ar FvNF X: most missing
72/5	27/1/26	3/4	5		Q-H	vl (2, vla)	Ar < last note = quaver X: some originally 1A
17/5	22/9/26	C	2		Q-H	vl (2, vla)	Ar FvNF/LP last note = quaver

Regular slur patterns in concerted vocal works (cont.)

Work (BWV)	Date	Metre	First instance 1: Score	2: Parts	Division of pulse	Instruments	Type
58/3	5/1/27	C	5		Q-H	v	As > last note = quaver
201/15	c. 1729	2/4	23		Q-H	fls, obl	As > AP last note = quaver DFU (parts) X: many 1A; vl has 1D + DFU
100/4	1732-5	2/4	3		Q-H	vl (2)	Cr FvNF/LP < last note = quaver
248/31	27/12/34	2/4	14	4	Q-H	v (bc)	Ar > last note = quaver
248/47	2/1/35	2/4	—	4	Q-H	obdm	As > last note = quaver
248/51		2/4	3		Q-H	v	Ar < last note = quaver
195/5	1735-50	3/4	[11]	9	Q-H	v2, ob2, fl2	As FvNF last note = quaver X: some 1A
244/20	30/3/36	C	4		Q-H	ob (bc)	Ar < last note = quaver
234/3	1735-50	3/4	1		Q-H	vl (bc)	Ar > last note = quaver X: many 1A

4C

47/2	13/10/26	3/8	—	8	Q	v (or org)	As > DFU

4D

114/2	1/10/24	3/4	—	11	Q	fl	As >
19/3	29/9/26	C	—	50	Q	ob2	As <
30a/1 (30)	28/9/37	2/4	5		Q	vl (fls, obs)	Ar FNF X: some 1D

4E

NONE

4F

151/1	27/12/25	12/8	—	28	Tw	fl	As > part of sequence of cross-beat slurs

4G

147/8	2/7/23	C	1		Q	obdc	Ar TNF + *superjectio* RFU X: obdm part shows 1D + 1C

Regular slur patterns in concerted vocal works (cont.)

Work (BWV)	Date	Metre	First instance 1: Score	2: Parts	Division of pulse	Instruments	Type
109/5	17/10/23	3/4	52	14	Q	ob2 (1)	Cr > SvNF RFU/tie
81/5	30/1/24	C	–	3	Q	obdm2 (1)	Ar > SvNF some LP tie for unslurred
245/13	7/4/24	3/4	..	14	Q	vl	As SvNF X: some 1D + 1A
245/16d		C	[–]	16	Q	vl, fls	As SvNF
245/18b		C	[–]	4	Q	vl, fls, obl	As SvNF
20/5	11/6/24	C	..	18	Q	obl	As <
124/3	7/1/25	3/4	–	3	Q	obdm	Cs FNF some arpeg TNF RFU/tie
92/2	28/1/25	C	[–]	5	Q	bc	As >
92/4		C	..	7	Q	obsdm	As < + Mes
249/2	1/4/25	3/4	17		Q	ob	Cr > + Mes arpeg tie for unslurred, some longer
249/5		3/4	48		Q	fl	As > +FNF X: some 1A
249/9		C	16	4	Q	obdm	Cr arpeg + > < > RFU; some extend to next beat
85/1	15/4/25	C	1		Q	ob (stgs)	Cr SvNF/LP FNF > some RFU/tied
103/1	22/4/25	3/4	103		Q	v (or picc)	Ar chromatic/LP RFU X: changed from 1A
103/3		6/8	44	9	Tw	v or fl	Ar SvNF/LP RFU or unslurred tied
108/2	29/4/25	3/4	46	33	Q	v	As < > most cover next semiquaver
187/5	4/8/26	C	7	4	E	ob	Ar FNF/LP DFU (parts)
47/4	13/10/26	C	9		Q	v, ob	Ar SvNF (Mes + FNF) some RFU
56/3	27/10/26	C	8		Q	ob	Cr TNF Mes FNF < some RFU
207/3	11/12/26	¢	–	44-5	E	obdm	As < > slur runs to next quaver X: slur shorter in score
232/2	21/4/33	C	3		Q	vl, 2	Ar SvNF (< or > + FNF) unslurred tied
248/19	26/12/34	2/4	52		Q	vl, obsdm (fl)	Cs < + > AP X: some parts 1A
14/4	30/1/35	C	–	24-5	Q	obs	Cs > SvNF/LP
11/3	19/5/35	C	8	–	Q	fls	As < X: most missing?

Regular slur patterns in concerted vocal works (cont.)

Work (BWV)	Date	Metre	First instance 1: Score	2: Parts	Division of pulse	Instruments	Type
100/6	1732-5	C	—	3	Q	obdm	Ar > +FNF DFU (strokes)
244/20	30/3/36	C	39		Q	ob	Cs < + >AP
244/57		C	5		E	vladg	Ar SvNF (FNF) DFU (stroke)
30a/7 (30)	28/9/37	C	1 later score (P 44)		Q	obs	Ar TNF+TNF/LP RFU last note = quaver (corta)
234/3	1735-50	C	29	24	Q	bc/v	As > some DFU/tied

4H

10/1	2/7/24	C	8		H	vl (obs)	Ar > crosses bar
5/5	15/10/24	C	—	5	Q	tr	As Mes, slurred constant DFU (parts)
5/3		3/4	5		Q	vla	Ar TNF some DFU (un)slurred constant
42/1	8/4/25	C	53		Q	vl	Ar < (un)slurred constant
85/2	15/4/25	C	1		Q	vcl	Ar TNF
108/2	29/4/25	3/4	—	12	Q	v	Cr TNF <
47/2	13/10/26	3/8	—	42	Q	v or org	As TNF (with 1B, 1D, 4M)
47/4		C	36	3	H	v, ob	Ar > some DFU (parts) X: 1D in score
100/1	1732-5	¢	17		E	fl	Ar TNF (Mes)
244/42	30/3/36	C	5		Q	v	Br <arpeg

4I

14/2	30/1/35		—	3	Q	vl, cor	Ar FNF unslurred = quavers, 1st tied DFU (2nd, parts):

30a/1 (30)	28/9/37	2/4	73	9	Q	bc	Ar < some DFU (quavers)

4J

121/4	26/12/24	C	39		Q	vl	As < 1st unslurred = quaver RFU

Regular slur patterns in concerted vocal works (cont.)

Work (BWV)	Date	Metre	First instance 1: Score	2: Parts	Division of pulse	Instruments	Type
108/2	29/4/25	3/4	..	3	H-Q	v	Ar syncopated:

4K

Work (BWV)	Date	Metre	1: Score	2: Parts	Division of pulse	Instruments	Type
81/5	30/1/24	C	–	2	Q	obdml (2)	Ar > + FNF some LP unslurred = quaver X: most missing?
20/5	11/6/24	C	—	28	Q	obl	As <
94/4	6/8/24	C	--	41	Q	bc	As > unslurred = quaver
121/2	26/12/24	3/4	--	57	Q	obdm	Ar < unslurred = quaver
133/2	27/12/24	¢	—	60	E	bc	As SNF unslurred = quaver
123/5	6/1/25	C	--	1	Q	fl (bc)	Ar < + > unslurred = dotted crotchet
92/2	28/1/25	C	41		Q	bc	As > unslurred = tied quaver
249/5	1/4/25	3/4	7		Q	fl	As > + LP unslurred = quaver/tie
85/1	15/4/25	C	10		Q	vl (stgs)	Cr > SNF RFU
176/4	27/5/25	C	--	12	Q	bc	Cr < + FNF > RFU
43/7	30/5/26	C	—	35	Q	bc	As > unslurred = quaver
36c/1 (36)	4-5/1725	3/4	—	7	Q	obsdm, fl	Ar < X: most obs slurs shorter or absent
110/4	25/12/25	3/4	—	26	Q	obsdm	As < > unslurred = dotted crotchet
43/9	30/5/26	3/4	—	2	Q	obs	Cr < + FNF > Mes RFU/quaver X: many too short
56/3	27/10/26	C	2		Q	ob	Ar > + FNF
98/5	10/11/26	¢	—	29	E	vl, 2	As > RFU, slur extends to next quaver
207/3	11/12/26	¢	--	7-8	E	vl, obdm	As > unslurred = syncopated crotchet; slur extends to next quaver

Regular slur patterns in concerted vocal works (cont.)

Work (BWV)	Date	Metre	First instance 1: Score	2: Parts	Division of pulse	Instruments	Type
112/3	8/4/31	C	1		Q	bc	Ar > unslurred = quaver
232/2	21/4/33	C	1		Q	vl, 2 (bc)	Ar > unslurred = quaver
248/31	27/12/34	2/4	---	12	Q	bc (v)	Ar < > unslurred = quaver
14/2	30/1/35	3/4	---	8	Q	cor (vl)	Cr < > SNF RFU/ tied quaver
11/3	19/5/35	C	2		Q	fls	Cr SNF (> + FNF) > unslurred = quaver; dots under slurs
244/20	30/3/36	C	5		Q	ob (bc)	Ar < > SNF unslurred = quaver; some DFU (parts)
30a/1 (30)	28/9/37	2/4	41		Q	fls, obs, vl	Ar < + > SNF DFU (part) or quaver
195/5	1735-50	3/4	| — |	9	Q	vl (stgs, obs, fls)	Ar SNF(< + FNF) unslurred = tied quaver X: most 1A in score and some parts

4L

249/2	1/4/25	3/4	---	41	Q	ob	As > (with 1E) X: longer in score
58/3	5/1/27	C	---	7	Q	v	Ar > (with 1E) X: 1C in score
11/4	19/5/35	C	3-4		H	v	Ar < > (with 1E)

4M

| 47/2 | 13/10/26 | 3/8 | — | 42 | Q | v (or org) | As > (with 1B, D, 4H) |

4N

NONE

Regular slur patterns in concerted vocal works (cont.)

Work (BWV)	Date	Metre	First instance 1: Score	2: Parts	Division of pulse	Instruments	Type

40

| 56/3 | 27/10/26 | C | 6 | – | Q | ob | As > + Mes X: slurs misplaced; 1D or 4K intended? |

5A

NONE

5B

96/1	8/10/24	9/8	–	7	T	obl (2, bc)	Br arpeg many cover 2 beats X: orig. 2B extended
249/11	1/4/25	C	–	10	T	obs	Ar TNF/LP + > X: altered from 2B slurs
110/1	25/12/25	9/8	49	25	T	v2, ob3 (1, 2, fag, stgs)	Cr < TNF/LP X: orig. 2A/B

5C/D

NONE

5E

32/3	13/1/26	3/8	9		T	v	Ar < > (+ extra beat) DFU (parts)
13/1	20/1/26	12/8	6		T	bc	As < > X: most 2C + 2A
100/5	1732-5	12/8	2		T	obdm	Cr < > TNF DFU (parts) most groups longer X: 2A/B in score
30a/5 (30)	28/9/37	C	4		T	vl, fl	Cr FvNF < > dots under slurs DFU tied

Regular slur patterns in concerted vocal works (cont.)

Work (BWV)	Date	Metre	First instance 1: Score	2: Parts	Division of pulse	Instruments	Type
				5F			
213/5	5/9/33	6/8	—	97·8	T	obdm	As > over bar X: 2A in score (98)
				5G			
176/5	27/5/25	3/8	—	1	H·W	obs	As across bar
				5H			
				NONE			

Notes

Introduction

1. Peter Williams (1986 p. 276) considers that 'The effect of every detail in any notation is to limit the performer's choice.'
2. For a survey of the pitfalls of diplomatic transcription of slurs, see Dadelsen 1982.
3. Slurs in Bach's Invention in D, BWV 774, indicate one accent per bar, according to Lohmann 1982 p. 72.

1 The primacy of singing

1. One of the earliest references is in Ganassi 1535; especially pp. 12, 87.
2. E.g. H. Faber's *Compendiolum Musicae*, first published in 1548 and reprinted well into the seventeenth century.
3. E.g. R. Descartes, *Les Passions de l'Âme* (Paris and Amsterdam, 1649).
4. The relationship with the terminology of rhetoric was noted by Spitta (1880 pp. 55–6).
5. '. . .auch sich bey mir gar *speciell* in *Clavier, General-Bass /* und denen daraus fließenden *Fundamental*-Regeln der *Composition informiren* laßen. . .'; NB only Bach's signature on this document is autograph.
6. '. . .in Betrachtung Selbiger nicht allein auf verschiedenen *Instrumen*ten sich wohl *habilitiret*, sondern auch *vocaliter* sich hören zu laßen, viele *specimina* hiesiges Ohrtes rühmlichst abgeleget, auch *in arte componendi* das seinige nach Verlangen zeigen dörffte'.
7. Bernhard, in Hilse 1973 pp. 90–1 (p. 184, note 32), begins '. . .in vorigem *Seculo*' and not '15 *Seculo*'.
8. 'Die *mechanischen Setzfiguren*. . .nehmen entweder aus der Zusammenziehung oder der Verkleinerung der Tacttheile ihren Ursprung.'
9. Walther: 'Die *Dissonantien* seyn die Nacht, die *Consonantien* der Tag; das Licht würde uns nimmermehr so angenehm seyn, wenn es immer Tag und niemahls Nacht wäre. Die *Dissonantien* seyn der Winter, die *Consonantien* der Sommer. Jene sind das bittere, diese das süße. Jene das Schwartze, diese das Weiße.'
10. 'Wenn die Noten entweder von der *Linea* zum *Spatio*, oder vom *Spatio* zur *Linea* gezogen werden. . .'

262

11. The cross-beat slurring of the *anticipatione della syllaba* is also described by Walther/Bernhard; the term *subsumptio post positiva* is used as an alternative; Walther 1708 p. 153.

12. 'Alle Vorschläge müssen an die Hauptnote geschleift (welches man den Abzug nennt) und allezeit stärker angegeben werden als die auf sie folgende Hauptnote.'

13. 'Heütiges tages. . .findet man. . .mehrere *Relationes Non-Harmonicas* hinter einander hergesetzet, es muß aber behutsam damit umgegangen werden, damit die unter solchen liegende *Affectus animi*, als Traurigkeit, Andacht, Liebe, Furcht, Verlangen *etc*: nicht zur Wiederwärtigkeit und Verdruß, ja gar zum *musical*. Teuffel werden mögen.' ('Nowadays one finds more non-harmonic relations set one after the other; one must be careful with this however, so that the underlying affects of the soul, such as sadness, devotion, love, fear, longing etc., do not lead to repulsiveness and frustration, yes, even to the devil in music.')

14. Cf. Mattheson's comments, p. 11 above.

15. H.-J. Schulze (1984 pp. 110-19) has recently identified this copyist as J. H. Bach. This scribe was previously termed 'Hauptkopist C' by Dürr (1976 pp. 31-4).

2 Articulation marks in string playing

1. For a general survey, see Boyden 1965 esp. pp. 157f.

2. E.g. J. J. Walther, *Scherzi da Violino Solo* (1676), Sonata 4, bb. 4 and 11.

3. 'Das gegenwärtige wird uns gänzlich überzeugen, daß der Bogenstrich die Noten belebe; daß er bald eine ganz modeste, bald eine freche, bald eine ernsthafte, bald eine scherzhafte, ist eine schmeichelnde, ist eine gesetzte und erhabene, ist eine traurige, ist aber eine lustige Melodie hervorbringe. . .'

4. 'Durch die geschleiften und nahe an einander liegenden Intervalle wird das Schmeichelnde, Traurige, und Zärtliche; durch die kurz gestoßenen, oder in entferneten Sprüngen bestehenden Noten. . .wird das Lustige und Freche ausgedrücket.'

5. 'Abermal ein in seinem Vatterlande berühmter Componist setzet ziemlich viel Bogenstriche drüber, allein die mehresten davon am unrechten Orte, welches seine Compositionen schlecht macht.'

6. Simpson 1659 p. 9: '. . .[the notes] would not have that Grace, or Ornament, if they were played severally'; Rousseau 1687 pp. 103-4: 'Des Agrémens'; Prelleur 1731, Violin, p. 7: 'Of the Usual Graces'.

7. '. . .il faut d'un seul coup d'archet articuler plusieurs nottes comme si elles etoient de coups d'archet differens. . .'

8. Brossard 1703 pp. 134, 135: 'spiccato/staccato'; Walther 1732 p. 575: 'staccato'; Grassineau 1740 p. 237: 'spiccato'; Chambers 1783 vol. 4: 'spiccato/staccato'.

9. 'Die Art. . .braucht er blos zum accompagnieren, und spricht, daß mittelst derselben die Haare des Violin-Bogens nur einen halben Messer-Rücken breit auf die Saiten stossen müssen, damit die singende *Principal*-Stimme sich wohl unterscheide. . .'

10. 'Steht aber nur über einer Note, auf welche etliche von geringerer Geltung folgen, ein Strichelchen: so bedeutet solches, nicht nur daß die Note halb so kurz seyn soll; sondern daß sie auch zugleich, mit dem Bogen, durch einen Druck markieret werden muß.'

3 Articulation marks in wind playing

1. Corrette 1735 p. 20: 'Les coups de langue sont sur la flute ce que les coups d'archet sont sur le violon'; la Borde 1780 p. 340: 'La langue fait aux instrumens à vent, ce que fait l'archet aux instrumens à corde.'

4 Articulation marks in keyboard playing

1. Schweitzer (1908 pp. 338-9) similarly suggests that the familiarity of the original performers with Bach's principles is reflected in the comparative paucity of articulation marks in Bach's keyboard works.
2. See J. J. Rousseau's entry on 'Phrase', in the *Encyclopédie* 1751-7, vol. 12 p. 530: 'C'est dans l'invention des *phrases* musicales, surtout dans leur liaison entr'elles & dans leur ordonnance selon de belles proportions, qui consiste la véritable beauté de la musique.'
3. 'Bey Figuren von 2 und 4 solcher Noten, kriegt die erste und dritte einen etwas stärckern Druck, als die zweyte und vierte, doch so, daß man es kaum mercket.'
4. 'Schleiffen aber heißet, den Finger von der vorhergehenden Note nicht eher aufheben, als bis man die folgende berühret.'
5. 'Es ist aber besser, daß man dergleichen Sätze ordentlich ausschreibt.'
6. 'Il y a des Instrumens, tels que le Clavecin, le Tympanon & c. sur lesquels le *Coulé* paroît presque impossible à pratiquer; & cependant on vient à bout de l'y faire sentir par un toucher doux & lié, très-difficile à décrire. . .'
7. 'Die kurtzen Noten nach vorgegangenen Puncten werden allezeit kürtzer abgefertiget als ihre Schreib-Art erfordert. . .'
8. See Fuchs 1985 p. 23: 'Bachs Gepflogenheiten bei Artikulationsangaben - Sparsamkeit bei den Tasteninstrumenten und Reichhaltigkeit bei Streich- und Blasinstrumenten - sind sicher stark spielpraktisch motiviert.'

5 Articulation marks and rhythmic inequality

1. 'ce qui lie le chant, & le rend plus coulant'. Couperin implies (1717 p. 41) that eligible notes are generally in conjunct motion: '. . .nous pointons plusieurs croches de suite par degrés-conjoints'.
2. Example in 2-time. '*Nottes egales*' are specified for an example with cross-beat slurring on the succeeding page.

6 Articulation marks within the compositional and notational procedure

1. Marshall's numbering of sketches is adopted here.
2. For a consideration of the significance of hand-position in Mozart's writing of dots and strokes, see Mies 1958.
3. For a study of Zelter's performances, see Neumann 1962.

8 Fundamentals of Bach's notated articulation

1. See also Brainard 1983.

2. The possibility of an original string/woodwind difference of articulation is suggested in *NBA* 2/7 KB, p. 74.

9 Bach's role in the preparation of printed sources

1. Two slurs only are evident in the parts (St Thom): b. 8 Alto (4–5), b. 9 Continuo (3–4).
2. All the readings for BWV 140 are based on *NBA* 1/27 *KB*, 131–2.
3. This source has not been examined by the present author.

10 Articulation marks in fair copies of works with instrumental ensemble

1. The watermark of the paper (double eagle with heart-shield) appears in works between 1739 and 1744, *NBA* 9 Addenda vol. 1, p. 60. Features of the hand suggest the latter end of this period: the crotchet rests tend to curve upwards; the downward stems on the minims are on the left rather than the right; some minims have open tops, a feature that appears regularly in the last decade of Bach's life. See Dadelsen 1958 esp. p. 110 for a survey of the development of Bach's hand.

11 Bach's keyboard articulation and the development of the keyboard idiom

1. The obbligato appears in an original separate organ part (St 106) in the hands of J. S. and C. P. E. Bach. This might suggest that the composer was not the soloist.
2. Emery (1957 pp. 52–4, 188–9) tentatively suggests that Bach's hand might be evident in some of the articulation marks and one small insert. Schulze (1984 p. 17) notes the presence of Bach's hand in this manuscript without qualification.

12 Bach and 'modern' articulation; slurs as 'phrase marks'

1. Grassineau 1767 p. 37: 'Phrase is a succession of melody or harmony, which forms, without interruption, a sense more or less complete, and which is terminated on a repose, by a cadence more or less perfect.'

13 Articulation marks in analysis and interpretation

1. See *NBA* 6/1 KB pp. 137f for a description of the primary source of BWV 1017 in P 229 (Altnickol); most of the other sources either omit the slurs or show them indeterminately placed.
2. See Dadelsen (1978 p. 103) for a distinction between *essential* (affective) and *accidental* (technical) articulation.

References

Agricola 1757 J. F. Agricola, *Anleitung zur Singkunst* (Berlin, 1757)

Allerup 1931 A. Allerup, *Die 'Musica Practica' des J. A. Herbst und ihre entwicklungs-geschichtliche Bedeutung*, Münsterische Beiträge zur Musikwissenschaft 1 (Kassel, 1931)

Bach 1753 C. P. E. Bach, *Versuch über die wahre Art das Clavier zu spielen*, vol. 1 (Berlin, 1753) (all references from 1759 edition)

Bach 1787 C. P. E. Bach, 1787 edition of Bach 1753

Bacilly 1668 B. de Bacilly, *Remarques curieuses sur l'art de bien chanter* (Paris, 1668), facsimile of 1679 edition (Geneva, 1971)

Barnett 1978 D. Barnett, 'Non-uniform slurring in 18th century music: accident or design?', *Haydn Yearbook* 10 (1978), 179-99

Beyer 1703 J. S. Beyer, *Primae Linae Musicae Vocalis* (Freiberg, 1703), facsimile (Leipzig, 1976)

Bodky 1960 E. Bodky, *The Interpretation of Bach's Keyboard Works* (Cambridge, Mass., 1960)

Boyden 1965 D. D. Boyden, *The History of Violin Playing from its Origins to 1761* (London, 1965)

Brainard 1983 P. Brainard, 'The aria and its ritornello: the question of "dominance" in Bach', *BAM*, 39-51

Brijon 1763 C. R. Brijon, *Réflexions sur la musique* (Paris, 1763), facsimile (Geneva, 1972)

Brossard 1703 S. de Brossard, *Dictionaire de musique* (Paris, 1703)

Butler 1980 G. G. Butler, 'Leipziger Stecher in Bachs Originaldrucken', *BJ* 66 (1980), 9-26

Chambers 1783 E. Chambers, *Cyclopaedia* (London, 1783)

Choquel 1762 H. L. Choquel, *La Musique rendue sensible par la méchanique* (Paris, 1762)

Collins 1967 M. Collins, 'Notes inégales: a re-examination', *JAMS* 20/3 (1967), 481-5

Corrette 1735 M. Corrette, *Methode pour apprendre aisément à jouer de la flute traversiere* (Paris, 1735)

Corrette 1738 M. Corrette, *L'Ecole d'Orphée* (Paris, 1738), facsimile (Geneva, 1972)

Couperin 1717 F. Couperin, *L'Art de toucher le clavecin* (Paris, 1717), *Œuvres complètes de François Couperin, Œuvres didactiques*, ed. M. Cauchie (Paris, 1933)

Crüger 1660 J. Crüger, *Musicae Practicae Praecepta Brevia* (Berlin, 1660)

Dadelsen 1958 G. von Dadelsen, *Beiträge zur Chronologie der Werke Johann Sebastian Bachs, TBSt* vol. 4/5 (Trossingen, 1958)

Dadelsen 1978 G. von Dadelsen, 'Die Crux der Nebensache. Editorische und praktische Bemerkungen zu Bachs Artikulation', *BJ* 64 (1978), 95-112

Dadelsen 1980 G. von Dadelsen, 'De confusione articulandi', *Ars Musica. Musica Scientia. Festschrift Heinrich Hüschen*, ed. D. Altenburg (Cologne 1980), 71-5

Dadelsen 1982 G. von Dadelsen, 'Über den Anteil der Interpretation an der Dokumentation', in *Quellenforschung in der Musikwissenschaft; Wolfenbütteler Forschungen* 15, ed. G. Feder (Wolfenbüttel, 1982), 33-56

Demoz 1728 [Demoz de la Salle], *Methode de musique* (Paris, 1728)

Donington 1974 R. Donington, *The Interpretation of Early Music* (London, 1963; rev. edn 1974)

Dreyfus 1985 L. D. Dreyfus, 'The metaphorical soloist: concerted organ parts in Bach's cantatas', *EM* 13/2 (1985), 237-47

Dreyfus 1987 L. D. Dreyfus, *Bach's Continuo Group* (Cambridge, Mass., 1987)

Dürr 1974 A. Dürr, 'De vita cum imperfectis', *Studies in Renaissance and Baroque Music in Honor of Arthur Mendel*, ed. R. L. Marshall (Kassel, 1974), 243-53

Dürr 1976 A. Dürr, *Zur Chronologie der Leipziger Vokalwerke J. S. Bachs* (Kassel, 1976; reprinted and edited version of *BJ* 1957)

Eggebrecht 1970 H. H. Eggebrecht, 'Über Bachs geschichtlichen Ort', *WF*, 247-89

Emery 1957 W. Emery, *Notes on Bach's Organ Works* 4-5, A Companion to the Revised Novello Edition, Six Sonatas for two Manuals and Pedal (London, 1957)

Encyclopédie 1751-7 D. Diderot and J. D'Alembert, *Encyclopédie, ou Dictionnaire* (Paris, 1751-7; references from 1765 edition)

Falck 1688 G. Falck, *Idea Boni Cantoris* (Nuremberg, 1688)

Finkel 1978 K. Finkel, *Musik in Unterricht und Erziehung an den gelehrten Schulen im pfälzischen Teil der Kurpfalz; Quellenstudien zur pfälzischen Schulmusik bis 1800*, vol. 3 (Tutzing, 1978)

Fuchs 1985 J. R. Fuchs, *Studien zu Artikulationsangaben in Orgel- und Clavierwerken von Joh. Seb. Bach* (Neuhausen-Stuttgart, 1985)

Galliard 1742 P. Tosi, *Opinioni de' cantori antichi e moderni* (Bologna, 1723), trans. J. E. Galliard (London, 1742)

Ganassi 1535 S. Ganassi, *Opera intitulata Fontegara* (Venice, 1535), ed. H. Peter (Berlin, 1956)

Ganassi 1542 S. Ganassi, *Regola Rubertina* (Venice, 1542), ed. H. Peter (Berlin, 1972)

Geminiani 1742 F. Geminiani, *Rules for Playing in a True Taste on the Violin, German Flute, Violoncello, Harpsichord, Particularly the Thorough Bass* (London, c. 1742)

Geminiani 1751 F. Geminiani, *The Art of Playing the Violin* (London, 1751), facsimile (Oxford, 1952)

Granom 1766 G. A. Granom, *Plain and Easy Instructions for Playing on the German-Flute* (London, 1766)

Grassineau 1740 J. Grassineau, *A Musical Dictionary* (London, 1740)

Grassineau 1767, 1767 edition of Grassineau 1740

Grüß 1988 H. Grüß, 'Über Stricharten und Artikulation in Streichinstrumentenstimmen Johann Sebastian Bachs', *IB V*, 331-40

Herbst 1642/53 J. A. Herbst, *Musica [Moderna] Prattica* (Nuremberg [Frankfurt], 1642/[53])

Herz 1974 G. Herz, 'Der lombardische Rhythmus im "Domine Deus" der h-Moll-Messe J. S. Bachs', *BJ* 60 (1974), 90-7

Hiller 1774 J. A. Hiller, *Anweisung zum musicalisch-richtigen Gesange* (Leipzig, 1774)

Hilse 1973 W. Hilse, 'The treatises of Christoph Bernhard', *The Music Forum* 3 (1973), 1-196

Hotteterre 1707 J. Hotteterre, *Principes de la flute traversiere* (Amsterdam, 1707), facsimile of 1728 edition (Kassel, 1973)

Hotteterre 1719 J. Hotteterre, *L'Art de preluder* (Paris, 1719), facsimile (Basel, n.d. [198?])

Houle 1987 G. Houle, *Meter in Music, 1600-1800* (Bloomington and Indianapolis, 1987)

Jablonsky 1717 J. T. Jablonsky, *Allgemeines Lexicon der Künste und Wissenschaften* (Leipzig, 1717), 1748 edition

Jenkins 1976 G. Jenkins, 'The legato touch and the "ordinary" manner of keyboard playing from 1750-1850', 2 vols. (Ph.D. thesis, Cambridge, 1976)

Kilian 1983 D. Kilian, 'Zur Artikulation bei Bach', *BB* 2 (Leipzig, 1983), 27-35

Kinsky 1937 G. Kinsky, *Die Originalausgaben der Werke Johann Sebastian Bachs* (Vienna, Leipzig and Zurich. 1937)

Kirnberger 1771 J. Kirnberger, *Die Kunst des reinen Satzes in der Musik*, vol. 1 (Berlin, 1771, page numbers from 1774 edition)

Kloppers 1965 J. Kloppers, 'Die Interpretation und Wiedergabe der Orgelwerke Bachs' (Ph.D. thesis, Frankfurt, 1965)

Koprowski 1975 R. Koprowski, 'Bach "fingerprints" in the engraving of the original edition', in 'Bach's "Art of Fugue": an examination of the sources', *CM* 19 (1975), 61-7

Kubik 1986 R. Kubik, 'Artikulation und Struktur', *Festschrift Martin Ruhnke* (Neuhausen-Stuttgart, 1986), 203-18

Kuhnau 1689 J. Kuhnau, *Neuer Clavier-Übung erster Theil* (Leipzig, 1689), *DDT* 4

Kürzinger 1763 I. F. X. Kürzinger, *Getreuer Unterricht zum Singen mit Manieren und die Violin zu spielen* (Augsburg, 1763)

la Borde 1780 J. B. de la Borde, *Essai sur la musique ancienne et moderne*, vol. 1 (Paris, 1780)

le Huray and Butt 1985 P. G. le Huray and J. A. Butt, 'In search of Bach the organist', *Bach, Handel, Scarlatti Tercentenary Essays*, ed. P. Williams (Cambridge, 1985), 185-206

Lohmann 1982 L. Lohmann, *Studien zu Artikulationsproblemen bei den Tasteninstrumenten des 16.-18. Jahrhunderts; Kölner Beiträge zur Musikforschung* 125 (Regensburg, 1982)

Loulié 1696 E. Loulié, *Eléments ou principes de musique* (Paris, 1696), trans. A. Cohen (New York, 1965)

Luther's Works 1972 *Luther's Works*, vol. 49, ed. G. G. Krodel and H. T. Lehmann (Philadelphia, 1972)

Mahaut 1759 A. Mahaut, *Nouvelle méthode pour apprendre. . .à jouer de la flûte traversiere* (Amsterdam and Paris, 1759)

Marais 1701 M. Marais, 'Avertissement', *Pieces de violes. . .2e livre* (Paris, 1701)

Marpurg 1755 F. W. Marpurg, *Anleitung zum Clavierspielen* (Berlin, 1755)

Marpurg 1758 F. W. Marpurg, *Anleitung zur Singcomposition* (Berlin, 1758)

Marpurg 1762 F. W. Marpurg, *Die Kunst das Clavier zu spielen* (Berlin, 1762)

Marpurg 1763 F. W. Marpurg, *Anleitung zur Musik überhaupt und zur Singkunst besonders* (Berlin, 1763), facsimile (Leipzig, 1975)

Marshall 1972 R. L. Marshall, *The Compositional Process of J. S. Bach*, 2 vols. (Princeton, 1972)

Marshall 1983 R. L. Marshall, 'Editore traditore: Ein weiterer "Fall Rust"?', *BAM*, 183-91

Mather 1973 B. B. Mather, *Interpretation of French Music from 1678 to 1775* (New York, 1973)

Mattheson 1731 J. Mattheson, *Grosse General-Baß-Schule* (Hamburg, 1731)

Mattheson 1739 J. Mattheson, *Der vollkommene Kapellmeister* (Hamburg, 1739)

Merck 1695 D. Merck, *Compendium Musicae* (Augsburg, 1695)

Mersenne 1636 M. Mersenne, *Harmonie universelle* (Paris, 1636)

Mies 1958 P. Mies, 'Die Artikulationszeichen Strich und Punkt bei Wolfgang Amadeus Mozart', *Mf* 11 (1958), 428-55

Minear 1975 P. S. Minear, 'J. S. Bach and J. A. Ernesti: a case study in exegetical and theological conflict', *Our Common History as Christians - Essays in Honor of Albert C. Outler*, ed. J. Deschner, L. T. Howe and K. Penzel (New York, 1975), 131-55

Mozart 1756 L. Mozart, *Versuch einer gründlichen Violinschule* (Augsburg, 1756)

Muffat 1698 G. Muffat, Introduction to *Florilegium Secundum* (Passau, 1698), *DTÖ* 2/2

Neumann 1978 F. Neumann, *Ornamentation in Baroque and Post-Baroque Music* (Princeton, 1978)

Neumann 1962 W. Neumann, 'Welche Handschriften J. S. Bachscher Werke besaß die Berliner Singakademie?', *Hans Albrecht in memoriam*, ed. W. Brennecke and H. Haase (Kassel, 1962), 136-42

Neumann 1981 W. Neumann, 'Das Problem "vokal-instrumental" in seiner Bedeutung für ein neues Bach-Verständnis', *Bachforschung und Bachinterpretation heute*, ed. R. Brinkmann (Kassel, 1981), 72-85

Newman 1969 W. S. Newman, 'Is there a rationale for the articulation of J. S. Bach's string and wind music?', *Studies in Musicology - Essays in the History, Style, and Bibliography of Music in Memory of Glen Haydon*, ed. J. W. Pruett (Chapel Hill, 1969), 229-44

Nivers 1665 G. Nivers, Introduction, *Livre d'orgue* (Paris, 1665)

O'Donnell 1979 J. O'Donnell, 'The French style and the overtures of Bach: 2', *EM* 7/3 (1979), 336-45

Petri 1782 J. S. Petri, *Anleitung zur praktischen Musik* (Leipzig, 1782; enlarged edition of 1769), facsimile (Giebing, 1969)

Petzoldt 1982 M. Petzoldt, 'Zwischen Orthodoxie, Pietismus und Aufklärung - Überlegungen zum theologiegeschichtlichen Kontext Johann Sebastian Bachs', *BS* 7 (Leipzig, 1982), 66-108

Petzoldt 1985 M. Petzoldt, '"Ut probus & doctus reddar". Zum Anteil der Theologie bei der Schulausbildung Johann Sebastian Bachs in Eisenach, Ohrdruf und Lüneburg', *BJ* 71 (1985), 7-42

Piani 1712 G. A. Piani, 'Avertissement', *Sonate a violino solo e violoncello col cimbalo* (Paris, 1712)

Pont 1979 G. Pont, 'A revolution in the science and practice of music', *Musicology* 5, Musicological Association of Australia (Sydney, 1979)

Praetorius 1619 M. Praetorius, *Syntagmatis Musici* vol. 3 (Wolfenbüttel, 1619)

Prelleur 1731 P. Prelleur, *The Modern Musick-Master* (London, 1731)

Printz 1678 W. C. Printz, *Musica Modulatoria Vocalis, oder Manierliche und zierliche Sing-Kunst* (Schweidnitz, 1678)

Printz 1696 W. C. Printz, *Phrynis Mitilenaeus, oder Satyrischer Componist* (Dresden and Leipzig, 1696; earlier versions Quedlinburg, 1676-7, 1679)

Quantz 1752 J. J. Quantz, *Versuch einer Anweisung die Flöte traversiere zu spielen* (Berlin, 1752)

Rameau 1724 J. P. Rameau, 'Ornaments table', *Pièces de clavecin* (Paris, 1724), facsimile (Kassel, 1958; rev. edn 1972)

Riepel 1757 J. Riepel, *Gründliche Erklärung der Tonordnung* (Frankfurt and Leipzig, 1757)

Robinson 1715 D. Robinson, *An Essay upon Vocal Music* (Nottingham, 1715)

Robinson 1981 S. L. Robinson, 'The Forquerays and the French viol tradition', 2 vols. (Ph.D. thesis, Cambridge, 1981)

Rousseau 1687 J. Rousseau, *Traité de la viole* (Paris, 1687)

Rousseau 1768 J. J. Rousseau, *Dictionnaire de musique* (Paris, 1768)

Saint-Lambert 1702 M. de Saint-Lambert, *Les Principes du clavecin* (Paris, 1702), facsimile (Geneva, 1974)

Scheidt 1624 S. Scheidt, *Tabulatura Nova*, 2 vols. (Hamburg, 1624), *DDT* 1

Schering 1926 A. Schering, *Musikgeschichte Leipzigs*, vol. 2 (Leipzig, 1926)

Schestakowa 1988 D. Schestakowa, 'Zur Problematik der Bogensetzung bei Bach – Beobachtungen bei der Edition der Brandenburgischen Konzerte', *IB V*, 315-22

Schickhardt 1710 J. C. Schickhardt, *Principes de la flûte* (Amsterdam, c. 1710)

Schmitz 1952 A. Schmitz, 'Die Figurenlehre in den theoretischen Werken Johann Gottfried Walthers', *AMw* 9 (1952), 79-100

Schmitz 1970 A. Schmitz, 'Die oratorische Kunst J. S. Bachs', *WF*, 61-84

Schneiderheinze 1985 A. Schneiderheinze, 'Johann Sebastian Bach, Johann Friedrich Doles und die "Anfangsgründe zum Singen"', *BB* 4 (Leipzig, 1985)

Schulze 1977 H.-J. Schulze, '". . .da man die besten nicht bekommen könne. . .". Kontroversen und Kompromisse vor Bachs Leipziger Amtsantritt', *Bericht über die Wissenschaftliche Konferenz zum III. Internationalen Bach-Fest der DDR*, ed. W. Felix, W. Hoffmann and A. Schneiderheinze (Leipzig, 1977), 71-7

Schulze 1984 H.-J. Schulze, *Studien zur Bach-Überlieferung im 18. Jahrhundert* (Leipzig, 1984)

Schünemann 1928 G. Schünemann, *Geschichte der deutschen Schulmusik* (Leipzig, 1928)

Schwarz 1972 V. Schwarz, 'Aufführungspraxis als Forschungsgegenstand', *ÖMZ* 27/6 (1972), 314-22

Schweitzer 1908 A. Schweitzer, *J. S. Bach* (Leipzig, 1908)

Seagrave 1959 B. A. G. Seagrave, 'The French style of violin bowing and phrasing from Lully to Jacques Aubert (1650-1730)' (Ph.D. thesis, Stanford, 1959)

Seaton 1975 D. Seaton, 'The autograph: an early version of the "Art of Fugue"', in 'Bach's "Art of Fugue": an examination of the sources', *CM* 19 (1975), 54-9

Simpson 1659 C. Simpson, *The Division Violist* (London, 1659)

Spitta 1880 P. Spitta, *Johann Sebastian Bach*, vol. 2 (1880), trans. C. Bell and J. A. Fuller-Maitland (London, 1884)

Stiller 1984 G. Stiller, *Johann Sebastian Bach and Liturgical Life in Leipzig*, ed. R. Leaver (St Louis, 1984)

Tarade 1774 T.-J. Tarade, *Traité du violon* (Paris, c. 1774), facsimile (Geneva, 1972)

Tartini 1760 G. Tartini; 'Lettera del defonto Signor Giuseppe Tartini alla Signora Maddalena Lombardini', (1760), trans. C. Burney (London, 1779), reprinted W. Reeves (London, 1913)

Walther 1708 J. G. Walther, *Praecepta der musicalischen Composition* (MS, 1708). ed. P. Benary (Leipzig, 1955)

Walther 1732 J. G. Walther, *Musicalisches Lexicon* (Leipzig, 1732), facsimile (Kassel, 1953)

Williams 1980 P. Williams, *The Organ Music of J. S. Bach*, vol. 1 (Cambridge, 1980)

Williams 1984 P. Williams, *The Organ Music of J. S. Bach*, vol. 3 *A Background* (Cambridge, 1984)

Williams 1986 P. Williams, 'The snares and delusions of notation', *J. S. Bach as Organist*, ed. G. Stauffer and E. May (London, 1986), 274-94

Wolff 1977 C. Wolff, 'Bachs Handexemplar der Schübler-Choräle', *BJ* 63 (1977), 120-9

Wolff 1979 C. Wolff, 'Textkritische Bemerkungen zum Originaldruck der Bachschen Partiten', *BJ* 65 (1979), 65-74

Wragg c. 1790 J. Wragg, *The Flute/Oboe Preceptor* (London, c. 1790)

Index of BWV works cited

(excluding entries in Appendix 2)

Index of names

('author' indicates a twentieth-century author)

276